Organizational Routines

Perspectives on Process Organization Studies

Series Editors: Ann Langley and Haridimos Tsoukas

Perspectives on Process Organization Studies is an annual series, linked to the International Symposium on Process Organization Studies, and is dedicated to the development of an understanding of organizations and organizing at large as processes in the making. This series brings together contributions from leading scholars, which focus on seeing dynamically evolving activities, interactions, and events as important aspects of organized action, rather than static structures and fixed templates.

Volume 1: Process, Sensemaking, and Organizing
Editors: Tor Hernes and Sally Maitlis

Volume 2: Constructing Identity in and around Organizations
Editors: Majken Schultz, Steve Maguire, Ann Langley, and Haridimos Tsoukas

Volume 3: How Matter Matters: Objects, Artifacts, and Materiality in Organization Studies
Editors: Paul R. Carlile, Davide Nicolini, Ann Langley, and Haridimos Tsoukas

Volume 4: Language and Communication at Work: Discourse, Narrativity, and Organizing
Editors: François Cooren, Eero Vaara, Ann Langley, and Haridimos Tsoukas

Volume 5: Organizational Routines: How They Are Created, Maintained, and Changed
Editors: Jennifer Howard-Grenville, Claus Rerup, Ann Langley, and Haridimos Tsoukas

Organizational Routines

How They Are Created, Maintained, and Changed

Edited by
Jennifer Howard-Grenville, Claus Rerup,
Ann Langley, Haridimos Tsoukas

OXFORD
UNIVERSITY PRESS

Great Clarendon Street, Oxford, OX2 6DP,
United Kingdom

Oxford University Press is a department of the University of Oxford.
It furthers the University's objective of excellence in research, scholarship,
and education by publishing worldwide. Oxford is a registered trade mark of
Oxford University Press in the UK and in certain other countries

First published 2016
First published in paperback 2017

Published in the United States of America by Oxford University Press
198 Madison Avenue, New York, NY 10016, United States of America

British Library Cataloguing in Publication Data
Data available

Library of Congress Cataloging in Publication Data
Data available

ISBN 978–0–19–875948–5 (Hbk.)
ISBN 978–0–19–880441–3 (Pbk.)

Contents

Contents

Acknowledgments

We thank Sophia Tzagaraki whose excellent administrative assistance made preparing this volume both possible and pleasurable. As well, we are grateful to the participants in the Sixth International Symposium on Process Organization Studies for their interest in how organizational routines are created, maintained, and changed, and their scholarly exchange at the symposium that reflected and inspired the themes in this volume.

We would like to express our great appreciation to the following colleagues who have generously offered their time to act as reviewers for the papers published in this volume.

Jennifer Howard-Grenville, Claus Rerup, Ann Langley, and Haridimos Tsoukas

Reviewers Listed Alphabetically

Helle Kryger Aggerholm, Aarhus University
Katherina Dittrich, University of Zurich
Jeannette Eberhard, Ivey Business School
Bertrand Fauré, University Toulouse
Vern Glaser, University of Alberta
Daniel Hjorth, Copenhagen Business School
Karen Locke, Mason School of Business
Philipe Lorino, ESSEC
Mazi Raz, Ivey Business School
Anja Schröder,TU
John Paul Stephens, Weatherhead School of Management
Mark Zbaracki, Ivey Business School
Mike Zundel, University of Liverpool

List of Figures

List of Tables

List of Contributors

Helle Kryger Aggerholm is Associate Professor at the Department of Business Communication, Business and Social Sciences, Aarhus University, Denmark. Overall, she is interested in studying how communication constitutes organizations from a micro-ethnographic perspective. Her major research areas are strategic communication, strategy communication within a strategy-as-practice context, organizational communication, as well as language as social interaction.

Birte Asmuß is Associate Professor at the Department of Business Communication, Business and Social Sciences, at Aarhus University, Denmark. Her research focuses on workplace interaction with a specific focus on strategy work, various meetings types (formal–informal), and performance appraisal interviews. She is interested in exploring the potential of micro-ethnographic research for organization studies.

Rebecca Bednarek is Lecturer at Birkbeck College, University of London. Her research interests include the study of financial markets through practice theory, and strategizing in pluralistic and paradoxical organizational settings. She has investigated these issues through qualitative studies of the (re)insurance industry and the New Zealand science sector. With Paula Jarzabkowski and Paul Spee she has authored an ethnographic monograph *Making Markets for Acts of God* on trading practices in the global reinsurance industry. She has also published in *Human Relations*, *Industrial Relations Journal*, *Long Range Planning* (forthcoming), *Research in the Sociology of Organizations*, and *Strategic Organization*.

Eugenia Cacciatori is Senior Lecturer in Management at Cass Business School, City University London. Her research interests center on coordination in knowledge-intensive work and the organizational processes of innovation.

Amy C. Edmondson is the Novartis Professor of Leadership and Management at the Harvard Business School. She is the author of *Teaming: How Organizations Learn, Innovate and Compete in the Knowledge Economy* (Jossey-Bass, 2012), *Teaming to Innovate* (Jossey-Bass, 2013), and more than seventy articles on leadership, teams, innovation, and organizational learning. Number 15 on the 2013 Thinkers 50 list of the world's most influential management thinkers, Edmondson teaches on topics including leadership, teamwork, and innovation at HBS and around the world. Before her academic career, she was Director of Research at Pecos River

Learning Centers, where she worked with founder and CEO Larry Wilson to design change programs in large companies. In the early 1980s, she worked as Chief Engineer for architect/inventor Buckminster Fuller, and her book *A Fuller Explanation: The Synergetic Geometry of R. Buckminster Fuller* (Birkauser Boston, 1987) clarifies Fuller's mathematical contributions for a non-technical audience. Edmondson received her PhD in Organizational Behavior, AM in psychology, and AB in engineering and design, all from Harvard University.

Martha S. Feldman is the Johnson Chair for Civic Governance and Public Management and Professor of Social Ecology (Department of Planning, Policy and Design), Business, Political Science and Sociology at the University of California, Irvine. She has written four books and dozens of articles on the topics of organization theory, public management, and qualitative research methods. Her current research on organizational routines explores the role of performance and agency in creating, maintaining, and altering these fundamental organizational phenomena. She is a Senior Editor for *Organization Science* and also serves on the editorial boards of the *Academy of Management Journal*, *Academy of Management Discoveries*, *International Public Management Journal*, *Journal of Management Studies*, *Organization Studies*, *Public Administration Review*, and *Qualitative Research in Organizations and Management*. She received the *Administrative Science Quarterly*'s 2009 award for Scholarly Contribution, the 2011 Academy of Management Practice Scholarship Award, and in 2014, she received an honorary doctorate in economics from St. Gallen University Business School and was listed by Thompson Reuters as a highly cited author. In 2015, she received the Academy of Management Distinguished Scholar Award from the Organization and Management Theory Division.

Jennifer Howard-Grenville is the Diageo Professor in Management Studies at the Judge Business School, University of Cambridge. She studies processes of organizational and institutional change and has explored the role of routines, issue selling, and culture in enabling and inhibiting change. She is particularly interested in how people change their organizations in response to environmental and social demands. Her work has been published in *Academy of Management Journal*, *Organization Science*, *Organization & Environment*, *Law & Social Inquiry*, *California Management Review*, and several other journals.

Paula Jarzabkowski is Professor of Strategic Management at Cass Business School, City University London, and EU Marie Curie International Outgoing Fellow. Her research takes a practice theory approach to strategizing in pluralistic contexts, such as regulated firms, third sector organizations, and financial services, particularly insurance and reinsurance. She is experienced in qualitative methods, having used a range of research designs, including cross-sectional and longitudinal case studies, and drawing on multiple qualitative data sources including audio and video ethnography interviews, observation, and archival sources. Her research has appeared in a numerous leading journals including *Academy of Management Journal*,

Journal of Management Studies, Human Relations, Organization Science, and *Organization Studies.*

Eun Ju Jung is Assistant Professor in the Department of Information Systems and Operations Management at George Mason University, USA. She earned her PhD in Business Information Systems from Michigan State University and a BBA from Kyungpook National University, South Korea. She worked at the Korea Institute for Defense Analyses (KIDA) as a researcher. Her current research interests include crowdfunding and open innovation, online social networks and online collaboration, and the impact of online community in business innovation and healthcare performance.

Ann Langley is Professor of Strategic Management at HEC Montréal, Canada, and holder of the Canada Research Chair in Strategic Management in Pluralistic Settings. Her research focuses on strategic change, inter-professional collaboration, and the practice of strategy in complex organizations. She is particularly interested in process-oriented research and methodology and has published a number of papers on that topic. In 2013, she was co-guest editor with Clive Smallman, Haridimos Tsoukas, and Andrew Van de Ven of a Special Research Forum of Academy of Management Journal on Process Studies of Change in Organizations and Management. She is also coeditor of the journal *Strategic Organization.*

Philippe Lorino is Distinguished Professor of Management Control and Organization Theory at ESSEC Business School (Paris and Singapore) and an advisor to the French Nuclear Safety Authority. He graduated (Sciences) from Paris École Polytechnique and École des Mines and was awarded Paris University PhD in Management in 1993. He served as a senior civil servant in the French Government, in charge of public industrial policies. From 1987 to 1993, as a director in the finance department of an international computer company, he was in charge of designing new control systems. He draws from Pragmatist philosophy and semiotics (Peirce, Dewey) and dialogism theory (Bakhtin) to develop a view of organizing as an ongoing process of dialogical inquiry, aimed at understanding and transforming collective activity, for example in the management of safety in hazardous activities. He is particularly interested in the role of management tools as mediating signs in this ongoing exploration of activity. He has published books, chapters, and journal papers in French and English.

C. Robert Mesle is the author of *Process Relational Philosophy: An Introduction to Alfred North Whitehead* (Templeton Press, 2008) and *Process Theology: A Basic Introduction* (Chalice Press, 1993). As a board member of the Institute for the Postmodern Development of China he has been a keynote speaker at many conferences on applied process thought in China since 2007, and has taught introductions to process philosophy in universities in China and at the International Whitehead Conferences in Bangalore, India, and Pomona, CA. He serves on the editorial board of *Process Studies,* and the boards of the Center for Process Studies and the

International Process Network. He is Professor of Philosophy and Religion at Graceland University, where his wife, Barbara, is Professor of English.

Sue Newell is Professor of Information Systems and Management at Sussex University and Head of the Department of Business and Management. She has most recently worked at Bentley University in the USA and at Warwick University in the UK. She has a BSc and PhD from Cardiff University, UK. Sue's research focuses on understanding the relationships between innovation, knowledge, and organizational networking—primarily from an organizational theory perspective. She was one of the founding members of IKON. Her research emphasizes a critical, practice-based understanding of the social and material aspects of innovation, change, knowledge management, and inter-firm networked relations. Sue has published over 100 journal articles in the areas of information systems, organization studies, and management, as well as numerous books and book chapters.

Brian T. Pentland is Professor in the Department of Accounting and Information Systems at Michigan State University. His publications have appeared in *Academy of Management Review, Accounting, Organizations and Society, Administrative Science Quarterly, JAIS, Journal of Management Studies, Management Science, MIS Quarterly, Organization Science, Organization Studies*, and on YouTube and elsewhere. He received his PhD in Management from the Massachusetts Institute of Technology in 1991 and an SB in Mechanical Engineering from the Massachusetts Institute of Technology in 1981.

Claus Rerup is Professor of Management at the Frankfurt School of Finance and Management, Germany. His research focuses on organizational sense-making, routine dynamics, and organizational learning. His publications have appeared in *Academy of Management Journal, Administrative Science Quarterly, Journal of Management, Journal of Management Studies*, and *Organization Science* among others. His PhD is in organization theory from the Aarhus School of Business, Denmark.

Maxine Robertson is Professor of Innovation and Organisation at Queen Mary University of London. She completed her PhD at Warwick University and is a founding member of IKON. Maxine's research interests focus primarily on three interrelated areas: networked innovation processes and practices, knowledge work, and professional identity. She has explored these domains in a variety of sectors and contexts, notably the biomedical sector (the development of radical therapeutics and the management of clinical trials); the IT sector (gender, expertise, and project working); the UK investment banking sector (careers and identity work); the UK legal sector (professional identity in mid-tier firms); and expert consulting firms (managing knowledge workers, autonomy and identity). She has published extensively across these areas.

Barbara Simpson is Professor of Leadership and Organizational Dynamics at Strathclyde Business School in Glasgow. Her PhD in Management, which was awarded by the University of Auckland in 1998, marked a sea change from her earlier career as a physics-trained geothermal scientist. Nevertheless, traces of this past experience remain evident in her work today, which brings the principles of action, flow, and movement to bear on the processes of creativity, innovation, leadership, and change. She has pursued these interests in diverse organizational settings including hi-tech businesses, professional firms, public utilities, arts companies, SMEs, and micro-enterprises involved in the manufacture of plastics and food products. Her current research is deeply informed by the philosophies of the American Pragmatists, especially George Herbert Mead's thinking on process and temporality. She has published her work in journals including *Organization Studies*, *Human Relations*, *Organization*, *R&D Management*, and *Journal of Management Inquiry*.

Paul Spee is Senior Lecturer at the University of Queensland Business School. Informed by social practice theory, his research interest revolves around the social dynamics of strategists and the way heuristics such as strategy tools are adopted and how they influence a firm's strategizing behavior. More recently, his work has expanded to investigate the practice of market making in the reinsurance industry, with a particular emphasis on the sociomateriality and calculative practices involved. His work has been published in leading journals on management and organization theory such as the *Academy of Management Journal*, *International Journal of Management Reviews*, *Organization Studies*, and *Strategic Organization*.

Jacky Swan is Professor of Organizational Behaviour at Warwick Business School, University of Warwick. She completed her PhD at Cardiff University. Her research interests are in linking innovation and networking to processes of creating and managing knowledge across different industry sectors and national contexts. She is Co-Director and co-founder of the IKON (Innovation, Knowledge and Organizational Networks) Research Centre at Warwick Business School (<http://www.warwick.ac.uk/fac/soc/wbs/research/ikon/>). She recently completed a major funded study of the use of evidence-based knowledge in healthcare commissioning management. She has published widely, including in *Organization Studies*, *Organization Science*, *Human Relations*, *Research Policy*, and is co-author of *Managing Knowledge Work* (Palgrave Macmillan, 2002).

Haridimos Tsoukas holds the Columbia Ship Management Chair in Strategic Management at the Department of Business and Public Administration, University of Cyprus, Cyprus, and is a Distinguished Research Environment Professor of Organization Studies at Warwick Business School, University of Warwick, UK. He is the co-founder and co-organizer of the International Symposium on Process Organization Studies (with Ann Langley). His research is informed by process philosophy, phenomenology, and neo-Aristotelian perspectives on reason and the social. His interests include: knowledge-based perspectives on organizations and management; organizational becoming; practical reason in management and policy studies; and meta-theoretical issues in organizational issues in organizational and management research.

Scott F. Turner is Associate Professor of Strategy at the Darla Moore School of Business at the University of South Carolina. His research focuses at the intersection of innovation, change, and organizational routines.

Tiona Zuzul is Assistant Professor of Strategy and Entrepreneurship at the London Business School. Her research explores the behavioral foundations of innovation and strategy in ambiguous settings, particularly new or nascent industries. Prior to joining academia, she worked as a consultant, advising firms and executives on expansion into new emerging markets. Zuzul received her doctorate in Strategy from Harvard Business School, MSc from the London School of Economics, and AB in Psychology from Harvard College.

Series Editorial Structure

Editorial Officer & Process Organization Studies Symposium Administrator

Sophia Tzagaraki, process.symposium@gmail.com

Endorsements

As we become more willing to convert reified entities into differentiated streams, the resulting images of process have become more viable and more elusive. Organization becomes organizing, being becomes becoming, construction becomes constructing. But as we see ourselves saying more words that end in "ing," what must we be thinking? That is not always clear. But now, under the experienced guidance of editors Langley and Tsoukas, there is an annual forum that moves us toward continuity and consolidation in process studies. This book series promises to be a vigorous, thoughtful forum dedicated to improvements in the substance and craft of process articulation.

(*Karl E. Weick*, Rensis Likert Distinguished University Professor of Organizational Behavior and Psychology, University of Michigan, USA)

In recent years, process and practice approaches to organizational topics have increased significantly. These approaches have made significant contributions to already existing fields of study, such as strategy, routines, knowledge management, and technology adoption, and these contributions have brought increasing attention to the approaches. Yet because the contributions are embedded in a variety of different fields of study, discussions about the similarities and differences in the application of the approaches, the research challenges they present, and the potential they pose for examining taken for granted ontological assumptions are limited. This series will provide an opportunity for bringing together contributions across different areas so that comparisons can be made and can also provide a space for discussions across fields. Professors Langley and Tsoukas are leaders in the development and use of process approaches. Under their editorship, the series will attract the work and attention of a wide array of distinguished organizational scholars.

(*Martha S. Feldman*, Johnson Chair for Civic Governance and Public Management, Professor of Social Ecology, Political Science, Business and Sociology, University of California, Irvine, USA)

Perspectives on Process Organization Studies will be the definitive annual volume of theories and research that advance our understanding of process questions dealing with how things emerge, grow, develop, and terminate over time. I applaud Professors Ann Langley and Haridimos Tsoukas for launching this important book series, and encourage colleagues to submit their process research and subscribe to *PROS*.

(*Andrew H. Van de Ven*, Vernon H. Heath Professor of Organizational Innovation and Change, University of Minnesota, USA)

The new series—*Perspectives on Process Organization Studies*—is a timely and valuable addition to the organization studies literature. The ascendancy of process perspectives in recent years has signified an important departure from traditional perspectives on organizations that have tended to privilege either self-standing events or discrete entities. In contrast, by emphasizing emergent activities and recursive relations, process perspectives take seriously the ongoing production of organizational realities. Such a performative view of organizations is particularly salient today, given the increasingly complex, dispersed, dynamic, entangled, and mobile nature of current organizational phenomena. Such phenomena are not easily accounted for in traditional approaches that are premised on stability, separation, and substances. Process perspectives on organizations thus promise to offer powerful and critical analytical insights into the unprecedented and novel experiences of contemporary organizing.

(*Wanda J. Orlikowski*, Alfred P. Sloan Professor of Information Technologies and Organization Studies, Massachusetts Institute of Technology, USA)

The recent decades witnessed conspicuous changes in organization theory: a slow but inexorable shift from the focus on structures to the focus on processes. The whirlwinds of the global economy made it clear that everything flows, even if change itself can become stable. While the interest in processes of organizing is not new, it is now acquiring a distinct presence, as more and more voices join in. A forum is therefore needed where such voices can speak to one another, and to the interested readers. The series *Perspectives on Process Organization Studies* will provide an excellent forum of that kind, both for those for whom a processual perspective is a matter of ontology, and those who see it as an epistemological choice.

(*Barbara Czarniawska*, Professor of Management Studies, School of Business, Economics and Law at the University of Gothenburg, Sweden)

We are living in an era of unprecedented change; one that is characterized by instability, volatility, and dramatic transformations. It is a world in which the seemingly improbable, the unanticipated, and the downright catastrophic appear to occur with alarming regularity. Such a world calls for a new kind of thinking: thinking that issues from the chaotic, fluxing immediacy of lived experiences; thinking that resists or overflows our familiar categories of thought; and thinking that accepts and embraces messiness, contradictions, and change as the *sine qua non* of the human condition. Thinking in these genuinely processual terms means that the starting point of our inquiry is not so much about the *being* of entities such as "organization," but their constant and perpetual *becoming*. I very much welcome this long overdue scholarly effort at exploring and examining the fundamental issue of *process* and its implications for organization studies. Hari Tsoukas and Ann Langley are to be congratulated on taking this very important initiative in bringing the process agenda into the systematic study of the phenomenon of organization. It promises to be a path-breaking contribution to our analysis of organization.

(*Robert Chia*, Professor of Management, University of Strathclyde, UK)

This new series fits the need for a good annual text devoted to process studies. Organization theory has long required a volume specifically devoted to process research that can address process ontology, methodology, research design, and analysis. While many authors collect longitudinal data, there are still insufficient methodological tools and techniques to deal with the nature of that data. Essentially, there is still a lack of frameworks and methods to deal with good processual data or to develop process-based insights. This series will provide an important resource for all branches of organization, management, and strategy theory. The editors of the series, Professors Ann Langley and Hari Tsoukas are excellent and very credible scholars within the process field. They will attract top authors to the series and ensure that each paper presents a high quality and insightful resource for process scholars. I expect that this series will become a staple in libraries, PhD studies, and journal editors' and process scholars' bookshelves.

(*Paula Jarzabkowski*, Professor of Strategic Management, Cass Business School, UK)

1

Introduction

Advancing a Process Perspective on Routines by Zooming Out and Zooming In

Jennifer Howard-Grenville, Claus Rerup,
Ann Langley, and Haridimos Tsoukas

1.1 Introduction

Routines are fundamental to accomplishing work (Cyert and March, 1963) and scholarship from different theoretical streams acknowledges how organizational routines, organizing, and change are connected (Parmigiani and Howard-Grenville, 2011). In this chapter, we summarize how organizational routines have been studied from a process perspective (Howard-Grenville and Rerup, Forthcoming). We start with Nelson and Winter who defined routines as "regular and predictable behavior patterns of firms" (Nelson and Winter, 1982: 14). Extending this definition, Feldman and Pentland (2003) defined routines as "repetitive, recognizable patterns of interdependent organizational actions carried out by multiple actors" (Feldman and Pentland, 2003: 95). This definition is consistent with a process perspective. First, it emphasizes how actions taken by specific individuals sustain or amend patterns over time. Second, it considers routines to be *emergent* (i.e. coming into being only through specific performances), and *generative* (i.e. capable of producing continuity or change in the actions they spawn) (Feldman, 2000; Rerup and Feldman, 2011) rather than as entities or "black boxes" that condense organizational knowledge (Salvato and Rerup, 2011). A process perspective does not see an organizational routine as "a fixed response to defined stimuli" (March and Simon, 1958: 142) but highlights how routines are "effortful accomplishments" (Pentland and Reuter, 1994: 488) that emerge, persist, or change.

For the Sixth International Symposium on Process Organization Studies, from which a number of the chapters in this volume were drawn, we sought to explore how process theorizing stands to advance understanding of organizational routines, and organizing in general, given routines' centrality to organizational action. While considerable work has been done to develop a processual understanding of routines (see Howard-Grenville and Rerup, Forthcoming, for a review), much still needs to be done to develop a richer account of how routines unfold over time, evolving or not as people perform them, and how routine dynamics contribute to other aspects of organizing. More generally, work also needs to better unpack processes by making action more visible in the boxes and arrows diagrams that we often use to depict process dynamics in conceptual models (Feldman, Forthcoming). In this chapter, we first elaborate on what constitutes a process perspective on organizational routines. Then we explore three themes that emerge from the various chapters, and provide an overview of each chapter as we discuss the themes. Finally, we close with a discussion of directions for future research that will further build a process perspective on routines.

1.2 A Process View of Routines

Over the past fifteen years a growing group of scholars have started to view routines as fundamentally performative accomplishments that are dynamic rather than stable (Howard-Grenville and Rerup, Forthcoming). This focus on process developed as organizational scholars started to move towards increasingly dynamic ways of understanding organizational phenomena (Tsoukas and Chia, 2002; Feldman and Orlikowski, 2011). Distinctively, "[p]rocess studies focus attention on how and why things emerge, develop, grow, or terminate over time... Process studies take time seriously, [and] illuminate the role of tensions and contradictions in driving patterns of change" (Langley et al., 2013: 1).

A process perspective explores how routines are performed by specific people in specific settings (Feldman, 2000). It shows how action, improvisation, and novelty are part of routine performances, and debunks the idea that routines are semi-automatic and mindless (Levinthal and Rerup, 2006; Salvato, 2009). As well, it departs from a view of routines as "black boxes" that transform inputs into organizational outputs and places attention on the actual actions and patterns that comprise routines (Feldman, this volume). Routines are both effortful accomplishments (Pentland and Reuter, 1994), in that it takes effort to perform, sustain, or change them, and emergent accomplishments, because sometimes the effort to perform routines leads to unforeseen change (Rerup and Feldman, 2011; Feldman, this volume). For instance, Feldman (2000) high-lighted how organizational routines can change continuously as a result of people's situated actions, and other work has demonstrated how it is by stretching and modifying routines that organizational work is accom-plished (Howard-Grenville, 2005; Canales, 2011; Turner and Rindova, 2012). Studying routines from a process perspective reduces "grain size" (Cohen et al., 1996) and introduces more moving parts because the routine is regarded as having interacting aspects, including performative and osten-sive aspects (Feldman and Pentland, 2003).

The performative and ostensive are created and re-created through action. Specific performances or actions accomplished by specific actors, at specific times, in specific places constitute the performative aspects whereas the ostensive aspects provide a "model of" and "model for" enacting the routine (see also Pentland and Feldman, 2007: 789). Similar to the idea that mind and body cannot be separated, the routine must comprise both aspects (Feldman, this volume). As such, the ostensive has meaning only when derived from performances; artifacts of a routine, like a standard operating procedure, or an espoused, envisioned routine can-not be regarded as a routine. Some scholars posit that a "single" ostensive can be shared across actors (Dionysiou and Tsoukas, 2013) while other scholars posit that the ostensive "may not be the same from person to person, from event to event or over time. Indeed, multiple and divergent understandings are probably more the norm than the exception" (Pentland and Feldman, 2005: 797). As noted by Howard-Grenville and Rerup (Forthcoming), divergence and struggle between different points of view can arise because (i) actions taken to enact an espoused ostensive are misaligned (Rerup and Feldman, 2011), (ii) the routine is performed differently from time to time (Feldman, 2004), (iii) the participants who enact the routine approach it from different perspectives (Zbaracki and Bergen, 2010; Turner and Rindova, 2012), or (iv) have differing goals and intentions for the routine (Howard-Grenville, 2005; D'Adderio, 2014). These observations lead to what some scholars refer to as "Cohen's Para-dox": how performative divergence is incorporated into the "same" rou-tine without the routine changing into a "new" routine. This paradox highlights how divergence in performances of a routine can lead to both

3

stability and change of the routine (Birnholtz et al., 2007; Cohen, 2007; Pentland et al., 2011).

For instance, when a group of people take action to accomplish the routine, they will note if the performances and the ostensive "model" of the routine align (Pentland and Feldman, 2007). If the "model" and the performances of the routine remain decoupled over multiple trials, people may not be able to enact the routine in a manner that is consistent with the ostensive. Eventually, if this misalignment persists, they will face two options. First, they can update or alter the ostensive to match their actions. Second, they can change their actions to match the ostensive. This matching may not be as conscious as it seems when described in this way. In fact, much of what happens in performing routines may be the result of people's dispositions, or their emotional, aesthetic, or bodily experiences, which we are only just beginning to conceptualize as they apply to routines (Feldman; Simpson and Lorino; Turner and Cacciatori; all this volume). Nonetheless, the encounter between performances and ostensives can lead to different patterns emerging over time, or the same pattern persisting despite variability in its performance. Process scholars interested in Cohen's Paradox (Cohen, 2007) are investigating how different mechanisms shape the interaction between performances and ostensives, and how these lead to stability or change in routines.

Feldman (this volume) and Simpson and Lorino (this volume) each advocate a stronger processual approach in which distinctions between the ostensive and the performative are reconceptualized, "de-emphasizing the entity-like features [of routines] and emphasizing more the continuity of becoming" (Feldman, this volume: 24). Indeed, when routines are regarded as responses to certain stimuli, there is a tendency to see them and their surrounds as disjointed parts, deflecting attention from the processes by which parts hang together (Simpson and Lorino, this volume). Feldman (this volume) asserts that a stronger processual account can be developed by attending to actions—the sayings and doings—that comprise routines. As well, she suggests a shift in the language we use to describe routines, from the performative and ostensive aspects to, respectively, performing and patterning. Such a shift draws attention to how patterning emerges from action, or, in other words, action is constitutive of routines.

In a recent review of the literature on organizational routines, Howard-Grenville and Rerup (Forthcoming) found that work to date from a process perspective can be grouped into several larger themes, including: Change in Routines, Artifacts, and Emergence of Routines.

Change in how routines are performed is the single most prevalent theme among scholars who use a process perspective. This observation is perhaps not surprising because a call for such work was made by Feldman (2000) and Feldman and Pentland (2003). As indicated earlier, change occurs for several reasons. First, routine participants might not perform the routine identically each and every time they enact it. Second, organizational routines are enacted by multiple people, and all routine participants might not agree on how to perform the routine. Differences in orientations, subjectivity, positions, and power create differences in actions and interactions. What is interesting is that variability in routine performances can lead to patterns of both stability and change in organizational routines.

Scholars have been keenly interested in the link between artifacts and organizational routines (Cacciatori, 2012). For instance, Pentland and Feldman (2008) noted that espousing and designing a routine by developing a set of artifacts (checklists, written procedures, or software encoded versions of these) reinforces the misunderstanding that routines are things, and that artifacts on their own can generate patterns of action. A key insight is that agency and artifacts are entangled and that each constrains and enables the dynamics of routines (D'Adderio, 2011, 2014).

Process scholars are also intrigued by how routines form and take shape because if routines cannot be accomplished by designing artifacts, where do they come from? Answers to this question are only emerging although we know that initial interactions between people play an important role (Dionysiou and Tsoukas, 2013; Miller et al., 2014), as do artifacts, technologies, and social settings more generally (Ribes and Bowker, 2009; Labatut et al., 2011; Bapuji et al., 2012). Calls for more research on "microfoundations" suggest that more work on how individuals influence the emergence of routines is needed (Felin et al., 2012; 2015: 4).

1.3 An Overview of the Chapters

While a process perspective has enabled scholars to open up the "black box" of routines (Parmigiani and Howard-Grenville, 2011; Salvato and Rerup, 2011) and explore their actions and patterns in fine-grained, dynamic ways, there is much more work to be done. Chapters in this volume make considerable further progress, in part by both "zooming out" and "zooming in" (Nicolini, 2009, 2012) on the black box of a single routine and thereby extending our processual understanding of routines. We see three main themes expressed across these chapters, and subsequently also consider additional themes that warrant further development.

1.3.1 Theme 1: Zooming Out to Understand Routines in Larger Contexts

One of the critiques of a process perspective on routines is that scholars peering deep into the black box may have an understandably myopic view of the organizational and other contexts that shape and are shaped by routine performances (Howard-Grenville and Rerup, Forthcoming). Indeed:

> Perhaps somewhat ironically, studies from a practice [process] perspective are so concerned with situated action—the specific actions of specific people in specific organizations—that they sometimes ignore fundamental organizational attributes that exist above the level of the routine but nonetheless affect its performance. (Parmigiani and Howard-Grenville, 2011: 443)

The chapters in this volume begin to correct for this, by attending closely to the situated performances of routines, as well as their embeddedness within organizations, institutions, industries, and professions. Whereas the concept of a routine's embeddedness was introduced "to capture the degree to which the use of a routine overlaps with the enactment of other organizational structures," such as cultures, hierarchies, and technologies (Howard-Grenville, 2005: 619), recent work develops a more processual account, asserting that "routines are not simply *embedded in* context, they are also *enacted through* context" (D'Adderio, 2014: 23). As well, contexts are not simply organizational, as single routines can span multiple organizations (Edmondson and Zuzul, this volume), professions (Jarzabkowski et al., this volume), and even industries (Swan et al., this volume). Indeed, performing certain routines, like the deal assessment routine (DAR) central to reinsurance underwriting, simultaneously performs a profession (Jarzabkowski et al., this volume). Further exploring the entanglement of routines in their contexts therefore contributes not just to a process perspective on routines, but also to a process perspective on organizing, linking the concerns of routines scholars to broader themes in the organization studies literature (see Salvato and Rerup, 2011).

Several of the chapters in the current volume illuminate ways of understanding routines as entangled with contexts. First, Pentland and Jung demonstrate the importance of attending to technological shifts that afford rapid, revolutionary change in routines. Technological changes, and changes in social practices afforded by new technologies, create opportunities for deliberate departure from existing routines, and for novel recombinations, suggesting that routines do not simply evolve through path-dependent mechanisms. Technology and social learning can enable the rapid diffusion of new routines, reminding us that contexts enable as much as they constrain routine change. Simpson and Lorino, drawing from Pragmatist philosophy, advance arguments for a more fundamentally processual theorization of routines, including, among other moves, the collapse of distinctions between micro and macro levels of analysis. In so doing, routine performances and context would no longer be regarded as separable. Simpson and Lorino assert that, if we take seriously that all actions are situated, routines "can never be adequately theorized as either purely individual or purely organizational endeavors" (Simpson and Lorino, this volume: 55). Such an approach would put process and flow at the center of attention, as scholars seek to understand how concrete situations give rise to options for action. Similarly, Feldman calls for routines as relational, that is, connected to and inseparable from "such phenomena as people, materiality, emotion, history, power, [and] time" (Feldman, this volume: 37).

Three other chapters empirically explore how specific routines are enacted within, and to varying degrees, constitutive of, organizations, professions, and industries. Edmondson and Zuzul explore how teaming routines were developed and enacted between multiple organizations engaged in a mega-project to develop a sustainability-focused community, including healthcare organizations, schools, and residential buildings. They find that leaders guided the emergence of routines that enabled learning and exploration across organizations, almost the antithesis of what we think of as "routine." These routines leveraged the multi-organizational context, characterized by diverse goals and limited prior collaborative experience, to guide the emergence of norms for exchange and experimentation. In a quite different setting, Swan, Robertson, and Newell find that routines can enable action in situations where industry norms place considerable constraints. They explore routines used by organizations in early stage drug development, where the industry is characterized by both extreme regulatory hurdles, which assume a linear development process, and significant commercial hurdles, where attracting financing and partnerships relies on the promise of swift, positive trajectories. In reality, drug development is shrouded with uncertainty, and organizations cope by enacting a series of "guesswork" routines, which bridge their day-to-day practices with the pressures experienced at the industry level. While such routines enable organizations to carry on, they trigger actions that appease stakeholders at the expense of advancing the science, signaling the pernicious effects of routines that are responsive to broader industry pressures. Finally, Jarzabkowski, Bednarek, and Spee advance the idea of professional routines, those spanning organizations and entangled with the enactment of professional practice. They show how the situated work of individual reinsurance underwriters, drawing on artifacts common to the profession, is connected to individual professional work and the collective work of the profession. In doing so, they demonstrate not only how a professional setting shapes routine performances, but equally importantly how professional knowledge is performed through specific routines.

These efforts to treat routines as entangled with their contexts, not only shaped by them but simultaneously enacting them, helps us zoom out of the black box of the inner workings of routines and better situate them in the flow of organizing. As well, it holds promise for expanding the conversation about routines to other concerns held by organizational scholars, including coordination and collaboration across boundaries, innovation in uncertain environments, technological change, and professional practice and jurisdiction, to name a few. This development is very promising, though care should be taken to continue to forge a processual account by putting situated action at the center and avoiding a tendency to artificially separate actions from contexts (Feldman; Simpson and Lorino, this volume). We like the metaphor of "zooming" (Nicolini, 2009, 2012) for this reason, as it suggests we can attend to entangled processes at continuous levels of zoom, rather than at discrete levels of analysis.

1.3.2 Theme 2: Zooming In to Reveal Actor Dispositions and Skill

The chapters in this volume also zoom *in* on routines and use this increased granularity to add insight into how people enact routines. The idea that people exercise agency in performing routines is central to Feldman and Pentland's (2003) paper and has become a major theme taken up in the routines literature from a process perspective (Howard-Grenville and Rerup, Forthcoming). Feldman and Pentland asserted that the capacity for routines to change endogenously was rooted in part in people's "ability to remember the past, imagine the future, and respond to present circumstances," and that, "while organizational routines are commonly portrayed as promoting cognitive efficiency, they also entail self-reflective and other-reflective behavior" (Feldman and Pentland, 2003: 95). In many ways, thinking of routines as enacted by self-reflective people was a challenge to the once-predominant view that routines were "dead" and comprised habitual action (Cohen, 2007; Winter, 2013). The chapters in this volume, by zooming in on people's dispositions, situated actions, and skills, reveal considerable additional nuance around how routines are shaped by the people who perform them.

First, Turner and Cacciatori review psychological and sociological literatures to reveal a richer conceptualization of habit than has been portrayed in much of the routines literature. Habitual action can include deliberation and mindfulness, as well as temporal orientations to the present and future, not just the past. Turner and Cacciatori offer a typology of four ways we might think of people acting habitually, depending on the degree of their deliberation when performing actions, and the variability of the surrounding conditions. Importantly, these perspectives on habit refine how we think about agency in the performance of routines; if habit is both deliberative and socially situated (as in Dewey's and Bourdieu's conceptualizations), then habit can be a source of variety or innovation in routines and offer new ways of theorizing about agency in routines. Similarly, Simpson and Lorino draw on the Pragmatist concepts of habit, inquiry, and conversational trans-action to explore how people's routine performances "may remain stable...be radically disruptive and creative, or...anything in between" (Simpson and Lorino, this volume: 65). Habit, they argue, is an acquired dispositional resource that is put to use through inquiry, which transforms the indeterminate into an emergent course of action. Habit and inquiry unfold within social and temporal realms (conversational transactions). As people act they draw on their socially, organizationally, and occupationally informed dispositions to address a series of "what next" questions. As a result, people with different roles or experiences may intervene very differently to fix a problem that arises in a routine.

A second set of insights in these chapters arises from zooming in and attending not to disposition or habit, but to situated interactions that reveal the exercise of power, or professional skill or judgment. In Aggerholm and Asmuß's chapter, we see how hierarchical power, relational power, and language used in micro-interactions—face-to-face conversations central to performance appraisals—shape the larger outcomes of the annual performance appraisal routine. Different forms of power, and language itself, are mobilized as resources by the people engaged in performance appraisal, and structural/hierarchical power need not trump the mobilization of other resources. Aggerholm and Asmuß's use of video-based micro-ethnography also sheds light on the kind of methods needed to continue to zoom in on routines to more deeply understand how people perform them (Salvato and Rerup, 2011: 480–1). Jarzabkowski, Bednarek, and Spee's chapter similarly draws on ethnographic engagement to attend to how reinsurance underwriters use artifacts (spreadsheets, in this case) in their performance of the deal assessment routine. As well, they show how experienced underwriters manipulate artifacts differently from their novice peers, suggesting that a degree of professional skill is brought to bear in situated routine performances.

Finally, Pentland and Jun's chapter offers another mechanism for exploring the fine-grained interactions underpinning routines, by using a narrative network approach to represent patterns of action (see also Pentland and Feldman, 2007). A narrative network is composed of fragments representing who does what (actions), often with what (artifact or technology). In other words, narrative fragments are subsets of actors/actions, that, when performed, connect with other narrative fragments to generate pathways, or specific routine performances. Typical pathways might be regarded as the ostensive aspect of routines, while an actual pathway is the performative aspect. Narrative network approaches have been used to model routines and explore their dynamics (Hayes et al., 2011; Goh et al., 2011).

1.3.3 Theme 3: Innovation, Creativity and Routines in Ambiguous Contexts

A final, and somewhat surprising, theme uniting many of the volume chapters is that of innovation through routines, or creativity and surprise in the use of routines (Joas, 1996). Given that the predominant perspective on routines has typically been that they are stable, predictable patterns of action (Howard-Grenville and Rerup, Forthcoming), the attention to how routines enable innovation and navigation of uncertain environments is an unusual twist. The chapters in this volume tackle issues of novelty by both zooming in to focus on individual actors, and zooming out to include larger contexts.

While earlier work has shown how novelty is introduced into routines through the unintended or intended actions of people performing them (Feldman, 2000; Howard-Grenville, 2005; Rerup and Feldman, 2011), the implicit model of change is an evolutionary one, in which variations to routine performances are taken up more broadly, leading to gradual change in how routines are enacted. Pentland and Jung offer a different way of thinking about routine change stemming from people's deliberate departures from typical patterns of action. This can result in bursts of rapid, revolutionary change in routines, for it relies on a logic of intentional recombination rather than variation and selection. As well, the chapters that reconceptualize habit and disposition (Turner and Cacciatori; Simpson and Lorino) emphasize how people infuse their routine performances with deliberation and inquiry, which enable skillful adaptation or even invention within a routine. In other words, novelty enters routine performances not simply through random variation or slippage, but through people's intentions and orientations based on their pasts and their social contexts. Unlike Pentland and Jung's model, such forms of agency do not necessarily lead to rapid, revolutionary change, but nonetheless offer a more nuanced way of understanding how routines are continuously emergent, subject to who performs them and how.

Zooming out, other chapters explore how routines can sustain novelty and innovation, or enable action in ambiguous contexts. Edmondson and Zuzul demonstrate how particular leader actions can shape effective teaming routines, where teaming spans multiple organizations attempting to collaborate on a large-scale, fundamentally novel built environment project. Teaming is characterized by "ad hoc coordination and collaboration among shifting participants, over unspecified periods of time" (Edmondson and Zuzul, this volume: 181) and a routine for teaming hence might be regarded as an oxymoron. Yet, Edmondson and Zuzul show how teaming routines emerged not through the espousal of routines that might serves as guides to action, but through the modeling of actions that "signaled the importance of flexibility, participation, and experimentation in the project" (Edmondson and Zuzul, this volume: 197). Modeling invited performances that eventually led to the emergence of ostensive aspects of the teaming routine, which supported ongoing learning and innovation. Swan, Robertson, and Newell consider how organizations engaged in drug development innovate within a restrictive regulatory and economic context. They find that a series of "guesswork" routines—hedging, compressing, and reprioritizing—enacted at the project level are pragmatic responses to the combination of scientific unknowability and regulatory and economic constraint that pervades this industry. As in Edmondson and Zuzul's chapter, these routines are inherently flexible and emergent from ad hoc performances. Yet, unlike the case of teaming routines, guesswork routines do not produce uniformly positive outcomes as they may actually hinder the innovation process through their acquiescence to industry and institutional pressures.

1.4 Reflections on Future Research

In addition to the three themes summarized here, we see three ways in which the chapters in this volume raise questions for further research. First, the move to zoom out holds promise for future work to consider how routines interact with each other, within an "ecology" of routines, as well as how they interact with organizational and other contexts. Second, the move to zoom in can be extended by scholars attending to additional dimensions of human experience in the performance of routines, which could include emotion, aesthetics, and power, alongside habit and disposition (see Salvato and Rerup, 2011: Figure 1). Finally, the zooming in and out metaphor itself might prove productive in helping to bridge the gap between historically distinct perspectives on the routines, the capabilities perspective, which regards them as whole entities that contribute to certain organizational outputs, and the practice perspective, which is in line with the processual accounts described here (Parmigiani and Howard-Grenville, 2011).

1.4.1 Zooming Out: Ecologies of Routines

While the chapters in this volume, and prior work, draw attention to how routines are embedded within and enacted through their contexts, the entanglement of routines with *other routines* is equally deserving of attention. For methodological and analytical traction, prior work has tended to deeply probe one routine at a time, whether it be a moving in routine (Feldman, 2000), a garbage collection routine (Turner and Rindova, 2012), a towel changing routine (Bapuji et al., 2012), a roadmapping routine (Howard-Grenville, 2005), or a lending routine (Canales, 2011). However, rarely would we expect moving in, lending, or even garbage collection routines to be performed in the absence of other organizational routines. Hence, a challenge for scholars is to attend, empirically and conceptually, to interactions between routines in an "ecology," that is, the idea that no routine is ever enacted in a vacuum of other routines. Routines exist within, are surrounded by, and entangled with other routines. Often routines are coupled or intertwined because actions, artifacts, or people in one routine are linked to those in other routines. The idea of an ecology of routines is different from the idea of embeddedness, which refers to how a single routine is embedded within other (enacted) structures, like hierarchies, cultures, and institutions (Howard-Grenville, 2005). One can imagine, for example, that routines within an ecology interact in patterned yet diverse ways, unfold at different temporal paces, and involve people and artifacts in different ways. In addition, scholars should investigate how routines in ecologies are either co-located at a particular level of analysis or stretch across various micro and macro level activities and actors (Salvato and

Rerup, 2011). So far routines scholars have focused on exploring process questions that help us to understand how routines are changed or sustained over time, and how this work is linked to other aspects of organizing. Taking an ecological view of routines would shed considerable new light on the interactions of routines with their contexts. As well, we urge further work that, like chapters in this volume (e.g. Jarzabkowski, Bednarek, and Spee), considers how the performance of routines is constitutive of other social structures (e.g. professions), rather than regarding routines as simply embedded in relatively independent and enduring contexts.

1.4.2 Zooming In: People and Routines

Work in this volume helpfully zooms in, deepening our understanding of the role of people in accomplishing routines by drawing attention to the many faces of habit, disposition, power, and skill. Future research can build on these insights and go further in considering how people shape routine performances. Past work perhaps overly emphasized the importance of cognition (deliberation) in performing routines, but building on the work of John Dewey calls have been made to also include emotions or "impulse" in research on routines (Cohen, 2007; Winter, 2013). As well as emotion, aesthetic (see Feldman, this volume) and embodied (Heaphy et al., Forthcoming) aspects of human experience and interaction deserve greater attention for how they influence people's performances of routines (Salvato and Rerup, 2011).

To link the specific actions taken by routine participants more holistically to their dispositions, skills, emotions, and power it is also necessary to update and elaborate our approach to studying organizational routines. For example, video micro-ethnography, as used by Aggerholm and Asmuß in this volume, is valuable for gaining access to very fine-grained interaction, in real time, and with the benefit of capturing facial expressions, gestures, bodily orientations, and manipulations of artifacts, in addition to conversation (LeBaron, 2005). However, this method is also very demanding analytically and can rightly shed most light at a very high degree of "zoom." Other promising approaches include using a narrative network approach (Pentland and Jun, this volume; Pentland and Feldman, 2007), which could even take advantage of the incredible flux of interaction patterns captured by "big data" to analyze multiple interactions; the limits of this method might be in capturing accurate proxies for actor disposition, power, or emotion, however. As a result, a favorite method of routines scholars who work from a process perspective, ethnography, will likely remain a workhorse to continue to study situated action and interaction, but the attention of ethnographers could be productively directed more fully to attending to dispositions, inquiry, and conversational trans-actions, as traces of the flow of routines (Simpson and Lorino, this volume). Last but not least, Feldman's emphasis in this volume on the interplay of patterning and performing (as opposed to ostensives and performances) provokes researchers to look for how patterning occurs, not as a simply cognitive abstraction of the ostensive, but as a narration of experienced patterns which, Feldman asserts "likely have a great deal to do with famil-iarity and attractiveness as well as with the utility of flexibility and stabil-ity" (Feldman, this volume: 40).

Zooming in to holistically appreciate the individual routine participants will potentially help generate new understanding of existing phenomena in the literature on routines. Take the role of artifacts as an example. Building on their earlier discussion (Feldman and Pentland, 2003), Pentland and Feldman (2005) made a call for the field to incorporate artifacts more carefully into the performative perspective. Ten years later, it is obvious that the field has heeded the call (e.g. D'Adderio, 2011, 2014; Cacciatori, 2012). The development in this domain will continue but to remain inter-esting the role of artifacts in routines needs to be coupled with other phenomena, as Jarzabkowski, Bednarek, and Spee do in their chapter that connects the use of an artifact to the enactment of the professional (as an individual) and the profession (as a collective). The zoom in to people (and artifacts) must therefore always be done with an awareness of the "bigger picture" outside the immediate confines of the lens.

1.4.3 Building Bridges from the Process Perspective

Finally, we see some promise to extend the metaphor of zooming out and zooming in and exploring how it might help us draw connections between two previously separate "camps" in the routines literature. Parmigiani and Howard-Grenville's (2011) review of the empirical work on routines revealed two distinct approaches: the capabilities perspective, which, grounded in economic theory, is concerned with "what" routines are and how they relate to firm performance, and the practice perspective, which, grounded in sociology and practice theory, is concerned with "how" rou-tines are performed and their dynamics. Because such different assump-tions and questions underpin each perspective, borrowing or integration between them should be done only with respect for these differences (Parmigiani and Howard-Grenville, 2011). However, each literature makes some surprisingly similar observations about how people matter to the performance of routines, and how contexts shape routines. Accordingly, there is scope for mindful and appropriately-bounded zooming—out or in—that can explore routines for both "what" they do and "how" they do it. Some chapters in this volume signal how this can be done. For example, Edmondson and Zuzul demonstrate how leaders' modeling of particular actions and methods of inquiry culminated in routines that facilitated the organizational outcomes of teaming and innovation in a novel, highly ambiguous context. As well, Turner and Cacciatori explicitly demonstrate how a more nuanced account of habit can inform work on routines from both a capabilities and practice perspective. Work in this vein might then help build bridges not walls, connecting work from the capabilities and practice perspectives at appropriate intersections.

1.5 Conclusion

Process theorizing offers many potential ways of enriching our understanding of organizational routines, and organizing in general, given routines' centrality to organizational action.

The chapters in this volume show the importance of tracing connections between various dimensions of routines at different levels of "zoom" across time and space because "[t]he separation of micro-organizational level work at the individual or group level from macro-organizational work at the organization ... level has left a need for an integrative theory of intra-organizational behavior" (Gavetti et al., 2012: 26). As this volume shows, process-oriented research on organizational routines richly and robustly contributes to building such theory and we hope will inspire further inquiry and insight.

References

Bapuji, H., Hora, M., and Saeed, A. M. (2012). "Intentions, Intermediaries, and Interaction: Examining the Emergence of Routines." *Journal of Management Studies*, 49/8: 1586–607.

Birnholtz, J. P., Cohen, M. D., and Hoch, S. V. (2007). "Organizational Character: On the Regeneration of Camp Poplar Grove." *Organization Science*, 18/2: 315–32.

Cacciatori, E. (2012). "Resolving Conflict in Problem-Solving: Systems of Artefacts in the Development of New Routines." *Journal of Management Studies*, 49/8: 1559–85.

Canales, R. (2011). "Rule Bending, Sociological Citizenship, and Organizational Contestation in Microfinance." *Regulation and Governance*, 5/1: 90–117.

Cohen, M. D. (2007). "Reading Dewey: Reflections on the Study of Routine." *Organization Studies*, 28/5: 773–86.

Cohen, M. D., Burkhart, R., Dosi, G., Egidi, M., Marengo, L., Warglien, M., and Winter, S. G. (1996). "Contemporary Issues in Research on Routines and other Recurring Action Patterns of Organizations." *Industrial and Corporate Change*, 5/3: 653–98.

Cyert, R. M. and March, J. G. (1963). *A Behavioral Theory of the Firm*. Englewood Cliffs, NJ: Prentice-Hall.

D'Adderio, L. (2011). "Artifacts at the Centre of Routines: Performing the Material Turn in Routines Theory." *Journal of Institutional Economics*, 7/02: 197–230.

D'Adderio, L. (2014). "The Replication Dilemma Unravelled: How Organizations Enact Multiple Goals in Routine Transfer." *Organization Science*, 25/5: 1325–50.

Dionysiou, D. D. and Tsoukas, H. (2013). "Understanding the (Re)Creation of Routines from Within: A Symbolic Interactionist Perspective." *Academy of Management Review*, 38/2: 181–205.

Feldman, M. S. (2000). "Organizational Routines as a Source of Continuous Change." *Organization Science*, 11/6: 611–29.

Feldman, M. S. (2004). "Resources in Emerging Structures and Processes of Change." *Organization Science*, 15/3: 295–309.

Feldman, M. S. (Forthcoming). Making Process Visible: Alternatives to Boxes and Arrows." In A. Langley and H. Tsoukas (eds.), *Sage Handbook of Process Organizational Studies*. Thousand Oaks, CA: Sage Publications.

Feldman, M. S. and Orlikowski, W. J. (2011). "Theorizing Practice and Practicing Theory." *Organization Science*, 22/5: 1240–53.

Feldman, M. S. and Pentland, B. T. (2003). "Reconceptualizing Organizational Routines as a Source of Flexibility and Change." *Administrative Science Quarterly*, 48/1: 94–118.

Felin, T., Foss, N. J., Heimeriks, K. H., and Madsen, T. L. (2012). "Microfoundations of Routines and Capabilities: Individuals, Processes and Structures." *Journal of Management Studies*, 49/8: 1351–74.

Felin, T., Foss, N. J., and Ployhart, R. E. (2015). "The Microfoundations Movement in Strategy and Organization Theory." *Academy of Management Annals*, 9/1: 575–632.

Gavetti, G., Greve, H. R., Levinthal, D. A., and Ocasio, W. (2012). "The Behavioral Theory of the Firm: Assessment and Prospects." *Academy of Management Annals*, 6/1: 1–40.

Goh, J. M., Gao, G., and Agarwal, R. (2011). "Evolving Work Routines: Adaptive Routinization of Information Technology in Healthcare." *Information Systems Research*, 22/3: 565–85.

Hayes, G. R., Lee, C. P., and Dourish, P. (2011). "Organizational Routines, Innovation, and Flexibility: The Application of Narrative Networks to Dynamic Workflow." *International Journal of Medical Informatics*, 80/8: 161–77.

Heaphy, E., Locke, K., and Booth, B. (Forthcoming). "Embodied Relational Competence: Attending the Body in the Boundary-Spanning Work of Patient Advocates." In K. Elsbach and B. Bechky (eds.), *Qualitative Organizational Research: Best Papers from the Davis Conference on Qualitative Research*, vol. 3. Charlotte, NC: Information Age Publishing.

Howard-Grenville, J. (2005). "The Persistence of Flexible Organizational Routines: The Role of Agency and Organizational Context." *Organization Science*, 16/6: 618–36.

Howard-Grenville, J. and Rerup, C. (Forthcoming). "A Process Perspective on Organizational Routines." In A. Langley and H. Tsoukas (eds.), *Sage Handbook of Process Organizational Studies*. Thousand Oaks, CA: Sage Publications.

Joas, H. (1996). *The Creativity of Action*. Chicago, IL: University of Chicago Press.

Labatut, J., Aggeri, F., and Girard, N. (2011). "Discipline and Change: How Technologies and Organizational Routines Interact in New Practice Creation." *Organization Studies*, 33/1: 39–69.

Langley, A., Smallman, C., Tsoukas, H., and Van de Ven, A. H. (2013). "Process Studies of Change in Organization and Management: Unveiling Temporality, Activity, and Flow." *Academy of Management Journal*, 56/1: 1–13.

LeBaron, C. D. (2005). "Considering the Social and Material Surround: Toward Microethnographic Understandings of Nonverbal Behavior." In V. Manusov (ed.), *The Sourcebook of Nonverbal Measures: Going Beyond Words*. Mahwah, NJ: Erlbaum, 493–506.

Levinthal, D. and Rerup, C. (2006). "Crossing an Apparent Chasm: Bridging Mindful and Less-Mindful Perspectives on Organizational Learning." *Organization Science*, 17/4: 502–13.

March, J. G. and Simon, H. (1958). *Organizations*. New York: Wiley.

Miller, K. D., Choi, S., and Pentland, B. T. (2014). "The Role of Transactive Memory in the Formation of Organizational Routines." *Strategic Organization*, 12/2: 109–33.

Nelson, P. R. and Winter, S. (1982). *An Evolutionary Theory of Economic Change*. Cambridge, MA: Harvard University Press.

Nicolini, D. (2009). "Zooming In and Out: Studying Practices by Switching Theoretical Lenses and Trailing Connections." *Organization Studies*, 30/12: 1391–418.

Nicolini, D. (2012). *Practice Theory, Work, and Organization: An Introduction*. Oxford: Oxford University Press.

Parmigiani, A. and Howard-Grenville, J. (2011). "Routines Revisited: Exploring the Capabilities and Practice Perspectives." *Academy of Management Annals*, 5/1: 413–53.

Pentland, B. T. and Feldman, M. S. (2005). "Organizational Routines as a Unit of Analysis." *Industrial and Corporate Change*, 14/5: 793–815.

Pentland, B. T. and Feldman, M. S. (2007). "Narrative Networks: Patterns of Technology and Organization." *Organization Science*, 18/5: 781–95.

Pentland, B. T. and Feldman, M. S. (2008). "Designing Routines: On the Folly of Designing Artifacts, while Hoping for Patterns of Action." *Information and Organization*, 18/4: 235–50.

Pentland, B. T., Hærem, T., and Hillison, D. (2011). "The (N)Ever-Changing World: Stability and Change in Organizational Routines." *Organization Science*, 22/6: 1369–83.

Pentland, B. T. and Reuter, H. H. (1994). "Organizational Routines as Grammars of Action." *Administrative Science Quarterly*, 39/3: 484–510.

Rerup, C. and Feldman, M. S. (2011). "Routines as a Source of Change in Organizational Schemata: The Role of Trial-and-Error Learning." *Academy of Management Journal*, 54/3: 577–610.

Ribes, D. and Bowker, G. C. (2009). "Between Meaning and Machine: Learning to Represent the Knowledge of Communities." *Information and Organization*, 19/4: 199–217.

Salvato, C. (2009). "Capabilities Unveiled: The Role of Ordinary Activities in the Evolution of Product Development Processes." *Organization Science*, 20/2: 384–409.

Salvato, C. and Rerup, C. (2011). "Beyond Collective Entities: Multilevel Research on Organizational Routines and Capabilities." *Journal of Management*, 37/2: 468–90.

Tsoukas, H. and Chia, R. (2002). "On Organizational Becoming: Rethinking Organizational Change." *Organization Science*, 13/5: 567–82.

Turner, S. F. and Rindova, V. (2012). "A Balancing Act: How Organizations Pursue Consistency in Routine Functioning in the Face of Ongoing Change." *Organization Science*, 23/1: 24–46.

Winter, S. G. (2013). "Habit, Deliberation, and Action: Strengthening the Microfoundations of Routines and Capabilities." *Academy of Management Perspectives*, 27/2: 120–37.

Zbaracki, M. J. and Bergen, M. (2010). "When Truces Collapse: A Longitudinal Study of Price-Adjustment Routines." *Organization Science*, 21/5: 955–72.

Part I
Theme Specific Chapters

Section A
Theorizing Routines from a Process Perspective

2

Routines as Process

Past, Present, and Future

Martha S. Feldman

Abstract: This chapter traces how scholarship over time has taken into consideration the process-oriented nature of routines. The tracing includes the behavioral theory of the firm, evolutionary economics, and routine dynamics. Elaborating and building on the routine dynamics perspective, the chapter suggests that further process orientation is possible through a deeper understanding of action as doings and sayings that display a spectrum of intentionality, control over the body, and social autonomy. Actions have three features that are particularly useful for a process orientation to routines: they are constitutive; they transcend dualisms; and they are relational. The theoretical, rhetorical, and methodological changes entailed in moving from one kind of process orientation to another are discussed.

2.1 Introduction

It has become increasingly common in organization theory to focus on process (Czarniawska, 2008; Hernes, 2008; Chia and Holt, 2009; Langley et al., 2013). The turn may have been most clearly signaled when Karl Weick added a gerund to the classic title—*The Social Psychology of Organization*—and created his own classic, *The Social Psychology of Organizing* (Weick, 1979). As gerunds proliferated, organizational scholars have reached into the philosophies of Dreyfus, Heidegger, Schatzki, Whitehead, and Wittgenstein among others and the social theories of Bourdieu, Foucault, Giddens, Latour, and Vygotsky among others.

This turn entails considerable rhetorical, methodological, and theoretical complications given the dominance of entities in our language, in our research methods, and in many of our theoretical assumptions (Czarniawska, 2008; Mesle, 2008). These difficulties raise two issues. One, why is the effort worth making? What is to be gained? Two, how can the move to process theorizing be made? How does one do process theorizing?

In this chapter, I explore these questions briefly as they relate to the study of organizational routines. Theorizing about routines has moved in recent years from focusing on the routine as an entity that constitutes organization to now including a focus on the parts that constitute routines (Salvato and Rerup, 2011; Parmigiani and Howard-Grenville, 2011). I suggest that the field is now positioned to explore more deeply the processual ontology of routines, de-emphasizing the entity-like features and emphasizing more the continuity of becoming.

2.1.1 A Brief History

Organizational routines are "repetitive, recognizable patterns of interdependent actions, carried out by multiple actors" (Feldman and Pentland, 2003: 95). Common examples of routines include hiring routines, budgeting routines, and routines for providing services, producing products, and developing new products. Organizational routines are enacted in order to do something in and for the organization, often to accomplish some task.

Routines are, by their nature, processual. Cyert and March (1963) likened routines to computer programs and depicted them through flow charts. In *A Behavioral Theory of the Firm*, Cyert and March (1963) rejected the notion that organizational outcomes (e.g. the establishment of things like prices) are established by unseen forces (e.g. markets or other forms of rationality or functionality) and instead emphasized the role that people (or at least behavior) play in transforming both internal and external complexity into organizational outcomes (Zbaracki and Bergen, 2015). Standard operating procedures or routines were a central form of behavior in this theory.

The next major development in studying these organizational processes occurred when routines played a central role in Nelson and Winter's (1982) argument against the "as if" assumption of economics, asserting that it is not enough for us to compare organizational inputs and outputs and assume that organizations act rationally and maximize utility. They argued that we need to understand the organizational mechanisms that underlie this process and identified routines as a, if not the, key mechanism. They proposed an evolutionary theory of economics and likened routines to organizational DNA. Routines, from this perspective, are the skills of organizations (Nelson and Winter, 1982: 72ff.). This evolutionary economics perspective on routines has provided the building blocks of research on dynamic capabilities (Zollo and Winter, 2002: 340).

The work of Nelson and Winter brought forward the importance of routines as organizational processes differently than did earlier work on routines by Cyert and March (1963), which focused more on the effects such processes have within organizations. Consistent with their economics orientation, Nelson and Winter focused on the economy of the firm and the role of routines as processes within that economy. While later work differentiated between operational and administrative routines (Zollo and Winter, 2002), routines in the evolutionary economics view are crucially important but relatively undifferentiated arrows connecting organizational inputs with organizational outputs within the economy of the firm. Though integrally related to organizational processes (thus the analogy to arrows), routines in this way of thinking are essentially entities or black boxes (Parmigiani and Howard-Grenville, 2011; Salvato and Rerup, 2011; Howard-Grenville and Rerup, Forthcoming). While the work of Cohen and his co-authors (Cohen and Bacdayan, 1994; Cohen et al., 1996) raised questions about the entity-like nature of routines, the theorizing left the black box intact.

Further elaboration of the processual nature of organizational routines was pushed forward in the late 1990s and early 2000s with the adoption of a different set of methodological and theoretical tools for studying routines. Working separately and then together, Feldman and Pentland studied routines ethnographically and analyzed their data using concepts from phenomenology, ethnomethodology, and practice theory (Pentland and Rueter, 1994; Feldman, 2000; Feldman and Pentland, 2003). While the definition of routine used in their 2003 paper was fully consistent with all previous work on routines, their approach differed from previous theorizing by taking as a central question the nature of the relation between actions and patterns. They proposed a new focus on the internal (or endogenous) process of routines, theorized as the mutual constitution of performative and ostensive aspects of routines. The identification of the ostensive aspect as constitutive of and constituted through actions showed that enacted patterns may be more or less consistent with either written or imagined patterns. This focus oriented attention to the potential for flexibility in routines and the role of routines in the production of organizational stability and change. Research following this re-orientation has focused on internal dynamics of routines and has come to be known as routine dynamics. Routine dynamics refers to research that orients to the internal dynamics of routines and takes as focal the actions of human and non-human agents and the patterns created through those actions. Though developed from a different theoretical standpoint, Cohen's rhetorical turn of "live routines" captures the essence of this processual turn in the study of routines (Cohen, 2007).

2.1.2 Routine Dynamics

Routine dynamics emerged to explain observations of stability and change in routines that could not be explained by exogenous forces (e.g. management demand, technology change, etc.). Scholars noted, for instance, that as people enacted routines they generated new patterns of action even when there was no apparent exogenous force that caused these changes (Pentland and Rueter, 1994; Feldman, 2000; Pentland et al., 2011). Scholars also observed that considerable exogenous efforts were resisted and that people enacting routines often exhibited considerable flexibility in the actions they took to maintain patterns of action (Feldman, 2000, 2003; Howard-Grenville, 2005; Pentland and Feldman, 2008; Salvato, 2009). Indeed, the relation of stability and change in routine is so central to routines that some have referred to it as the "paradox of the (n)ever changing world" (Birnholtz et al., 2007; Cohen, 2007; Pentland et al., 2011). The process orientation of routine dynamics has helped us address these issues by refocusing on enactment rather than representation, on process and potentiality rather than likelihood, and on relationality rather than correlation.

The move to routine dynamics marks a shift in theoretical focus. While earlier theories of routines were based in theories with a correlational orientation, routine dynamics is based in theories with a relational orientation. Note that relationality in this context is not an orientation to people and their relationships but an orientation to the "dynamic unfolding" processes through which "the very terms or units involved in a transaction take on meaning, significance and identity" (Emirbayer, 1997: 287). Relationality proposes that process is ontologically primary and entities emerge from process. Theories of practice are the principal source of relational theorizing used in routine dynamics (Feldman and Orlikowski, 2011; Parmigiani and Howard-Grenville, 2011). By taking a relational approach to routines, routine dynamics has expanded the questions being asked about routines and fundamentally altered some of the assumptions about routines.

The development of routine dynamics entailed not only a theoretical shift, but also changes in methodology and rhetoric. The move to relational theorizing was enabled in part by the shift to ethnographic methods of studying routines. Ethnographies altered the grain size (Cohen et al., 1996) or granularity of analysis and moved the unit of investigation from the firm and the routines that constitute them to the routines and the actions that constitute them (Pentland and Rueter, 1994; Feldman, 2000; Howard-Grenville, 2005; D'Adderio 2008, 2014; Salvato, 2009; Zbaracki and Bergen, 2010; Rerup and Feldman, 2011; Turner and Rindova, 2012). Workflow data have also been used to explore the relationship between observable actions and patterns of action (Pentland et al., 2010, 2011) and agent-based modeling has been used to simulate the effects of actions over time (Pentland et al., 2011).

Rhetorically, routine dynamics introduced the performative and ostensive aspects of routines. Though sometimes mistaken as separate entities (see Simpson and Lorino, this volume), the term "aspects" indicates the connectivity of performance and pattern in constituting what we see as a routine. The introduction of the term "ostensive" drew attention to the relationality of performances and patterns and the constitutive nature of action in patterns. Similar to Wittgenstein's use of the term (2001), ostensive implies that patterns are constituted of specific instances that can be pointed to. This is different from an underlying generative layer such as a disposition or a genotype that is posited as having an existence independent of the phenotype or actions (Pentland et al., 2010). As Latour has suggested, the problem with ostensive definitions is that they become imbued with independence and mistaken as a cause—people mistake "what is glued for the glue" (Latour, 1986: 276). Incorporating the ostensive aspect as part of a routine and relationally interconnected with performance allows routine dynamics to acknowledge abstract patterns without giving them priority over the actions that are integral to them (Feldman, Forthcoming a).

D'Adderio (2011) portrayed the evolution in our current theorizing of routine dynamics through a series of boxes and arrows diagrams. These diagrams show that the early conceptualization focused on the performative and ostensive aspects with artifacts gradually making their way to become a more central part of the theorizing. Though the empirical work in routine dynamics has always acknowledged the role of various kinds of things in routines (e.g. Pentland and Rueter, 1994; Feldman, 2000, 2003; Howard-Grenville, 2005), the early theorizing of routine dynamics separated artifacts from the performative and ostensive aspects in particular to make the point that written rules and standard operating procedures are not to be confused with either the ostensive or performative aspects though such artifacts (as well as many other artifacts) have important interactions with both. As research has continued and scholars have come to understand that in particular the ostensive aspect is different from written rules and standard operating procedures, artifacts have been more fully incorporated into the relationship between performative and ostensive aspects (D'Adderio, 2008; Bapuji et al., 2012; Cacciatori, 2012; Turner and Rindova, 2012).

2.1.3 Process Theorizing and Routines

Theories of routines, thus, represent several points on a continuum of process theorizing. One way to talk about the ends of this continuum is as weak or strong process theory (Chia and Langley, 2005; Van de Ven and Poole, 2005, both cited in Hernes, 2008). The distinction between weak and strong is not a valuation of the importance of the theory or the significance of its contribution but of the ontological role of process and entity. "Whereas, according to a weak view, processes form part of the world under consideration, according to a strong view the world *is* process" (Hernes, 2008: 23). Another way of describing this distinction is that process theories "can be viewed from different ontologies of the social world: one a world made of things in which processes represent change in things (grounded in a substantive metaphysics) and the other a world of processes, in which things are reifications of processes (Tsoukas and Chia, 2002) (grounded in process metaphysics)" (Langley et al., 2013: 4).

Through the theoretical, methodological, and rhetorical moves used in routine dynamics, our understanding of routines has occupied new territory on the continuum of process theorizing. Occupying this new territory has been productive in providing new questions about routines and new ways of exploring these questions. Understanding the role of acting and enacting has been critical to the development of routine dynamics and the emergence of these new questions. Would moving further along the continuum of process theorizing have a similar effect? What might moving further look like? What kind of theory, method, and rhetoric will be required as we explore further the process ontology of routines?

One way forward entails exploring action and its creative potential more fully. While action has been central to developing routine dynamics, this concept has potential we have not fully tapped. Exploring more deeply the constitutive and creative nature of action holds potential for further developing the processual nature of routines. In the following section, I explore the concept of action with an eye to the role it has played and the untapped potential it has for routine dynamics and the processual orientation to routines.

2.2 Theorizing Action in Routines

> We say, "The wind is blowing", as if the wind were separate from its blowing, as if a wind could exist which did not blow.

This quote from Norbert Elias (1978: 111–12, cited in Emirbayer, 1997: 283) captures an important difficulty in theorizing the dynamic nature of routines. In everyday language as well as in much organization theory, routines are discussed as if they were things that can be stored somewhere and brought out for use when needed. But like the wind—a routine doesn't exist without being enacted. We can see the effects of a routine, we can remember enacting a routine, we can write down what we did or what we would like to have someone do, but none of these constitute a routine without action.

Unlike the wind, however, where we can only see the effects—we can only see the flag waving in the breeze but we cannot see the high and low pressure that creates the wind—there are two things about routines that can be readily observed: (1) rules that are written or otherwise articulated and other materialities and (2) action. Standard operating procedures (SOPs), or organizational if-then statements, for example, are a particular instantiation that have at times been used as proxies for routines (Cyert and March, 1963; Becker, 2004; Miner et al., 2008). SOPs, however, are representations of routines or sometimes aspirational or espoused routines. Using them as a proxy for routines is much like taking a dictionary or a style guide as a proxy for language. For some questions such proxies work well. Substituting the representation for the routine, however, certainly emphasizes the static nature of routines and diminishes the ability to observe dynamism.

Action is another observable part of routines and forms the basis for the processual orientation of routine dynamics. A focus on actions moves us from explaining routines as based on invisible forces to exploring the "specific actions by specific people at specific times and places that bring the routine to life" (Feldman and Pentland, 2003: 94). The action or traces of the action may be subtle and analyzing them may take a great deal of subtlety. Indeed, action may be recognized in the breaches and in the gaps (Garfinkel, 1967; Feldman, 1995; Silverman, 2007) or in the material traces (Latour, 2005; Orlikowski and Scott, 2008; D'Adderio, 2014). As Latour has said, the evidence of the action "might be indirect, exacting, complicated, but you need it. Invisible things are invisible. Period" (Latour, 2005: 150).

Focusing on action and particular ways of understanding action have allowed us to enhance the processual orientation of our theorizing about organizational routines and have unlocked a large number of new questions. But it is not just their observability that makes actions important to understanding routines. Actions have three features that are particularly useful in a process orientation to routines and routine dynamics. (1) Actions are constitutive. (2) Actions transcend dualisms. (3) Actions are relational. In the following sections I discuss each of these as they relate to developing our knowledge of the dynamic nature of routines and seeing the potential for developing further our understanding of the processual nature of routines. I start, however, by exploring the nature of action.

2.2.1 What is Action?

Actions are simply *doings and sayings*. Schatzki (2012) refers to doings and sayings as constitutive of practices. He also notes that these doings and sayings take place in time and space. This is consistent with the performative aspect of routines—actions taken in specific times and specific places. Actions are generally taken by people, but this does not preclude materiality. As scholars of sociomateriality have argued, materiality and acting are mutually constituted and, thus, inseparable in practice (Orlikowski and Scott, 2008; D'Adderio, 2014) or at the very least entangled and imbricated (Leonardi and Barley, 2008; Leonardi, 2011). Moreover, in an increasingly automated world some things (e.g. computers and the algorithms they run) increasingly take action (Dourish, 2013; Gillespie, 2013).

While the term "action" has long been included in the ways scholars have written about routines, the term has many meanings. For instance, with respect to organizational routines, action has often been theorized as organizational outcome as when it is conceptualized as skill (Nelson and Winter, 1982) or as individual regularity as when it is conceptualized as habit (cf. Turner and Cacciatori, this volume). Moreover, action is often assumed to be synonymous with rationality or rational action, which entails three limiting assumptions: means–end intentionality, control over the body, and social autonomy (Joas, 1996: 147). In the following, I briefly explore these three assumptions, discussing how they limit the concept of action and how they affect the study of routines.

Means–end intentionality (the first assumption) entails a sense of destination or goal but also obliviousness to the many ways that our actions are conditioned by history and by relations of power and the often unintended ways that our actions contribute to what comes next. To be clear, people do often take action in order to accomplish some goal. But goal orientation is just one part of understanding action. Unintended consequences have been a staple of social science since Merton's work (1936) and practice theorists suggest that action never accomplishes only what we intend but also constitutes it in multiple ways (Giddens, 1984; Bourdieu, 1990; Sewell, 1992; Gherardi, 2006). So, for example, we may intend to engage in a hiring routine but we may not intend the many ways in which our actions produce and reproduce the organization and associated institutions.

Research has shown that a hiring routine (Feldman, 2000; Rerup and Feldman, 2011) or a pricing routine (Zbaracki and Bergen, 2010) or a garbage collection routine (Turner and Rindova, 2012) or a roadmapping routine (Howard-Grenville, 2005) is often enacted with intentions to accomplish hiring, pricing, garbage collecting, and roadmapping and even to accomplish them in certain ways. When these aspirations are thwarted, people notice. But it is also important to remember that in the midst of accomplishing these tasks, there is much else that is accomplished that is unintended and often unnoticed.

Beyond recognizing that there is much that is unintended, it is also important to acknowledge that there are many ways in which what is intended is conditioned by what has happened before and what might happen next (Emirbayer, 1997). Action is always related to the flow of history and embedded power structures (Gherardi, 2006; Chia and Holt, 2009) and also to what has become thinkable and unthinkable (Bourdieu, 1984, 1990), familiar or unfamiliar, aesthetic or repugnant (Johnson, 2007). Scholars of routines have long noted that routines may preserve parts of old patterns as when British artillery crews noted that a three-second delay before firing was a remnant from times when someone had to make sure that the horses were secured before firing (Cohen and Bacdayan, 1994). The anticipation-guiding (Shotter, 2008) quality of the future, however, has been less recognized (Simpson and Lorino, this volume).

The second assumption is control over the body. This assumption entails a split between mind and body and suggests that mind is primary. Mind is what has control over body. This assumption also rules out emotion, particularly strong or "overwhelming" emotion (Joas, 1996: 170). The mind–body split is pervasive in the social sciences and in organization theory. Organization theory reflects the mind–body split by implicitly or explicitly portraying management as the mind of the organization and workers as the body (Taylor, 1911; cf. Michel, 2011). The broader assumption of the mind–body split has been questioned by recent research showing not only that action without mind is robotic behavior but also that our bodies are integral to how and what we think (Joas, 1996; Heaphy and Dutton, 2008; Johnson, 2012; Heaphy, Locke, and Booth, Forthcoming).

In work on routines the assumption of control over the body is reflected by a focus on routines espoused by management and concerns about why changes thought to be useful are not enacted or not enacted appropriately by people in the organization. Ironically, while theorized as mind controlling body at this macro level, theorizing about the enactment of routines themselves has at times been portrayed as mindless or automatic (Ashforth and Fried, 1988; cf. Cohen and Bacdayan, 1994). This portrayal has been refuted by work showing that routines are enacted with more or less mindfulness (Levinthal and Rerup, 2006).

The third assumption is social autonomy or the idea that action emerges from a self that is not connected to others. This assumption always brings to mind a letter to the editor I once read in which the letter-writer proudly proclaimed that he had never benefited from any government program. I wondered where he thought the roads he drove on and sidewalks he walked on came from. It is easy to imagine one is autonomous when roads and sidewalks (to say nothing of financial systems or clean air and water) have become taken for granted.

Joas finds this third assumption to be the least problematic as it has been thoroughly debunked in sociology (1996: 184). It is, nonetheless, still evident in work on routines whether in the form of managerial intention or in assertions that the practice perspective on routines separates the micro and macro as distinct levels of action (Simpson and Lorino, this volume). The assertion is that action that is consequential can somehow spring from an individual without any connection to the social. The practice perspective on routines has sometimes, for instance, been critiqued as emphasizing individual action over institutional structures. But, of course, action is consequential *because* of its relation to the social and social reality. Action in organizational routines is especially bound up in what others do.

Clarifying these assumptions about action is important to moving forward in a processual orientation to routines. Action, as doings and sayings, neither implies nor precludes intentionality, control over the body, or social autonomy. While the term action may to some denote rational individualism at the expense of both collectivity and history, this is not an essential trade-off (Joas, 1996). As Chia and Holt have pointed out, action may be purposive without necessarily being purposeful (2009: 109). Indeed, action—not as an imagined construct but as enacted in time and space—tends to display a spectrum of intentionality, control over the body, and social autonomy. Engaging this full spectrum provides a basis for a broader exploration of both what routines are and of their effects in organizations and in the world. The collective nature of action and the connections across time and space situate doings and sayings and are important to understanding their consequentiality in and through organizational routines.

Having clarified what I mean by action, we are in a better position to understand its potential and creativity. The following features of actions are important to developing our knowledge of the dynamic nature of routines and seeing the potential for developing further our understanding of the processual nature of routines.

2.2.2 Action as Constitutive

One reason to focus on action in routines is that actions constitute the world in which we live. Marx said, "Men make their own history." But Marx's quote continues: "Men make their own history, but they do not make it as they please; they do not make it under self-selected circumstances, but under circumstances existing already, given and transmitted from the past" ("18th Brumaire of Louis Bonaparte," 1852, quoted in Giddens, 1984: xxi). In other words, when we say that action is consequential or constitutive, we are not just talking about the intended outcomes of actions—indeed, that may be much or very little of what we are talking about.

When we say that action in routines is consequential, we are at one level talking about the mere fact that routines must be enacted. Without action, routines are empty formalizations or what might be referred to as espoused routines (Rerup and Feldman, 2011). At another level, action in routines is constitutive of other organizational structures. Since so much of what people do in organizations is done in the context of enacting routines, these actions are constitutive of how the organization operates and solves specific problems (Salvato, 2009; Rerup and Feldman, 2011; Jarzabkowski et al., 2012; D'Adderio, 2014). Action in routines constitutes professions (Jarzabkowski, Bednarek, and Spee, this volume), professional practice (Bruns, 2009), and types of organizations (Canales, 2011, 2014). Action in routines is constitutive of the structured relations between organizations and clients, customers, stakeholders, constituents (Turner and Rindova, 2012), and the relations and interactions of ecologies or systems of multiple routines (Howard-Grenville, 2005; Birnholtz, Cohen, and Hoch, 2007). Action in routines is even constitutive of the models, rules, and algorithms

33

that were once thought to determine and define routines (Zbaracki and Bergen, 2010).

2.2.3 Action Transcends Dualisms

Another reason to focus on action is the ability of action to transcend dualisms. A dualism is a dichotomy in which the two sides are seen as mutually exclusive. Two dualisms are particularly relevant to research on routines. One of these has been central to much of the work on routine dynamics while the other has potential that has not been as developed.

2.2.3.1 STABILITY AND CHANGE

The first dualism is stability and change. Rather than seeing stability and change as two alternative states of being, focusing on action in routines and specifically on how routines are enacted has allowed researchers to see that change is part of stability and stability is part of change. We have been supported in this work by others working on process approaches to understanding organizations (Tsoukas and Chia, 2002; Farjoun, 2010). The influential paper by Hari Tsoukas and Robert Chia has portrayed the image of the acrobat who achieves equilibrium by making many small adjustments and the relevance of this to routines:

> The apparent stability of the acrobat does not preclude change; on the contrary it presupposes it. Similarly, in the case of organizational routines, at a certain level of analysis—that of the routine itself—a synoptic account highlights the routine's self-contained, thing-like, and stable character. However, at another level of analysis—that of individual action and interaction through which routines are implemented—a process-oriented, or "performative" (Feldman 2000, p. 622) account, which takes human agency seriously, would show that routines are situated "ongoing accomplishments" (p. 613) and, as such, they keep changing, depending on the dynamic between ideals, action, and outcomes. (Tsoukas and Chia, 2002: 572)

In the study of routines we have referred to this process of adjustment as an effortful accomplishment (Pentland and Rueter, 1994). It often takes considerable effort to produce "the same routine." In the language of the performative-ostensive, it is flexibility of performance that allows us to maintain and sustain some stability in the ostensive patterns created (Howard-Grenville, 2005; Canales, 2011, 2014; Turner and Rindova, 2012; Turner and Fern, 2012).

Effortful accomplishments represent changes in the context of what appears to be overall stability but there is also relative stability in what appears to be change. These are emergent accomplishments (Feldman, 2000). While effortful accomplishments result from people taking different actions in order to produce the same or similar pattern, emergent accomplishments result from people taking the same or similar actions and producing new patterns.

An example of stability in change or emergent accomplishments appears in MacIntyre's book *After Virtue* in which he relates the emergence of changes in portrait painting between the late middle ages and the eighteenth century (2007: 189ff.). He suggests that the proliferation of portrait painting created a variety of experiments that produced new patterns of portrait painting. These changes illustrate what he refers to as internal goods based on the development of practices recognized by the practitioners and available to outsiders only if they submit to the expertise and values of insiders. Thus, portrait painting changed not because changes were demanded by outsiders but through the painting of many, many portraits and the changes in what excellence in portrait painting entailed for the practitioners of portrait painting.

While experimenting has long been understood to be a source of change in organizational routines, the reasons for experimentation were traditionally thought to be exogenous forces and the changes were to the entire routine. Seeing routines as generative systems that have dynamics has opened the potential for seeing the endogenous processes of change represented by both effortful and emergent accomplishment. Such endogenous processes include using the specific actions taken within or in relation to routines as a way of learning about and addressing problems in the routine and in the organization. Turner and Rindova (2012), for instance, have shown how the performance of routines enables the coordination of service delivery and customer satisfaction; D'Adderio (2014) has shown that action within routines can help people in even highly technical fields respond to unexpected challenges and opportunities; and Rerup and Feldman (2011) have shown that action in routines may literally be a trial in a trial and error process of organizational problem-solving.

2.2.3.2 MIND AND BODY

The second dualism is the mind–body dualism already discussed in relation to the assumption of control over the body. With respect to research on routines, we have made less progress on this dualism, and it has much potential. But we have made some progress, particularly in relation to the notion that thinking precedes doing or that there is a mind that thinks which then directs the body to act.

In Cyert and March's idea of sequential attention to goals, there is the implicit assumption that enacting a routine is separated from the work involved in addressing conflict. "Organizations resolve conflict among goals, in part, by attending to different goals at different times" (Cyert and March, 1963: 118). And when Nelson and Winter or later Winter talk of truces, there is clearly a sequentiality of first we have conflict which we resolve before we take action in routines (Nelson and Winter, 1982: 107–12; Winter in Cohen et al., 1996: 662).

> The "routine as truce" story is helpful here: once upon a time there was overt conflict, but in most cases it is largely over when the observer comes on the scene. What the observer sees is therefore the "product of cognitive functioning constrained by sensitivity to the sources of conflict." (Winter in Cohen et al., 1996: 662)

By contrast, routine dynamics suggests that the enactment of routines does not imply that conflicts have been resolved or that they have been put to one side, but that conflicts can be and are enacted through routines. The work by Zbaracki and Bergen on pricing routines, for instance, shows that routines are integral to the working out of truces, that conflict is not something separate from routines but is brought up through the enactment of routines and that working through conflict is part of that enactment (Zbaracki and Bergen, 2010). Similarly, recent work by D'Adderio on replicating shows that replicating is not a process of first getting a vision and then creating routines that enact the vision, but it is a process in which the ways we think about what we do are affected by the doing of it. Replication in this view involves the working out of differences through the doing of the work routines (D'Adderio, 2014).

The performative-ostensive distinction has sometimes been interpreted as if the performative aspect represents action or body and the ostensive aspect represents mind or cognition (see for example Simpson and Lorino, this volume). Given the prevalence of the Cartesian assumptions in scholarship, language, and everyday life, this is an easy mistake to make, but resisting the temptation to split mind and body has the potential to enrich our ways of thinking about routines. The ostensive aspect as it represents the process of patterning, for instance, has everything to do with aesthetics and familiarity or what we might refer to as embodied patterns. And emotion is an integral part of any performance and, thus, of patterning as well.

While routine dynamics has shown that performing routines involves orienting to patterns (conceptualized as ostensive aspects), the aesthetic qualities of routines have just begun to be explored. And while the concept of habit relates to familiarity and, through reference to Dewey's pragmatism, it has been expanded beyond automaticity (Cohen, 2007; Simpson and Lorino, this volume; Turner and Cacciatore, this volume), the work of familiarity and aesthetics, even in this expanded view of habit, has tended to disappear in the concepts of disposition and character.

2.2.3.3 ACTION IS RELATIONAL

By focusing on action, I am not trying to make an argument for action as the foundation (or micro-foundation) of routines. In fact, part of the attraction of action is its inherent relationality. A foundational approach seeks to identify the fundamental component out of which all else can be built. In relationality, by contrast, there are no fundamental elements. The focus is on relations within which things become. Relationality is not just about relationships among people but about the fluid positioning of such phenomena as people, materiality, emotion, history, power, and time. Dewey and Bentley referred to this as "trans-action," in which "systems of description and naming are employed to deal with aspects and phases of action, without final attribution to 'elements' or other presumptively detachable or independent 'entities,' 'essences,' or 'realities,' and without isolation of presumptively detachable 'relations' from such detachable 'elements'" (1949: 108, cited in Emirbayer, 1997: 286).[1] In relationality, "the very terms or units involved in a transaction derive their meaning, significance, and identity from the (changing) functional roles they play within that transaction. The latter, seen as a dynamic, unfolding process, becomes the primary unit of analysis rather than the constituent elements themselves" (Emirbayer, 1997: 287). The notion of a flat ontology (Schatzki, Forthcoming) is another way of conceptualizing relationality.

Actions are inherently relational because they are connectors. Actions make connections that create such things as identities (Czarniawska, 2008) and narratives (Pentland and Feldman, 2007). Action draws our attention to the arrows and insists that we examine not just the fact (the correlation) but also the how (the process) of connecting (Hernes, 2008).

A focus on action enhances our ability to see and explore the ways that such phenomena as people, materiality, emotion, history, power, and time are connected in enacting organizational routines. As a result, a focus on action allows us to bring in many other features of routines—

and that, it seems to me is the point: to be able to bring in the features of routines that are relevant to our empirical contexts and to the questions we are exploring.

2.3 Implications for Future Directions in Routine Dynamics

Action has clearly been at the center of routines research from the beginning. The focus on action became more intense with the development of routine dynamics. I am now suggesting further intensification would allow us to understand more about the potential of organizational routines. Doing so requires an understanding of the creative potential of action and an appreciation of how critical this creative potential is for organizational routines. While in some sense just an intensification of routine dynamics, deepening the commitment to action in organizational routines does entail some theoretical, rhetorical, and methodological changes.

Part of the work of this chapter has been to begin articulating the theoretical underpinnings of this shift. Making action even more focal in our study of routines would entail being aware of the assumptions described here that often limit the concept of action and incorporating more fully the constitutive nature of action, the ability of actions to transcend dualisms, and the relationality of action.

Making action more focal in our study of routines would also entail theorizing the performative and ostensive aspects as actions. The performative aspect of routines has already been largely understood as specific actions that people and sometimes machines take. Continued movement to engage the process ontology, therefore, seems most likely to affect the way we understand the ostensive aspect.

There are at least two ways that the ostensive aspect can be theorized as action. One of these is already present in routine dynamics. This is the idea that patterns are constituted through actions. Though some interpreters of routine dynamics continue to portray the ostensive aspect as cognition separated from action or as standard operating procedure (see Simpson and Lorino, this volume), a central point of routine dynamics is the inseparability or mutual constitution of acting and patterning. Mutual constitution of performing and patterning, indeed, is necessary for the conceptualization of routine as emergent and the claim that routine dynamics produce both stability and change.

The second way that the ostensive aspect can be theorized as action involves moving from talking about aspects to talking about patterning.

While the rhetorical move of focusing on performative and ostensive aspects of routines has shown that we can open up the entity of routines and explore the processes therein, the identification of aspects and particularly the ostensive aspect has, for some, simply shifted the entities to a different level (see Simpson and Lorino, this volume) leading them to portray the aspects as independent of action. What we need, instead, is to explore the specific actions (doings and sayings) involved in creating patterns or patterning. How do we create recognizability? The relevant question is "How do we do patterning?"

Current scholarship identifies possibilities. Czarniawska's work shows that interpreting is acting and refers specifically to narrating as a "constitutive action mode" (1997: 180). The work of Weick and many others on sense-making may provide another useful starting point (Weick, 1995; Christianson and Maitlis, 2014). Though sense-making is sometimes used primarily to denote cognition, actors do things, often in the form of discursive practices to "construct intersubjective meaning" (Christianson and Maitlis, 2014: 81). Sandberg and Tsoukas (2015) call for a revised perspective on sense-making, which would take action (and embodiment) more seriously. They assert: "sense is not an object to be passed on but a skillful activity to be engaged in" (2015: S24). Role-taking is one of those actions that has been explored specifically in the process of patterning (creating ostensive aspects) in organizational routines (Dionysiou and Tsoukas, 2013).

Another potential source of ideas for exploring processes of patterning is the idea of translation developed within the actor-network theory approach; scholars propose translating as a generalized term for actions "between mediators that may generate traceable associations" (Latour, 2005: 108). Translation is contrasted with diffusion by pointing out that projects (sometimes referred to as "tokens") do not move of their own accord, but must be taken up and engaged (Latour, 1986, 1996). In the taking up, they inevitably change even if the change is only slight. Czarniawska describes this translation as "a collective act of creation" (2008: 89). Translating as a *collective* act is particularly relevant to processes of patterning in organizational routines, which are not individual but collective acts.

Rhetorically, this shift would entail moving away from the identification of aspects of entities and an emphasis on the doing involved in the creating of both performative and ostensive aspects. Engaging instead the terms performing and patterning might suffice. The rhetorical difference here would be particularly noticeable in the shift from ostensive aspect to

Figure 2.1 Routine as performing and patterning

ostensive patterning or just patterning. This shift in language suggests even more profoundly that patterning is not something that goes on in the head but is also embodied. Patterns are constituted in and through action and emphasizing the constitutive nature of action in the process of patterning draws our attention to the work of recognizing and articulating or narrating these patterns. Such processes likely have a great deal to do with familiarity and attractiveness as well as with the utility of flexibility and stability.

A diagram of the routine as a whole might look something like Figure 2.1, a diagram of arrows without boxes. Understanding what is going on within this tangle of action would entail a methodological shift with an emphasis on tracing action rather than identifying entities.

Methods for doing such tracing already exist in the form of actor-network theory, action nets, and narrative networks. The first has been developed by many people but is most closely associated with Latour (2005). The second has been developed by Czarniawska (2004, 2008) and the third by Pentland and Feldman (2007).[2] Despite the difference in names, all three are described by their authors as methods. While each of these methods allow us to see routines from different perspectives, because of the radical nature of the tracing they allow us to see the constitutive work of action in routines as well as the situated relationality. Moreover, by tracing action these methods do not reify entities but show us stability as an ever-emergent process.

2.4 Conclusion

I promote action as a useful focus for the study of routines because of its observability, consequentiality, and ability to transcend dualisms, but not because I think it is the only thing we should study. Indeed, for me the attraction of action is the ability to draw in new concepts and to open up new questions. As with the move to theorizing routines as generative systems, the focus on action here is not intended to rule out or be an alternative to a focus on things but is instead consistent with a move toward materializ*ing* proposed in recent work on sociomateriality (Orlikowski and Scott, 2014).

Increasing the intensity of the process approach to studying routines has clearly opened the field of routines to a wide range of questions and to a wide range of scholars who were not formerly studying routines (Howard-Grenville and Rerup, Forthcoming). I hope that we will move forward in our theorizing and continue to develop a processual conceptualization of routines without succumbing to the pressures of theoretical, rhetorical, or methodological purity.

Notes

1. Simpson and Lorino, this volume, also discuss the concept of trans-action.
2. For further discussion of these methods, see Feldman (Forthcoming b).

References

Ashforth, B. E. and Fried, Y. (1988). "The Mindlessness of Organizational Behaviors." *Human Relations*, 41/4: 305–29.

Bapuji, H., Hora, M., and Saeed, A. M. (2012). "Intentions, Intermediaries, and Interaction: Examining the Emergence of Routines." *Journal of Management Studies*, 49/8: 1586–607.

Becker, M. C. (2004). "Organizational Routines: A Review of the Literature." *Industrial and Corporate Change*, 13/4: 643–78.

Birnholtz, J. P., Cohen, M. D., and Hoch, S. V. (2007). "Organizational Character: On the Regeneration of Camp Poplar Grove." *Organization Science*, 18/2: 315–32.

Bourdieu, P. (1984). *Distinction: A Social Critique of the Judgement of Taste*. Cambridge, MA: Harvard University Press.

Bourdieu, P. (1990). *The Logic of Practice*. Stanford, CA: Stanford University Press.

Bruns, H. C. (2009). "Leveraging Functionality in Safety Routines: Examining the Divergence of Rules and Performance." *Human Relations*, 62/9: 1399–426.

Cacciatori, E. (2012). "Resolving Conflict in Problem-Solving: Systems of Artefacts in the Development of New Routines." *Journal of Management Studies*, 49/8: 1559–85.

Canales, R. (2011). "Rule Bending, Sociological Citizenship, and Organizational Contestation in Microfinance." *Regulation & Governance*, 5/1: 90–117.

Canales, Rodrigo (2014). "Weaving Straw into Gold: Managing Organizational Tensions between Standardization and Flexibility in Microfinance." *Organization Science*, 25/1: 1–28.

Chia, R. and Holt, R. (2009). *Strategy without Design*. Cambridge: Cambridge University Press.

Chia, R. and Langley, A. (2005). Call for papers to the First Organizational Studies Summer Workshop on Theorizing Process in Organizational Research, June 12–13, 2005, Santorini, Greece.

Cohen, M. D. (2007). "Reading Dewey: Reflections on the Study of Routine." *Organization Studies*, 28/5: 773–86.

Cohen, M. D. and Bacdayan, P. (1994). "Organizational Routines are Stored as Procedural Memory: Evidence from a Laboratory Experiment." *Organization Science*, 5/4: 554–68.

Cohen, M. D., Burkhart, R., Dosi, G., Egidi, M., Marengo, L., Warglien, M., and Winter, S. (1996). "Routines and other Recurring Action Patterns of Organizations: Contemporary Research Issues." *Industrial and Corporate Change*, 5/3: 653–98.

Cyert, R. M. and March, J. G. (1963). *A Behavioral Theory of the Firm*. Oxford: Basil Blackwell.

Czarniawska, B. (1997). *Narrating the Organization: Dramas of Institutional Identity*. Chicago, IL: Chicago University Press.

Czarniawska, B. (2004). "On Time, Space and action nets." *Organization Studies*, 11/6: 773–91.

Czarniawska, B. (2008). *A Theory of Organizing*. Cheltenham: Edward Elgar.

D'Adderio, L. (2008). "The Performativity of Routines: Theorising the Influence of Artefacts and Distributed Agencies on Routines Dynamics." *Research Policy*, 37/5: 769–89.

D'Adderio, L. (2011). "Artifacts at the Centre of Routines: Performing the Material." *Journal of Institutional Economics*, 7/2: 197–230.

D'Adderio, L. (2014). "The Replication Dilemma Unraveled: How Organizations Balance Multiple Goals in Routines Transfer." *Organization Science*, 25/5: 1325–50.

Dewey, J. and Bentley, A. F. (1949). *Knowing and the Known*. Boston, MA: Beacon Press.

Dionysiou, D. and Tsoukas, H. (2013). "Understanding the (Re)Creation of Routines from Within: A Symbolic Interactionist Perspective." *Academy of Management Review*, 38/2: 181–205.

Dourish, P. (2013). Closing remarks. Governing Algorithms: A Conference on Computation, Automation, and Control, New York University, Friday, May 17. <http://vimeo.com/69342822>.

Elias, N. (1978). *What Is Sociology?* Trans. S. Mennell and G. Morrissey. New York: Columbia University Press.

Emirbayer, M. (1997). "Manifesto for a Relational Sociology." *American Journal of Sociology*, 103/2: 281–317.

Farjoun, M. (2010). "Beyond Dualism: Stability and Change as a Duality." *Academy of Management Review*, 35/2: 202–25.

Feldman, M. S. (1995). *Strategies for Interpreting Qualitative Data*. Thousand Oaks, CA: Sage Publications.

Feldman, M. S. (2000). "Organizational Routines as a Source of Continuous Change." *Organization Science*, 11/6: 611–29.

Feldman, M. S. (2003). "A Performative Perspective on Stability and Change in Organizational Routines." *Industrial and Corporate Change*, 12/4: 727–52.

Feldman, M. S. (Forthcoming a). "Theory of Routine Dynamics and Connections to Strategy as Practice." In D. Golsorkhi, L. Rouleau, E. Vaara, and D. Seidl (eds.), *Cambridge Handbook of Strategy as Practice*, 2nd edition. Cambridge: Cambridge University Press.

Feldman, M. S. (Forthcoming b). "Making Process Visible." In A. Langley and H. Tsoukas (eds.), *The Sage Handbook of Organization Process Studies*. Thousand Oaks, CA: Sage Publications.

Feldman, M. S. and Orlikowski, W. J. (2011). "Theorizing Practice and Practicing Theory." *Organization Science*, 22/5: 1240–53.

Feldman, M. S. and Pentland, B. T. (2003). "Reconceptualizing Organizational Routines as a Source of Flexibility and Change." *Administrative Science Quarterly*, 48/1: 94–118.

Garfinkel, H. (1967). *Studies in Ethnomethodology*. Englewood Cliffs, NJ: Prentice-Hall.

Gherardi, S. (2006). *Organizational Knowledge*. Malden, MA: Blackwell.

Giddens, A. (1984). *The Constitution of Society*. Berkeley, CA: University of California Press.

Gillespie, T. (2013). "The Relevance of Algorithms." In T. Gillespie, P. Boczkowski, and K. Foot (eds.), *Media Technologies: Essays on Communication, Materiality, and Society*. Cambridge, MA: MIT Press, 167–94.

Heaphy, E. and Dutton, J. E. (2008). "Positive Social Interactions and the Human Body at Work: Linking Organizations and Physiology." *Academy of Management Review*, 33/1: 137–62.

Heaphy, E., Locke, K., and Booth, B. (Forthcoming). "Qualitative Organizational Research: Best Papers from the Davis Conference on Qualitative Research." In K. Elsbach and B. Bechky (eds.), *Embodied Relational Competence: Attending the Body in the Boundary-Spanning Work of Patient Advocates*. Charlotte, NC: Information Age Publishing.

Hernes, T. (2008). *Theory for a Tangled World*. Abingdon: Routledge.

Howard-Grenville, J. A. (2005). "The Persistence of Flexible Organizational Routines: The Role of Agency and Organizational Context." *Organization Science*, 16/6: 618–36.

Howard-Grenville, J. A. and Rerup, C. (Forthcoming). "A Process Perspective on Organizational Routines." In A. Langley and H. Tsoukas (eds.), *The Sage Handbook of Organization Process Studies*. Thousand Oaks, CA: Sage.

Jarzabkowski, P., Lê, J., and Feldman, M. S. (2012). "Toward a Theory of Coordinating: Creating Coordination Mechanisms in Practice." *Organization Science*, 23/4: 907–27.

Joas, H. (1996). *The Creativity of Action*. Chicago, IL: University of Chicago Press.

Johnson, M. (2007). "'The Stone that was Cast Out shall become the Cornerstone': The Bodily Aesthetics of Human Meaning." *Journal of Visual Art Practice*, 6/2: 89–103.

Johnson, M. (2012). *The Meaning of the Body: Aesthetics of Human Understanding*. Chicago, IL: University of Chicago Press.

Langley, A., Smallman, C., Tsoukas, H., and Van de Ven, A. (2013). "Process Studies of Change in Organization and Management: Unveiling Temporality, Activity and Flow." *Academy of Management Journal*, 56/1: 1–13.

Latour, B. (1986). "The Powers of Association." In J. Law (ed.), *Power, Action and Belief: A New Sociology of Knowledge?* London: Routledge & Kegan Paul, 264–80.

Latour, B. (1996). *Aramis or The Love of Technology*. Cambridge, MA: Harvard University Press.

Latour, B. (2005). *Reassembling the Social: An Introduction to Actor-Network Theory*. Oxford: Oxford University Press.

Leonardi, P. M. (2011). "When Flexible Routines Meet Flexible Technologies: Affordance, Constraint, and the Imbrication of Human and Material Agencies." *MIS Quarterly*, 35/1: 147–67.

Leonardi, P. M. and Barley, S. R. (2008). "Materiality and Change: Challenges to Building Better Theory about Technology and Organizing." *Information and Organization*, 18/3: 159–76.

Levinthal, D. and Rerup, C. (2006). "Crossing an Apparent Chasm: Bridging Mindful and Less-Mindful Perspectives on Organizational Learning." *Organization Science*, 17/4: 502–13.

MacIntyre, A. (2007). *After Virtue*, 3rd edition. Notre Dame, IN: University of Notre Dame Press.

Maitlis, S. and Christianson, M. (2014). "Sensemaking in Organizations: Taking Stock and Moving Forward." *Academy of Management Annals*, 8/1: 57–125.

Marx, K. (1852). "The Eighteenth Brumaire of Louis Bonaparte." <https://www.marxists.org/archive/marx/works/1852/18th-brumaire/ch01.htm>.

Merton, R. K. (1936). "The Unanticipated Consequences of Purposive Social Action." *American Sociological Review*, 1/6: 894–904.

Mesle, R. C. (2008). *Process-Relational Philosophy: An Introduction to Alfred North Whitehead*. Westconshohocken, PA: Templeton Foundation Press.

Michel, A. (2011). "Transcending Socialization: A Nine-Year Ethnography of the Body's Role in Organizational Control and Knowledge Workers' Transformation." *Administrative Science Quarterly*, 56/3: 325–68.

Miner, A. S., Ciuchta, M. P., and Gong, Y. (2008). "Organizational Routines and Organizational Learning." In M. C. Becker (ed.), *Handbook of Organizational Routines*. Cheltenham: Edward Elgar, 152–86.

Nelson, R. R. and Winter, S. J. (1982). *An Evolutionary Theory of Economic Change*. Cambridge, MA: Harvard University Press.

Orlikowski, W. J. and Scott, S. V. (2008). "Sociomateriality: Challenging the Separation of Technology, Work and Organization." *Academy of Management Annals*, 2/1: 433–74.

Orlikowski, W. J. and Scott, S. V. (2014). "What Happens When Evaluation Goes Online? Exploring Apparatuses of Valuation in the Travel Sector." *Organization Science*, 25/3: 868–91.

Parmigiani, A. and Howard-Grenville, J. (2011). "Routines Revisited: Exploring the Capabilities and Practice Perspectives." *Academy of Management Annals*, 5/1: 413–53.

Pentland, B. T. and Feldman, M. S. (2007). "Narrative Networks: Patterns of Technology and Organization." *Organization Science*, 18/5: 781–95.

Pentland, B. T. and Feldman, M. S. (2008). "Designing Routines: On the Folly of Designing Artifacts, while Hoping for Patterns of Action." *Information and Organization*, 18/4: 235–50.

Pentland, B. T., Haerem, T., and Hillison, D. (2010). "Comparing Organizational Routines as Recurrent Patterns of Action." *Organization Studies*, 31/7: 17–40.

Pentland, B. T., Haerem, T., and Hillison, D. (2011). "The (N)Ever Changing World: Stability and Change in Organizational Routines." *Organization Science*, 22/6: 1369–83.

Pentland, B. T. and Rueter, H. H. (1994). "Organizational Routines as Grammars of Action." *Administrative Science Quarterly*, 39/3: 484–510.

Rerup, C. and Feldman, M. S. (2011). "Routines as a Source of Change in Organizational Schemata: The Role of Trial-and-Error Learning." *Academy of Management Journal*, 54/3: 577–610.

Salvato, C. (2009). "Capabilities Unveiled: The Role of Ordinary Activities in the Evolution of Product Development Processes." *Organization Science*, 20/2: 384–409.

Salvato, C. and Rerup, C. (2011). "Beyond Collective Entities: Multilevel Research on Organizational Routines and Capabilities." *Journal of Management*, 37/2: 468–90.

Sandberg, J. and Tsoukas, H. (2015). "Making Sense of the Sensemaking Perspective: Its Constituents, Limitations, and Opportunities for Further Development." *Journal of Organizational Behavior*, 36/S1: S6–S32.

Schatzki, T. (2012). "Primer on Practice." In J. Higgs, R. Barnett, S. Billett, M. Hutchings, and F. Trede (eds.), *Practice-Based Education*. Rotterdam: Sense Publishers, 13–26.

Schatzki, T. (Forthcoming). "Practice Theory as Flat Ontology." In H. Schaefer (ed.), *Praxistheorie. Ein Forschungsprogramm*. Bielefeld: Transcript-Verlag.

Sewell, W. (1992). "A Theory of Structure: Duality, Agency and Transformation." *American Journal of Sociology*, 98/1: 1–29.

Shotter, J. (2008). "Dialogism and Polyphony in Organizing Theorizing in Organization Studies: Action Guiding Anticipations and the Continuous Creation of Novelty." *Organization Studies*, 29/4: 501–24.

Silverman, D. (2007). *A Very Short, Fairly Interesting and Reasonably Cheap Book about Qualitative Research*. Thousand Oaks, CA: Sage Publications.

Taylor, F. (1911). *The Principles of Scientific Management*. New York: Harper & Brothers.

Tsoukas, H. and Chia, R. (2002). "On Organizational Becoming: Rethinking Organizational Change." *Organization Science*, 13/5: 567–82.

Turner, S. F. and Fern, M. J. (2012). "Examining the Stability and Variability of Routine Performances: The Effects of Experience and Context Change." *Journal of Management Studies*, 49/8: 1407–34.

Turner, S. F. and Rindova, V. (2012). "A Balancing Act: How Organizations Pursue Consistency in Routine Functioning in the Face of Ongoing Change." *Organization Science*, 23/1: 24–46.

Van de ven, A. and Poole, M. S. (2005). "Alternative Approaches for Studying Organizational Change." *Organization Studies*, 26/9: 1377–404.

Weick, K. (1979). *The Social Psychology of Organizing*. Reading, MA: Addison-Wesley.

Weick, K. E. (1995). *Sensemaking in Organizations*. Thousand Oaks, CA: Sage Publications.

Wittgenstein, L. (2001). *Philosophical Investigations*. Trans. G. E. M. Anscombe. London: Blackwell [Orig. pub. 1953].

Zbaracki, M. J. and Bergen, M. (2010). "When Truces Collapse: A Longitudinal Study of Price-Adjustment Routines." *Organization Science*, 21/5: 955–72.

Zbaracki, M. J. and Bergen, M. (2015). "Managing Market Attention." In G. Gavetti and W. Ocasio (eds.), *Advances in Strategic Management: Cognition and Strategy*. Bingley: Emerald Group Publishing, 371–405.

Zollo, M. and Winter, S. (2002). "Deliberate Learning and the Evolution of Dynamic Capabilities." *Organization Science*, 13/3: 339–51.

3

Re-Viewing Routines through a Pragmatist Lens

Barbara Simpson and Philippe Lorino

Abstract: The practice-based view that currently dominates the routines literature is based on an ostensive-performative duality. However, from the perspective of process philosophy, this duality, or at least the manner in which it is applied, presents four key obstacles to a more processual theorization of routines. This chapter offers an alternative approach that builds on Pragmatist philosophy, especially the ideas of John Dewey and George Herbert Mead, which inform a performative rather than a representational approach to understanding ordinary everyday actions. The argument provides an account of the social and temporal situatedness of human conduct in terms of the interrelated processes of habit, inquiry, and conversational trans-actions.

CompCo is a leading global manufacturer of computer hardware. The company's reputation for excellence is grounded in its strict adherence to the principles of Total Quality Management (TQM) and Just in Time (JIT) production. Some years ago, the Board sought to further improve CompCo's competitive position by investing in a cutting edge, completely automated, computer-integrated manufacturing system (CIM) for its printed circuit assemblies factory, which not only provided JIT supplies to CompCo, but also to a number of other computer assembly factories across Europe. CIM is a manufacturing concept that aims to eliminate human error and to enhance productivity by fully automating factory production processes. Depending entirely on real-time closed-loop feedback from automatic sensors and computerized monitoring to control production, CIM has been mythologized as the intelligent "lights-out" factory that needs no human presence other than a Controller who remotely monitors (rather than controls) the manufacturing processes.

> *CIM was implemented at CompCo using an "intelligent" software system in which links between the physical (automated workstations and belt conveyors) and software "layers" of the CIM were facilitated by means of barcodes. All the components necessary for any scheduled product were picked up and loaded by robots into bar-coded plastic trays. Automated belt conveyors connected a central dispatching station with the various workstations where robotic systems used these components to assemble the required products. Because of the complexity of CompCo's product range and production processes, the prototype CIM initially retained a few manually operated workstations. This human presence was tolerated as a temporary aberration that would be replaced by full automation within a matter of months. One day during this interim period, the whole system stopped working for no apparent reason; carefully planned production routines were thrown into complete disarray. It took the combined efforts of designers, engineers, computer scientists, and technicians over several (very costly) days to discover the problem. A rogue plastic components tray had introduced an unexpected bar-code that the intelligent factory could not interpret, and another plastic tray with a monitored bar-code had altogether vanished.*

These events were experienced by one of us (Philippe) some twenty years ago, while he was working as a management controller at CompCo. He was fully engaged as a participant in this episode, contributing to the analysis and feedback processes that ensued. Over the following five years, he continued to discuss the episode with others who had been involved in this situation, then later he extended his exploration with academic colleagues. To us, it is a story that invites questions about often invisible and taken-for-granted assumptions regarding human action at the human–machine interface, and in particular about the situated actions that emerge through social interactions. There is an element of unanticipated human intervention that must be unraveled if lessons are to be learned from the CompCo experience. How are we to understand what happens when well-planned actions fall apart, and how should we theorize the improvisational actions that inevitably arise in such situations (Suchman, 1987)?

Routines theory has potential to open up some useful insights into the CompCo story. For instance, it might seek to understand how production routines changed while at the same time persisting throughout the introduction of the new CIM system (Howard-Grenville, 2005). It might demonstrate how patterns of action were varied, retained, and selected in the evolution of production routines (Pentland et al., 2012). Or it might map the learning processes that accompany this evolving process (Rerup and Feldman, 2011). More generally, a practice-based theorization of routines (Feldman, 2000; Feldman and Pentland, 2003) may be very helpful in understanding how people's actions intervene in the processes of creating, maintaining, disrupting, and changing routines, where these are understood as "repetitive, recognizable patterns of interdependent actions, carried out by multiple actors" (Feldman and Pentland, 2003: 95). This definition not only recognizes human agency in the performance of routines, but it also acknowledges the relationality of social (and material) interactions. What is missing, though, is a thoroughgoing theorization of the temporal dimensions of those situated actions that comprise routines. This is precisely where process theory might very productively intersect with contemporary understandings of routines.

In this chapter, we pursue this opportunity for theory development first by investigating the ontological and epistemological status of routines in organizing processes. Analyzing the limits of routines theory, both in its historical behaviorist form (March and Simon, 1993) and in its later practice-based form (Feldman and Pentland, 2003), we uncover four obstacles to a more processual appreciation of human conduct. Next, we propose an alternative theorization inspired by Pragmatist thinking about human action as a continuously emerging social process of meaning-making. Taking human conduct as the motive force for social change, the Pragmatists developed a practical and fundamentally processual understanding of those movements that shape, and are shaped by, our everyday experiences of living. We focus particularly on the ideas of John Dewey and George Herbert Mead, both of whom are already known to the routines community (Cohen, 2007; Dionysiou and Tsoukas, 2013; Winter, 2013), but here we go further by exploring three specific dimensions (habit, inquiry, and conversational trans-action) in their Pragmatist theory of creative action (Joas, 1996). As we unfold each of these dimensions, we will return to CompCo to illustrate and deepen our practical understandings of the situation. We argue that these three dimensions, taken in combination, offer fresh insights into the relational and temporal dynamics of routines.

3.1 A Processual Critique of Routines Theory

Scholarly interest in routines as mechanisms for the accomplishment of organizational work has been growing steadily for the past three decades (Becker, 2004; Parmigiani and Howard-Grenville, 2011), but arguably it was the seminal work of March and Simon, first published in 1958, that opened this topic up to organizational researchers. They suggested that the activities associated with problem-solving may be routinized "to the degree that choice has been simplified by the development of a fixed response to defined stimuli" (1993: 163). They further recognized that the "rationality" of the chooser is always bounded by the specifics of both past experience and current situation. Thus for them, a routine is a "response . . . that has been developed and learned at some previous time as an appropriate response for a stimulus of this class" (1993: 160). The behaviorist language of stimulus–response is pervasive in March and Simon's argument. It implies that routinized activity is determined by some sort of environmental stimulus, and that the learned response to this stimulus is immediately available without further cognitive intervention. There is a clear causal sequence—first stimulus, then response—so routines are understood as automatically triggered responses to previously experienced stimuli. Problem-solving activities are invoked only by exception, when the available repertoire of routine responses, or performance programs, proves inadequate for a given stimulus. Even in this situation though, March and Simon envisage the execution of procedural plans based on pre-existing procedures for problem-solving.

This stimulus–response model is underpinned by a representational theory of mind. That is, it assumes the classic Cartesian separation of mind and body, which understands thinking as a way of forming cognitive representations of the experienced world, and acting as the execution of already formed representations. This dualistic formulation is, however, a serious point of contention for process theorists, who see it as cutting across the very processes that are of interest, reducing movement to static representations, and thereby failing to account for the relational and temporal dynamics of practical organizational situations (Simpson, 2009). As far back as 1896, Dewey was arguing that the only way to overcome dualisms such as stimulus–response is by *not* starting from disjointed parts (i.e. stimuli, processing, responses), but by asking how these parts hang together. In his view, it is not that the stimulus sets the organism in motion, but rather the organism, as long as it is alive, is always already in motion. Living means moving. Stimulus and response are then each understood as complete acts that are mutually constituting in the processes of living rather than being related in a strictly causal sequence (Burbules, 2004). This re-conceptualization of stimulus and response as an ongoing and dynamic interplay requires an ontological shift away from the substantialist assumptions of a representational idiom, towards the processual assumptions of a performative idiom (Pickering, 1995), which emphasizes way-finding rather than navigation (Suchman, 1987; Chia and Holt, 2009), and novelty emergence rather than predictability of outcomes (Garud et al., 2015).

Perhaps anticipating this critique, March and Simon stressed the subjective and social nature of their subjects' rationality which, far from being a purely physiological reflex, they saw as rooted in social experience. But then the very notion of "stimulus" becomes problematic. In psychological theories, a stimulus is a mere perceptual phenomenon but, giving the example of customer order management, March and Simon stretched this concept into a much thicker and more complex idea that comes close to the notion of a constructed narrative. Responding to these definitional issues, Feldman and Pentland (2003) re-framed routines as complex systems of action that engage both ostensive and performative aspects:

> The ostensive aspect is the ideal or schematic form of a routine. It is the abstract, generalized idea of the routine, or the routine in principle. The performative aspect of the routine consists of specific actions, by specific people, in specific places and times. It is the routine in practice. Both of these aspects are necessary for an organizational routine to exist. (Feldman and Pentland, 2003: 101)

Feldman and Pentland took their inspiration for this re-theorization from their reading of Latour (1986), who contrasted ostensive and performative approaches to the problem of power and its functioning in society. However, he argued that the ostensive and the performative are ontologically distinct and incommensurable perspectives that defy efforts of integration into a single unified theory. His definition of the ostensive says "*In principle* it is possible to discover properties which are typical of life in society and could explain the social link and its evolution, though *in practice* they might be difficult to detect" (1986: 272), while he defined the performative saying "It is impossible *in principle* to define the list of properties that would be typical of life in society although *in practice* it is possible to do so" (1986: 273). Whilst either definition might be adopted to study power, like oil and water, the ostensive and performative cannot be blended together.

Drawing these threads of critique together, we see four key obstacles to a more processual theorization of routines:

Obstacle 1: Duality or dualism?

Dualisms are a recognized problem for those theories of action that seek to account for the mutually constituting dynamics of human conduct (Giddens, 1984; Bourdieu, 1990; Joas, 1996). A dualism separates systems of action into discrete entities, each of which is defined in opposition to the other, each therefore being immanent in the other (e.g. mind is that aspect of human experience that is not body, and vice versa). There is thus an underlying commonality (the system of action itself) that allows opposing aspects to be unified in an inclusive theory, but one that necessarily lacks dynamism because it is built out of stable entitative units. Both Giddens and Bourdieu rejected dualistic accounts in favor of the numerical notion of duality which, like Latour's distinction between ostensive and performative definitions, is based on two alternative ways of being in, and knowing about, the world. The social worlds in which we live are, of course, whole and continuous; they appear to have dual, or plural, natures only because of the limitations of our theoretical (and philosophical) assumptions (Dewey, 1917). There is no possibility of unifying these different natures, at least not at the same level of experience as that which created the duality. Nevertheless, the alternative positions are useful to the extent that they offer radically different insights into human action.

Feldman and Pentland presented their ostensive-performative framing of routines in terms of a duality, which calls for "a new ontology of the underlying phenomenon" (2003: 95). In their description of academic hiring practices in universities they recognized the paradox inherent in this duality whereby routines are both infinitely variable and yet easily identifiable. However, in proposing a unifying "ostensive-performative ontology" (2003: 103), it is not clear how Feldman and Pentland have tackled the profound ontological differences implied by this duality. Furthermore, they have argued that the ostensive and the performative are "two related parts" (2003: 95), or aspects, of organizational routines. "Each part is necessary, but neither part alone is sufficient to explain (or even describe) the properties of the phenomenon we refer to as 'organizational routines'" (2003: 95). This seems to suggest a slippage towards the sort of dualistic thinking that would admit both terms, ostensive and performative, as qualifiers of the same underlying concept, namely routines. Latour is very clear that in his view, ostensive theories of society have run their course, so now "we have to shift from an ostensive to a performative definition of society" (Latour, 1986: 272). He does not suggest that this approach can be bolted on to existing, representational notions of practice. His advice would seem to be that more effort is required to better theorize the performative view.

Obstacle 2: A variance-based theory of learning and organizing

A further implication of dualistic thinking is that it tends to suggest a causal connection between the ostensive and performative aspects of routines such that the performative generates new ideas that transform the

Figure 3.1 Dual learning systems of routines (adapted from Pentland and Feldman, 2005: 795)

ostensive, while the "best practice" and guidance implications of the ostensive encourage modifications in actual performances (Feldman, 2000). This leads to routines being conceived as dual learning systems that engage both ostensive and performative aspects (see Figure 3.1). The resulting scheme of learning and organizing is variance-based: it is the perceived gap between the ostensive and the performative that motivates ongoing change. Following this logic, a good fit between ostensive and performative aspects would generate a high level of stability, or even resistance to change. "A close match seems likely to indicate and predict stability and perhaps inertia. More disparate matches seem likely to indicate the existence of flexibility or change" (Pentland and Feldman, 2005: 805). Langley (1999) critically contrasted variance-based theories with process theories, arguing that the former are concerned with explaining efficient causal relationships between discrete variables amongst which time ordering is immaterial to the outcomes (Mohr, 1982), while the latter are more appropriate for mapping the probabilistic patterns of time-ordered events. Whereas variance-based theories provide a perspective on planned actions *over* time, process theories seek to engage in a continuous rethinking and adaptation of action *in* time. We argue it is this processual perspective that needs to be further developed within the routines literature.

Obstacle 3: The temporal problem

Although routines are seen as "an important source of flexibility and change" in organizations (Feldman and Pentland, 2003: 94), the literature remains largely mute about their timing and temporality. We can, however, infer a strong logical (cause–effect) and temporal (sequential) link between the ostensive and performative aspects of routines. The ostensive refers to cognitive representations expressed as artifacts such as plans and operating procedures, while the performative is concerned with situated action (Suchman, 1987). The ostensive is assumed to shape and direct performance (or vice versa), implying a sequential theory of time: there are successive phases of thought (modeling, programming, representing) and action (performing, executing). However, in making a separation between thought and action, this theoretical perspective denies the active function of the situation, as a potential source of doubt, beyond minor adjustments: "There are always contextual details that remain open—and that must remain open—for the routine to be carried out" (Feldman and Pentland, 2003: 101).

Whilst representationalism may be a useful fiction to analyze simple situations, it does not work in complex situations (Maturana and Varela, 1992). A more processual approach would situate action in the ongoing and entangled constructions that develop within thinking by/in doing, and doing by/in thinking. There can still be representations, but they do not have the same status as in cognitivist theories. They are just iconic mediations that serve as resources for situated action, but not the (determining) source of that action. As stressed by Weick (1998: 553), "[t]he process that animates these artifacts (structure, control, authority, planning, charters, and standard operating procedures) may well consist of ongoing efforts to rework and reenact them in relation to unanticipated ideas and conditions encountered in the moment." Thus performance, situated in the present moment and circumstances, has an emergent and improvisational quality that is often "tacit, taken-for-granted" but nevertheless "part of the infrastructure present in all organizing" (Weick, 1998: 553). The future then appears to actors as an open horizon of possibilities to explore, while the past is a rich, diverse, and often contradictory source of inspiration. We suggest, therefore, that routines theory would benefit from the explicit inclusion of more processual understandings of time and temporality.

Obstacle 4: The micro–macro problem

The micro–macro dualism is pervasive and well-recognized as a problem in the social sciences. The issue is, once a system has been separated into discrete levels of analysis, how is it then possible to reassemble the dynamic relationships between these levels? Routines theory faces a paradox: actual situated performances are generally viewed as occurring at the level of the individual, while the routine is an organization-level pattern involving multiple actors. However, "[e]ven an abstract and presumed collective understanding of a routine is not invariable because actors' understanding of a routine will vary with their role and perspective... [in a way] that makes sense only to the individual in that setting" (Howard-Grenville, 2005: 627). How then are we to move from subjective representations to organizational repetitive schemes? In the routines literature, it is often taken for granted that sociality is based on the commonality of representations: shared mental images, shared artificial/instrumental representations, shared discourses. Differences can then appear as imperfections which can raise difficulties: "If individual orientations differ, we may see contests over the use of routines" (Howard-Grenville, 2005: 627), implying that the normal use of routines is based on individual orientations that do not differ. If we take seriously the notion that all actions and all experiences are socially situated (Howard-Grenville, 2005), then they can never be adequately theorized as either purely individual or purely organizational endeavors. Process theorists reject the practice of separating systems into discrete levels of analysis, arguing instead that processes flow across all levels of a system. Their concern is how these processes emerge through practical engagements within concrete situations.

3.2 Pragmatism: A Processual Approach to Human Social Experience

Pragmatist thinking first arose as a trenchant critique of Descartes' exhortation that, in order to find absolute and universal truths, everything should be subjected to doubt. Charles Sanders Peirce, who is often cited as the father of Pragmatism, rejected the primacy that this Cartesian view affords the individual doubting thinker, isolated from the material and social world. Instead, he anchored his understanding of doubt in the local situated actions of ordinary day-to-day living, through which we discover together practical ways of coping with life's vicissitudes (Locke et al., 2008). Doubt arises when our actions meet with some form of resistance, and it may be resolved by reconstructing the meanings of either the self or the situation, or rather their relationship. This reconstructive activity, which Peirce called *Inquiry*, is a creative accomplishment that continuously injects the possibilities of novelty and change into the otherwise recurring patterns of social experience (Joas, 1996). The ontological category that underpins this Pragmatist position is process. That is, Pragmatists are more concerned with flow, movement, and the passage of events in time than with variables such as cognitive representations, objects, or the stuff of life more generally. Epistemologically their knowing is accomplished through relational engagement in conversations that transcend the usual dualisms permeating the organizational literature (e.g. stimulus–response, subject–object, individual–organizational). Furthermore, Pragmatism invites methodological innovation as researchers seek to go with the flow, themselves transforming as their research situations unfold.

Of course it is not possible to articulate the whole of the Pragmatist canon in this short chapter. Instead we will focus on three interrelated Pragmatist concepts, habit, inquiry, and conversational trans-action,[1] which we find particularly useful in our re-viewing of routines theory. Although we will now elaborate each of these concepts in turn, in a performative idiom they are intimately engaged together in the unfolding of experience and should not be considered as separate in practice, where habits are continuously involved in lived experience as a resource and mediation of ongoing inquiry, which is achieved collectively through conversational trans-action.

3.2.1 Habit

Within the routines literature, and organization studies more generally, the notion of habit is often presented as an idiosyncratic and purely individual mode of conduct (Nelson and Winter, 1982; Hodgson, 1993) that is contrasted to routines, which are taken to be organization-level phenomena. For instance, Becker (1992: 328) defines habit in terms of mechanical behavior that displays "a positive relation between past and current consumption," where the focus is very much on the micro-level. Such habits are stimulus–response reflexes that "require no thought; they are automatic" (Feldman and Pentland, 2003: 97). Pragmatists, however, see habit as much more than a mere tool in efficient and rational decision-making. For them, the defining quality of habit is its dispositional, rather than behavioral, orientation. "[T]he essence of habit is an acquired predisposition to ways or modes of response" (Dewey, 1957 [1922]: 32). It is embedded in social experience as "an attitude of response" (Mead, 1938: 3). "What habit is depends on when and how it causes us to act" (Peirce, 1878: 257). This dispositional understanding of habit continues to be valued by contemporary writers such as Bourdieu, Elias, and Deleuze (Crossley, 2013).

Dewey put particular effort into re-defining habit as a Pragmatist concept. For him, habits are acquired and continuously modified through experience, but they never fully determine the course of action. They are simultaneously object, resource, and outcome of inquiries that are both situated and recursive. A habit is neither a representation of actual action nor the actual performance of an action, but rather it is an acquired resource that mediates between the particular action situation and its organizational, social, and temporal contexts. To be precise, it is an inherently social, lively, and mutable (Cohen, 2007) organizing resource, a form of social language that makes action recognizable, repeatable and debatable.

> At CompCo, we see two different habits in play. Firstly, the rogue plastic components tray appeared in the system due to the actions of a human operator at one of the few remaining manual work stations. The operator noticed that one of the trays on the conveyor belt was damaged—one side was torn and twisted. Fearing that this tray could jam one of the machines, he found some unused trays in a corner of the workshop, he transferred the contents of the broken tray into a new tray, and placed the new tray on the conveyor belt. Understanding the operator's actions is neither straightforward nor obvious. He found himself immersed in an entirely unfamiliar environment populated by many robots but very few of the human beings more usually associated with his experience of manufacturing operations. What he did is surprising in this unfamiliar "science-fiction" setting because he chose to act on his own initiative, rather than asking for help. However, his actions must be understood in the context of existing habits used by skilled workers in that factory.

> The operator's actions reflected his well-established habit born of intensive and long-term training in TQM, which encourages taking initiative whenever possible to prevent defects and lost production. In engaging a habit from his experience (fixing incidents immediately and locally), he is qualifying the situation as an "incident" in the ordinary processes of production: there is an established and stabilized production system; there are incidents; a competent operator fixes incidents whenever possible within the existing system. The practical language of TQM is involved in the understanding and the resulting enactment of the situation.

> Secondly, the CIM experts engaged different habits drawn from their cultural and professional experience in CIM. They are faced with an inexplicable difficulty when the system shuts down. From their perspective, the problem appears as a technical issue, either at the "physical level" (sensors, actuators, robot mechanics, communication infrastructures, a broken part that has jammed a machine, an electrical incident, etc.) or at the "informational level" (a bug in some part of the complex software and telecommunication architecture). The engineers use well-established habits calling for detailed technical analyses and the resolution of error protocols. In doing so, they qualify the situation as a prototyping issue: this assembly workshop is an experimental unit; there may still be defects and bugs in the design of the system; and they must be fixed.

The TQM habit engaged by the operator arises as he imagines the potential future situation of a machine jammed by the broken tray (temporal context) and seeks to avoid difficulties for downstream operators (social context). The habit also transforms the primary meaning and definition of apparently simple objects, such as plastic trays, which prove much more complex and polysemous than at first glance. Should the plastic tray be considered a physical object characterized as broken or not broken, or is it rather an informational object that conveys vital systems information in the form of a bar-code? How this question is answered completely changes the way actors look at and engage with the object.

Habits translate diffusely teleological social motives into immediate actions. They translate mediating "whys" into detailed and specific "hows."

> As soon as we have projected [an end], we must begin to work backward in thought. We must change what is to be done into a how, the means whereby. The end thus reappears as a series of 'what nexts,' and the what next of chief importance is the one nearest the present state of the one acting... Now the thing which is closest to us, the means within our power, is a habit. (Dewey, 1957 [1922]: 36–7)

In CompCo, distinct habits translate distinct ends into distinct immediate actions. Running technical diagnostics is a "how" that translates the "why": "we must debug an innovative production technology," while replacing the broken tray is a "how" translating the "why": "we should fix production incidents."

Habits must be reassessed in each present moment, even in apparently simple situations. At what point should a broken plastic tray be considered a prototyping event instead of an ordinary production incident? The intelligence of the situation must be built continuously; it is not an automatic, Pavlovian reflex (Dewey and Bentley, 2008 [1949]). Habit transforms a singular act performed here and now into a socially meaningful gesture. Therefore, crucially, habit involves ongoing judgment so it cannot be equivalent to mindless repetition.

> We must protest against the tendency in psychological literature to limit [habit's] meaning to repetition. It assumes from the start the identity of habit with routine. Repetition is in no sense the essence of habit. Tendency to repeat acts is an incident of many habits but not of all. The essence of habit is an acquired predisposition to ways or modes of response, not to particular acts. (Dewey, 1957 [1922]: 41–2)

3.2.2 Inquiry

"Inquiry" is the term Pragmatists use to describe the process in which habits are mobilized and continuously adapted to new and emerging "what nexts" (Lorino et al., 2011). It is an evolving and transformational process in which selves and situations are mutually engaged and always in-the-making (Elkjaer and Simpson, 2011). Dewey (1986 [1938]) defined inquiry very specifically as the process that transforms an indeterminate, or doubtful situation into one that is sufficiently unified that a coherent course of action can be anticipated. However, inquiry is not necessarily visible and neither does it always involve a perceptible rupture in habits.

> Some forms of common sense inquiries, which aim at determining what is to be done in some practical predicament, are neither exceptional nor infrequent. For the stock and staple of common sense inquiries and judgments are of this sort. The deliberations of daily life concern in largest measure questions of what to make or to do. Every art and every profession is faced with constantly recurring problems of this sort . . . Farmer, mechanic, painter, musician, writer, doctor, lawyer, merchant, captain of industry, administrator or manager, has constantly to inquire what is better to do next. (Dewey, 1986 [1938]: 162–3)

Neither are the mechanisms of living reducible to "unintelligent automatism" (Dewey, 1957 [1922]: 70). Human action involves both habit and inquiry: habit-based inquiries develop inquiry-based habits, and vice versa. Retrospectively the process of action may appear as the implementation of some predetermined plan, but in the present the possibilities for action are manifold, the future is open, and even when uncertainty seems very low, options for action are still contingent.

> The CompCo story illustrates two distinct inquiry processes in relation to the breakdown of the CIM system. Firstly, the human operator was confronted with a problem—a broken plastic tray, which he assumed could cause a jam in the production system. At that point, several options were available to him—he might have pressed the emergency stop and brought the whole system to an immediate halt until a maintenance technician could be located; he might have called a member of the design team for advice; or he might have simply turned a blind eye to what he perceived to be a minor problem. In the event, he chose to use his own initiative, something that is very much encouraged in a TQM culture, replacing the broken tray on the conveyor belt. In choosing this action, he was responding to the justified expectations of the company, his peers, and the general TQM orientation towards "doing a good job." He interpreted the problematic situation as an ordinary production incident, which then allowed him to move quickly to find a solution. In particular, since he was able to find a new tray, he assumed he had solved the problem immediately and locally, remaining the only actor involved in the inquiry. He was not aware of the function of the bar-coding of the plastic components trays, so when the system broke down, it never occurred to him that his actions may have been the cause. As far as he was concerned, his actions had ensured the continuity of the process. He had translated a "why" into a "how" through a quick, albeit barely visible inquiry.

Secondly, the inquiry that was triggered for the CIM experts when the prototype production system unaccountably stopped working, was quite visible and formally organized. It started from an implicit characterization of the problematic situation as a technical defect of the new production unit. This was a critical step, which required them to find a hypothetical explanation, which in turn defined what actors should be involved as inquirers (i.e. designers and engineers). There is (or should be) no opportunity for human error to affect the operation of a CIM system, so they looked for a breakdown in either the technical hardware or in the complex software that operates the system. Although the experts understood that a few human operators were still engaged in the process, these people were regarded as "honorary robots" whose habits of action were all supposed to be pre-programmed and predictable. Eventually they discovered that one of the bar-coded trays did not match any planned order in the production schedule, and further that one other tray that was part of the scheduled production had disappeared, and could not be located by any of the multiple sensors. How could the designers have anticipated that a plastic tray could vanish, and that an unknown plastic tray could burst in from nowhere?

Inquiry does not start from a structured problem that needs solving. Rather, the first critical phase of inquiry entails the transformation of a "felt difficulty" into a problem.

There is nothing intellectual or cognitive in the existence of such situations, although they are the necessary condition of cognitive operations or inquiry. In themselves they are precognitive. The first result of evocation of inquiry is that the situation is taken, adjudged, to be problematic ... without a problem, there is blind groping in the dark. The way in which the problem is conceived decides what specific suggestions are entertained and which are dismissed; what data are selected and which rejected. (Dewey, 1986 [1938]: 111–12)

We would add that it also decides which actors are involved as inquirers and which are left out, as well as the temporal and spatial scope of the inquiry (Lorino and Tricard, 2012).

At CompCo the indeterminate situation first has no intellectual status, it is just an existential unease: a broken tray on the production line; the assembly line stops working. The first phase of the inquiry, often tacit and rarely verbalized, transforms this existential unease into a structured problem: the broken tray needs to be fixed or replaced, and the bug that stopped the system must be traced.

Once a problem has been constructed, its resolution is sought by engaging abductive, deductive, and inductive logics of reasoning (Lorino et al., 2011). Firstly, a plausible hypothesis accounting for the problematic situation is abductively inferred in order to restore intelligibility. Then the hypothesis is translated into empirically testable propositions through deductive reasoning. Finally, induction develops an empirical protocol to test the propositions (Peirce, 1998: 441–2). The entire reasoning of inquiry is expressed through active experimentation in which thinking and acting are simultaneous and confluent dynamics. Of course the inquiry steps described here in a sequential way for the purposes of presentation, are inevitably iterative and entangled as they grope for new forms of understanding.

> Both inquiries at CompCo were framed by particular, but different problem definitions. Whereas the operator was able to conclude his inquiry quickly by problematizing the situation as a production incident, abducting an efficient solution, and then implementing it, the engineers repeatedly cycled through a series of inquiries because they were unable to abduct a plausible explanation for the system breakdown. Limited by their initial problem definition, they could not imagine any sensible hypotheses. This inquiry was eventually resolved only when the experts expanded their inquiry to include the workstation operators (i.e. "non-experts").

3.2.3 Conversational Trans-Action

The purpose of inquiries and their associated habits is to make sensible the present situation so that practical actions may be discerned. This mobilization of habits and inquiries is situated within social and temporal contexts in what the Pragmatists term "the act" (Mead, 1938). Arising in the interplay between habit, inquiry, and the transformation of organizational or social situations, the act carries within itself "a consoling and supporting consciousness of the whole to which it belongs and which in some sense belongs to it" (Dewey, 1957 [1922]: 331). Situating the whole act within the flow of experience emphasizes both the relational and temporal extensiveness of the ongoing experience that structures organizing actions (Simpson, 2014). Evidently agency is in play in this process as choices are made about what and how adjustments are made, but in the Pragmatists' view, this agency is explicitly social rather than individualistic in its expression. It is a form of agency that arises in conversation, and as such, it pervades the social situation (Emirbayer and Mische, 1998; Simpson, 2009).

Mead (1934) did not conceive "conversation" as the mere transmission and reception of vocal utterances, but as an ongoing dynamic of gesture and response, within which situations are continuously reconstructed as conversants come to see what is happening through each other's eyes. It is then the very medium of inquiry. Each gesture in a conversation (whether it be vocal utterance, silence, body language, or mood) is a way of probing the meanings of the situation and of testing out what may happen next. When we gesture, we are not simply sending a message, we are also trying to anticipate the possible responses that our gesturing may engender. By reflexively standing in the other's shoes, we build and maintain sociality so that we can be open to a range of potential responses. Mead understood the conversational flow as a mutually constituting dynamic that engages the meanings of conversants' situations and conversants' selves. Describing this process as a mere interaction between distinct entities is inadequate, whereas Dewey and Bentley's (2008 [1949]) term "trans-action" is intended to indicate that all entities participating in an inquiry are involved on an equal footing and that their very definition and delineation is completely contingent on the progress of the inquiry.

In a conversational situation, this trans-actional approach implies that meaning-making cannot be attributed to any individual, but rather it emerges continuously from the very processes of conversing (see also Bakhtin, 1981; Shotter, 2008; Tsoukas, 2009). Any act is always addressed by and addresses other acts, and its meaning depends upon the responses it evokes. Conversation can thus be understood as a continuous process of usually quite subtle, mutual re-orientations. Of course, we carry our habits with us into every conversation, and it is here that these dispositional attitudes are tested and adjusted to bring better, more practically useful understandings of the evolving situation. Ultimately it is selves, and their dispositions to act, that are transformed in conversation, so in Mead's words, "selves exist only in relation to other selves" (1925: 278).

The conversational trans-action is not only relational, but also temporal. In Mead's view (1932), social agency engages both the past and the future as resources that give meaning and direction to actions in the present moment. As we proceed in our living and acting together, we rebuild both past experiences and anticipated futures to continuously re-author our understandings in response to what seems to be going on in the present moment (Simpson, 2014). Presents, then, are emergent turning points in the flow of living; they are events that arise whenever something happens. They are the creative confluence of two or more different temporalities. It is in the interweaving of pasts and futures that temporal experience is continuously constituted in the present moment (Tsoukas and Chia, 2002; Hernes et al., 2013; Lorino and Mourey, 2013).

Examining the CompCo story through the lens of conversational trans-actions allows us to step back and take a wider view of the social and temporal dynamics of the situation. We see that the operator and the CIM experts were engaged in quite different temporalities where each had a history of experience that led to different anticipated futures. The operator's experience led him to imagine a potential future in which the damaged tray might cause a major problem in the automated production system, and then to resolve this problem using his initiative. The tacit characterization of the situation as an ordinary production incident led to the specific temporal and social configuration of this inquiry. The time horizon of the inquiry was very short—usually production incidents are resolved within a matter of minutes. Potential legitimate inquirers are the normal participants in manufacturing operations: the operator, possibly his/her supervisors and quality controllers, but certainly not system designers.

In contrast, the CIM experts brought deep technical experience to bear on this critical situation. Their tacit characterization of the situation as a system design issue—the debugging of a technical prototype—led to a specific temporal and social configuration over a time horizon spanning the life cycle of the equipment. Legitimate actors were those who would normally be involved with design issues: automation designers and software engineers, but not operators. As a result, the designers' conversational trans-action did not at first involve the operators— equally, the operator's decision to replace the tray had not involved the designers.

In a later phase of inquiry, the designers did involve the operators, but only as potential witnesses—had they observed some sign that might be meaningful from a design point of view? In taking this action, however, a new conversational configuration was opened up, and the designers discovered the operator's "communicative gesture" only in the slowly emergent course of the conversation. Both the operator and the CIM experts had been functioning within closed and separate social and temporal frames. It was only when conversations began to span these boundaries that new understandings were generated and the problem was eventually identified and remedied.

There is a close link between the conversational form of sociality and temporality (Roth, 2014). The conversational trans-action is not the "joint" or "common" production of several participants, but the ongoing re-generation of differences. Conversant A moves the situation in a direction which makes it new for B; B responds to A by moving the situation in a direction that makes it new for A . . . and so on. The present is fleshed out through this recurrent turn-taking as successive turns lead to the gradual emergence of a mediate shape, a kind of discourse in acts (Lorino, 2014). Just as music can never be fully appreciated as a mere sequence of sounds, it is the conversational flow that communicates the overall tone of coordinated action. Hypothetical accounts of the past, invisible expectations of the future, and the gradual emergence of sense in the dialogical dynamics of trans-action are thus temporally linked and interdependent.

At CompCo we can imagine that operators may report no specific observation that could put engineers on a relevant track to find the bug. But equally, one of the operators might have mentioned that the only problem he met was fortunately a problem that he could easily solve by himself, which in turn may have triggered a new abductive phase in the inquiry leading the engineers to a new hypothesis.

3.3 Discussion

This chapter is motivated by a desire to explore what, if anything, a processual view of organizing might add to the currently flourishing literature on organizational routines, especially to the extent that they are seen as "source[s] of flexibility and change" (Feldman and Pentland, 2003: 94). Looking through the lens of process philosophy and theory, we see four key obstacles to a more fluid understanding of how routines are created, maintained, disrupted, and changed. Firstly, we challenge the assumption that ostensive and performative aspects of routines can be united under a single theoretical umbrella. We agree with Latour (1986) that a more productive way forward could be to focus exclusively on developing routines theory within a performative idiom. Of course we acknowledge that this is the road less traveled, but for this very reason it is a path that offers great opportunity to adventurous researchers. Secondly, we point to implicit variance-based assumptions that relate the ostensive and the performative to each other through mutually causal mechanisms. There are two central tenets of variance-based theories that conflict with more processual approaches: (i) they assume the situation being examined is sufficiently stable that any timing differences amongst variables will have no material influence on outcomes; and (ii) they assume that all action is preceded by cognition. By contrast, process theories assume that the situations in which we find ourselves are continuously and endlessly unfolding, and within this flow, thinking and acting reside together as mutually constituting dynamics.

Thirdly, we observe that there is no explicit theorization of temporality in the routines literature. Of course the importance of time as an independent variable as routines unfold from their antecedents to their outcomes, is well recognized (Turner, 2014), and there is also increasing scholarly interest in the temporal orientations of actors in routines (Howard-Grenville, 2005), but in these examples, and in the routines literature more generally, time remains the abstract time of measuring, dating, and sequencing. It articulates the past as an already known and determined history, while the future is extrapolated from past experience. However, this time-reckoning perspective cannot describe the temporality of the performative flow of living with its characteristics of emergence, unpredictability, and irreversibility. For example, how can we appreciate the temporality of an ordinary conversation that leads to new understandings, the temporality of winegrowers nursing their vineyard through uncertain weather, or the temporality of a football game with its many twists and turns? Whilst routines are undeniably present in each of these examples, they are situated within the flow of temporality rather than simply marching to the external rhythm of time. The inherently processual nature of the performative idiom demands a temporal understanding of the present moment as continuously emergent in the interplay between remembered pasts and imagined futures. Finally, distinctions such as micro–macro, but also individual–organizational, stimulus–response, and stability–change, may function as dualisms that arrest the flow of action, and reduce dynamic situations to static representational forms. Process theory, by contrast, seeks a "'*practical* holism' that eschews the primacy of mentalism, cognitivism or even intentionality in engaging with the day-to-day affairs of the world" (Chia and MacKay, 2007: 228).

To move forward from these critiques, we have proposed an alternative theorization that resonates particularly with the performative idiom. Drawing on Pragmatist thinking, we have developed an argument that frames the social and temporal dimensions of ordinary everyday practice in terms of the mutually embedded and practically inseparable dynamics of habit, inquiry, and conversational trans-action. We see the performativity of routines, then, as provisionally constituted in the intelligent engagement of inquiry, understood as a continuously emergent conversational process in which habitual predispositions to act in certain ways in certain situations are constantly exposed to the experimental logics of abduction, deduction, and induction. The existential doubt that initiates an inquiry generates actions, out of which the problem and the solution co-emerge. This is a very different approach from the stimulus–response of March and Simon (1993), where a routine is understood as being triggered by an already fully structured problem. It is holistic experience, rather than reflexes or cognitions, that allows us to connect particular types of situations to arrays of potential options for action. Further, because actors choose amongst their abducted hypotheses in deciding "what next," their practice may remain stable, it may be radically disruptive and creative, or it may be anything in between. Actions, then, are generative to the extent that different histories of experience may coincide to produce alternative anticipated futures. By positioning inquiry alongside conversational trans-action, our performative view of routines is fundamentally temporal as it locates actions in the perpetually unfolding present.

The Pragmatist approach we are advocating is concerned primarily with the flow of experience and processes of mutual transformation. As such, it is both ontologically processual, and epistemologically conversational and relational. These foundational assumptions invite new methodological approaches that engage with underlying processual dynamics, not only through historical analyses, but also by participating directly in the social and temporal presents of practice and engaging with the "practical holism" of the situation. This requires us to step away from "levels of analysis" or other dualistic framings, and to immerse ourselves in the confluence of multiple, socially and temporally situated flows of action. It also invites us to carefully re-language the ways we talk about action in order to avoid the stasis of representations and keep the dynamics alive in our analytical framings (Mesle, 2008). Whilst this need is well recognized in, for instance, Weick's (1979) entreaty to replace nouns with verbs in our research descriptions, the rush towards the gerund-ing of everything has perhaps now been overdone in the organizational literature. A more subtle re-languaging is called for. We suggest that the confluence of habits, inquiries, and conversational trans-actions as defined by the Pragmatists offers just such a re-languaging of familiar ideas in ways that open up new possibilities for analysis and research more generally.

In reviewing the routines literature, we are conscious that the field itself is in a state of dynamic emergence. Step by step, the initial behaviorist account of routines has been deconstructed and replaced by an increased recognition that situated (performative) action is not the same as planned or programmed action. What we are proposing here is yet another step in this process, a step that is timely given recent developments in the field. At the conference that informed this edited volume, Martha Feldman (2014) proposed a new action-based model of routines built on processes of "patterning" and "performing." We see this as a very exciting move that sits remarkably comfortably with our Pragmatist argument, which allows us to understand patterning and performing, not as contrasting constructs, but as two mutually constituting flows within the same process, that of inquiry. We hope, therefore, that the Pragmatist take on habits, inquiry, and conversational trans-actions will resonate with further developments that advance the performative idiom in routines theory.

Ultimately, the real strength of the Pragmatist approach we have articulated is that it accounts for both the situatedness of actions in terms of the social and relational contexts in which they arise, and also for the continuous reconstruction of pasts and futures in the flow of present experience. In doing so, it holds the potential for new theory that integrates the social and the temporal in a thoroughgoing performative exposition of the means by which the work of organizing is accomplished.

Note

1. Here we follow Dewey and Bentley (2008 [1949]) in hyphenating this word to differentiate its meaning from other common usage, especially in economics and psychoanalysis.

References

Bakhtin, M. M. (1981). *The Dialogical Imagination: Four Essays*. Austin, TX: University of Texas Press.
Becker, G. S. (1992). "Habits, Addictions and Traditions." *Kyklos*, 45/3: 327–46.
Becker, M. C. (2004). "Organizational Routines: A Review of the Literature." *Industrial and Corporate Change*, 13/4: 643–77.
Bourdieu, P. (1990). *The Logic of Practice*. Cambridge: Polity Press.
Burbules, B. (2004). *Pragmatism and Educational Research*. Lanham, MD: Rowman & Littlefield.
Chia, R. and Holt, R. (2009). *Strategy without Design: The Silent Efficacy of Indirect Action*. Cambridge: Cambridge University Press.
Chia, R. and MacKay, B. (2007). "Post-Processual Challenges for the Emerging Strategy-as-Practice Perspective: Discovering Strategy in the Logic of Practice." *Human Relations*, 60/1: 217–42.
Cohen, M. (2007). "Reading Dewey: Reflections on the Study of Routines." *Organization Studies*, 28/5: 773–87.
Crossley, N. (2013). "Habit and Habitus." *Body & Society*, 19/2–3: 136–61.
Dewey, J. (1917). "Duality and Dualism." *Journal of Philosophy, Psychology and Scientific Methods*, 14/18: 491–3.
Dewey, J. (1957 [1922]). "Human Nature and Conduct." In *Middle Works*, vol. 14, ed. J. A. Boydston. Carbondale and Edwardsville, IL: Southern Illinois University Press).
Dewey, J. (1986 [1938]). "Logic: The Theory of Inquiry." In *The Later Works, 1925–1953*, vol. 12, ed. J. A. Boydston. Carbondale, IL: Southern Illinois University Press).
Dewey, J. and Bentley, A. (2008 [1949]). "Knowing and the Known." In *The Later Works, 1925–1953*, vol. 16, ed. J. A. Boydston. Carbondale, IL: Southern Illinois University Press.
Dionysiou, D. D. and Tsoukas, H. (2013). "Understanding the (Re)Creation of Routines from Within: A Symbolic Interactionist Perspective." *Academy of Management Review*, 38/2: 181–205.

Elkjaer, B. and Simpson, B. (2011). "Pragmatism: A Lived and Living Philosophy. What Can It Offer to Contemporary Organization Theory?" In H. Tsoukas and R. Chia (eds.), *Research in the Sociology of Organizations: Special Volume on Philosophy and Organization Theory*, vol. 32. Bingley, UK: Elsevier, 55–84.

Emirbayer, M. and Mische, A. (1998). "What is Agency?" *American Journal of Sociology*, 103/4: 962–1023.

Feldman, M. (2000). "Organizational Routines as a Source of Continuous Change." *Organization Science*, 11/6: 611–29.

Feldman, M. (2014). "Understanding Action in Routines." Paper presented at the 6th International Symposium on Process Organization Studies, Rhodes, Greece.

Feldman, M. and Pentland, B. (2003). "Reconceptualizing Organizational Routines as a Source of Flexibility and Change." *Administrative Science Quarterly*, 48/1: 94–118.

Garud, R., Simpson, B., Langley, A., and Tsoukas, H. (2015). "Introduction: How Does Novelty Emerge?" In R. Garud, B. Simpson, A. Langley, and H. Tsoukas (eds.), *Process Research in Organization Studies: The Emergence of Novelty in Organizations*. Oxford: Oxford University Press, 1–24.

Giddens, A. (1984). *The Constitution of Society: Outline of the Theory of Structuration*. Cambridge: Polity Press.

Hernes, T., Simpson, B., and Söderlund, J. (2013). "Managing and Temporality." *Scandinavian Journal of Management*, 29/1: 1–6.

Hodgson, G. M. (1993). "Institutional Economics: Surveying the 'Old' and the 'New'." *Metroeconomica*, 44/1: 1–28.

Howard-Grenville, J. (2005). "The Persistence of Flexible Organizational Routines: The Role of Agency and Organizational Context." *Organization Science*, 16/6: 618–36.

Joas, H. (1996). *Creativity of Action*. Chicago, IL: University of Chicago Press.

Langley, A. (1999). "Strategies for Theorizing from Process Data." *Academy of Management Review*, 24/4: 691–710.

Latour, B. (1986). "The Powers of Association." In J. Law (ed.), *Power, Action and Belief*. London: Routledge & Kegan Paul, 264–80.

Locke, K., Golden-Biddle, K., and Feldman, M. S. (2008). "Making Doubt Generative: Rethinking the Role of Doubt in the Research Process." *Organization Science*, 19/6: 907–18.

Lorino, P. (2014). "From Speech Acts to Act Speeches: Collective Activity, a Discursive Process Speaking the Language of Habits." In F. Cooren, E. Vaara, A. Langley, and H. Tsoukas (eds.), *Perspectives on Process Organization Studies*, vol. 4: *Language and Communication at Work: Discourse, Narrativity, and Organizing*. Oxford: Oxford University Press, 95–124.

Lorino, P. and Mourey, D. (2013). "The Experience of Time in the Inter-Organizing Inquiry: A Present Thickened by Dialog and Situations." *Scandinavian Journal of Management*, 29/1: 48–62.

Lorino, P. and Tricard, B. (2012). "The Bakhtinian Theory of Chronotope (Time-Space Frame) Applied to the Organizing Process." In M. Schultz, S. Maguire, A. Langley, and H. Tsoukas (eds.), *Perspectives on Process Organization Studies*, vol. 2:

Constructing Identity in and Around Organizations. Oxford: Oxford University Press, 201–34.

Lorino, P., Tricard, B., and Clot, Y. (2011). "Research Methods for Non-Representational Approaches to Organizational Complexity: The Dialogical Mediated Inquiry." *Organization Studies*, 32/6: 769–801.

March, J. and Simon, H. A. (1993). *Organizations.* New York: Wiley.

Maturana, H. R. and Varela, F. J. (1992). *The Tree of Knowledge: The Biological Roots of Human Understanding.* Boston and London: Shambhala Publications.

Mead, G. H. (1925). "The Genesis of the Self and Social Control." *International Journal of Ethics*, 35/3: 251–77.

Mead, G. H. (1932). *The Philosophy of the Present.* La Salle, IL: Open Court.

Mead, G. H. (1934). *Mind, Self and Society.* Chicago, IL: University of Chicago Press.

Mead, G. H. (1938). *The Philosophy of the Act.* Chicago, IL: University of Chicago Press.

Mesle, C. R. (2008). *Process-Relational Philosophy: An Introduction to Alfred North Whitehead.* West Conshohocken, PA: Templeton Foundation Press.

Mohr, L. B. (1982). *Explaining Organizational Behavior.* San Francisco, CA: Jossey-Bass.

Nelson, R. R. and Winter, S. G. (1982). *An Evolutionary Theory of Economic Change.* Cambridge, MA: Belknap Press/Harvard University Press.

Parmigiani, A. and Howard-Grenville, J. (2011). "Routines Revisited: Exploring the Capabilities and Practice Perspectives." *Academy of Management Annals*, 5/1: 413–53.

Peirce, C. S. (1878). "How to Make our Ideas Clear." In *Collected Papers of Charles Sanders Peirce*, vol. 5, ed. C. Hartshorne and P. Weiss. Cambridge, MA: Belknap Press/Harvard University Press), 248–71.

Peirce, C. S. (1998). *The Essential Peirce.* Bloomington, IN: Indiana University Press.

Pentland, B. and Feldman, M. (2005). "Organizational Routines as a Unit of Analysis." *Industrial and Corporate Change*, 14/5: 793–815.

Pentland, B., Feldman, M., Becker, M., and Liu, P. (2012). "Dynamics of Organizational Routines: A Generative Model." *Journal of Management Studies*, 49/8: 1484–508.

Pickering, A. (1995). *The Mangle of Practice: Time, Agency and Science.* Chicago, IL, and London: University of Chicago Press.

Rerup, C. and Feldman, M. (2011). "Routines as a Source of Change in Organizational Schemata: The Role of Trial-and-Error Learning." *Academy of Management Journal*, 54/3: 577–610.

Roth, W. M. (2014). "Working Out the Interstitial and Syncopic Nature of the Human Psyche: On the Analysis of Verbal Data." *Integrative Psychological & Behavioral Science*, 48/3: 283–98.

Shotter, J. (2008). "Dialogism and Polyphony in Organizational Theorizing: Action Guiding Anticipations and the Continuous Creation of Novelty." *Organization Studies*, 29/4: 501–24.

Simpson, B. (2009). "Pragmatism, Mead, and the Practice Turn." *Organization Studies*, 30/12: 1329–47.

Simpson, B. (2014). "George Herbert Mead." In J. Helin, T. Hernes, D. Hjorth, and R. Holt (eds.), *The Oxford Handbook of Process Philosophy and Organization Studies*. Oxford: Oxford University Press, 272–86.

Suchman, L. A. (1987). *Plans and Situated Actions: The Problem of Human–Machine Communication*. Cambridge: Cambridge University Press.

Tsoukas, H. (2009). "A Dialogical Approach to the Creation of New Knowledge in Organizations." *Organization Science*, 20/6: 941–57.

Tsoukas, H. and Chia, R. (2002). "On Organizational Becoming: Rethinking Organizational Change." *Organization Science*, 13/5: 567–82.

Turner, S. F. (2014). "The Temporal Dimension of Routines and their Outcomes: Exploring the Role of Time in the Capabilities and Practice Perspectives." In A. J. Shipp and Y. Fried (eds.), *Time and Work: How Time Impacts Groups, Organizations and Methodological Choices*, vol. 2. Hove: Psychology Press, 115–45.

Weick, K. E. (1979). *Social Psychology of Organizing*. Reading, MA: Addison-Wesley.

Weick, K. E. (1998). "Improvisation as a Mindset for Organizational Analysis." *Organization Science*, 9/5: 543–55.

Winter, S. (2013). "Habit, Deliberation, and Action: Strengthening the Microfoundations of Routines and Capabilities." *Academy of Management Perspectives*, 27/2: 120–37.

4

The Multiplicity of Habit

Implications for Routines Research

Scott F. Turner and Eugenia Cacciatori

Abstract: This chapter explores habit as a foundational concept for routines research. The authors examine how habit and habitus have been conceptualized in psychology and sociology, giving particular attention to the role of deliberation and mindfulness. Drawing on this work, they develop a typology of habit that is based on the extent of deliberation by the individual performing an activity, and the variability in the conditions in which he or she performs it. The chapter considers the implications of these insights on habit for two central perspectives of organizational routines, the capabilities perspective and the practice perspective, arguing that both can be advanced by closer attention to the idea of routines as interlinked habits.

4.1 Introduction

The concept of habit has drawn considerable attention in research on organizational routines. Routines, as repetitive patterns of interactions (Becker, 2004), have been described as the organizational analogue of individual habits (Hodgson, 2003). Scholars have also explored the idea that routines result from the interlinking of individual habits, reflecting connections between individual learning and organizational routines (Cohen, 1991; Cohen and Bacdayan, 1994). This work has recently received renewed attention as part of efforts to strengthen the micro-foundations of organizational routines (Felin et al., 2012; Winter, 2013; Cohen et al., 2014).

While the value of habit as a core element of the micro-foundations of routines is viewed differently across central perspectives in the literature (i.e. routines as capabilities, routines as practice), these perspectives have tended to adopt a similar view of habit as the automatic response dispositions of individuals (Knudsen, 2008; Parmigiani and Howard-Grenville, 2011). But in recent work, Cohen (2007, 2012) has been critical of this view of habit and has argued in favor of drawing upon conceptualizations of habit that see it as more flexible and generative. Whereas traditional views of habit as automatic emphasize its independence from conscious thought and its tendency to fire (and misfire), alternative conceptualizations tend to characterize habit as "pre-reflective," but entirely compatible with intentional and intelligent behavior. These differences in approaches and terminology across disciplines have made it difficult to understand the role of habit in individual behavior, which in turn inhibits the potential for habit to strengthen our understanding of organizational routines.

In this chapter, we aim to contribute to this understanding by clarifying some of the relationships between habit, deliberation, and mindfulness that are part of current debates in routines research (Levinthal and Rerup, 2006; Winter, 2013; Laureiro-Martinez, 2014). To do so, we review how habit has been conceptualized in different research traditions. While work on habit in routines has primarily drawn from psychology (e.g. James, 1914 [1890]; Dewey, 2002 [1922]), we examine a wider spectrum of perspectives, encompassing both psychology and sociology. Drawing on this work, we develop a typology of habit that takes a broader and more integrative look at the concept. This typology provides an avenue for further understanding how routines unfold over time (e.g. Langley et al., 2013), suggesting that the stability and dynamics of routines as interaction patterns depend, in no small part, on the different types of habits that shape the behavior of routine participants. In the discussion section, we consider the implications of these insights on habit for the capabilities and practice perspectives of routines (Parmigiani and Howard-Grenville, 2011; Turner, 2014). While these perspectives differ in many ways, we argue that both can be advanced, and perhaps drawn closer together, through a broader conceptualization of habit.

4.2 Literature Background

4.2.1 Routines as Interlinked Habits

Research on routines as interlinked habits views routines as sequential patterns of action that are based in the interconnected, reciprocally-triggering habits of routine participants. The roots of this view are based in earlier efforts to draw connections between organizational routines and individual learning (e.g. Cohen and Bacdayan, 1994), drawing primarily on psychological research examining procedural and declarative memory. Procedural memory, which is viewed as central for habits, involves remembering how to perform actions; this form of memory tends to persist, has little accessibility to language and conscious thought, and has limited tolerance for novel conditions. Because it is not easily accessible to conscious thought, procedural memory provides an important mechanism that supports individuals' dispositions to act in similar ways in response to similar circumstances without going through a deliberative process. By contrast, declarative memory centers on facts and concepts, and it tends to be more subject to decay, more accessible for conscious thought (e.g. deliberating among alternative courses of action), and more tolerant of novel conditions (Cohen, 1991).

The idea of routines as interlinked habits suggests that routines emerge through a process of gradual learning by participants in the routine, and become stored in procedural memory (Cohen et al., 1996). In experimental research, Cohen and Bacdayan (1994) found evidence consistent with the idea of routines being stored as procedural memory; specifically, the researchers found that as pairs of individuals formed routines for playing a card game, the routines were not impacted by the introduction of time delays (i.e. decay), but were impaired when novel conditions were introduced. In this manner, a routine can be viewed as a concatenation of individual habits, each stored in procedural memory (Cohen et al., 1996), with the corresponding actions of participants primed by and priming the actions of others. This is similar to the notion of "habit meshing," which Weick (1969: 58) described as how "each person's habits are part of the environment of others" within organizations.

Thus, as the routine forms, the initially distinct action dispositions of individuals tend to coalesce into a cohesive whole, such that the routine in aggregate represents a collective disposition (Hodgson, 2003; Knudsen, 2008), which can result in the performance of "seemingly automated" sequences of actions (Narduzzo et al., 2000: 37). In related research, Dionysiou and Tsoukas (2013) argue that the formation and interlinking of these action dispositions coincide with the development of shared schemata among routine participants; specifically, their work emphasizes that stability in routines reflects the development of shared schemata that guide meaningful interactions among participants, and action dispositions stored in procedural memory that contribute to participant responses in more automatic and unreflective ways.

While the idea of routines as interlinked habits may suggest a rather automatic, machine-like view of routines, a key issue is the way in which the underlying habits are conceptualized. Some scholars (e.g. Knudsen, 2008) have viewed habit as automatically triggered by contextual cues, consistent with contemporary research in psychology (Wood and Neal, 2007), while others (e.g. Cohen, 2007) have drawn upon a broader conceptualization of habit as proposed by Dewey (2002 [1922]), which emphasizes that habits can be mindless and automatic in the extreme, but they can also exhibit dynamic and mindful qualities. What is habit, then, and how is it viewed in different research traditions in psychology and sociology?

4.2.2 Habits

Although the term "habit" has been used in different ways across different disciplines, Camic (1986: 1044) proposes that habit has a common core meaning: "a more or less self-actuating disposition or tendency to engage in a previously adopted or acquired form of action." Around this common core, scholars of habit vary in their views, particularly regarding whether the form of action is simple, circumscribed, and automatic versus generalized, complex, and deliberate (Camic, 1986).

While consideration of habit was common in early work in psychology and sociology, the evolution of the disciplines led to psychologists focusing largely on the automatic notion of habit, and the virtual disappearance of habit from sociological discourse (Camic, 1986).[1] More recently, though, sociology has seen a reemergence of scholarly attention in this area, focusing largely on the notion of habitus and general/complex forms of behavior (Bourdieu, 1990).

In this section, we provide a brief review of three related areas of research. First, we consider the dominant view in psychology on habit, where habits are defined as response dispositions that are automatically triggered by cues in the performance context (Wood and Neal, 2007). Second, we examine recent work in sociology on habitus, which arose in opposition to the traditional view of habit in psychology[2] (Bourdieu, 1990). Last, we consider earlier work in psychology by Dewey (2002 [1922]), and related phenomenological work by Merleau-Ponty (1962), that has received less attention and argues for a broader conceptualization of habit.

4.2.2.1 DOMINANT VIEW IN PSYCHOLOGY ON HABIT

Psychologists have long relied on the concept of habit for understanding our daily lives. William James (1939) argued that individuals are "mere bundles of habits," and suggested that 99 percent, perhaps 99.9 percent, of daily activity is habitual.

Concept of habit. In psychology, much of the attention directed to habits has focused on fairly simple and automatic actions. Early roots of this line of thought can be found in the work of James (1914 [1890]), who argued that with habit formation comes diminishment in the conscious attention with which individuals perform their activities, and further spoke of habits in terms of "automatic agency" (1914 [1890]: 31). In more recent work in psychology, scholars have defined habits as response dispositions that are automatically triggered by cues in the performance context. In this sense, habits represent learned associations between stable contextual features and responses (Neal et al., 2006). In diary studies, Wood, Quinn, and Kashy (2002) classified habits as behaviors that participants report performing "just about every day" and "usually in the same location" (Wood et al., 2002: 1285).

Habit development and performance. According to this view, habits develop gradually as individuals do the same things in the same context. In this process, associations are formed in memory between the actions/responses and the stable features of the context in which they are performed (Wood and Neal, 2009). As these associations in memory form, there is greater integration of actions within sequences, resulting in the cueing and implementation of larger units of behavior that require little conscious control to proceed to completion (Neal et al., 2006). While the pursuit of prior goals may have led individuals to perform activities similarly under similar conditions, once habits are established, they are automatically triggered by cues in the performance context. In this work, scholars highlight that the physical location where responses are performed provides the cues that trigger many everyday behaviors (Wood and Neal, 2009). Research by Wood et al. (2005) found that a number of everyday habits can transfer/persist across settings—specifically for students transferring from one university to another—when aspects of performance context are similar in both settings.

While habits have a persistent memory trace in general, scholars in psychology have also considered how cognitive resources may strengthen or weaken the likelihood of engaging in such behaviors. For example, when individuals are distracted, they have less working memory available to generate alternative courses of action, and as such, they are more likely to act habitually (Wood and Neal, 2009). Recent work has also focused on the role of self-control/willpower resources, which Wood and Neal (2009: 583) describe as a "domain-general resource that functions like a muscle in that it is temporarily depleted with use and regenerates with rest." In related diary studies, scholars have found that the most effective strategy for inhibiting habitual responses is one of vigilant resistance using self-control/willpower resources (Quinn et al., 2010); however, when such resources are low, individuals are typically unable to inhibit the habitual response or choose other courses of action (Neal et al., 2013). Scholars also suggest that efforts to change habitual behaviors are more likely to be effective when they are based in or coincide with interventions that disrupt the environmental cues that would otherwise automatically trigger the habit (Verplanken and Wood, 2006).

4.2.2.2 REEMERGENT VIEW IN SOCIOLOGY ON HABITUS

Concept of habitus. While the field of sociology ceded the study of habit to psychology in the early twentieth century, prominent contemporary scholars in sociology like Mauss (1973) and Bourdieu (1990) have refocused attention in this area, particularly on the notion of habitus. For Mauss and Bourdieu, habitus differs from habit, in that habitus focuses on intelligent dispositions and practical understanding while habit refers to mechanical, stimulus–response forms of behavior (Crossley, 2013a).

While the concept of habitus has evolved over time (Crossley, 2013b), in general, it refers to a system of stable dispositions, which are based in past experiences. Habitus are generative systems with the capacity to produce an infinite number of practices, but the range of such practices is limited in diversity by the corresponding embodied schemata that guide perception, appreciation, and action (Bourdieu, 1990; Bourdieu and Wacquant, 1992). A habitus can be viewed as an acquired ability to do certain sorts of things, i.e. a form of competence, and represents a prereflective and embodied mastery of certain types of situations. Using the analogy of sport, Bourdieu (1990: 66) sees habitus as the "feel for the game" that enables players to act in intelligent ways even when the speed of the game inhibits their ability to think reflectively about their next move (Crossley, 2013b). In this way, habitus "captures the skilled activity of the expert player rather than the conditioned response of the lab rat" (Crossley, 2013a: 139).

Habitus development and performance. According to Bourdieu (1990: 53), habitus are "structured structures predisposed to function as structuring structures." In this sense, the habitus is produced by a particular class of conditions, and the habitus as a system of dispositions serves as the basis for perceiving, appreciating, and acting. The primary structuring influences on habitus are based in social class and historical era (Crossley, 2013b). Given that individuals of the same class or era tend to be exposed to the same conditions, they tend to develop the same habitus (Bourdieu, 1990). As a result, habitus "captures the way in which the individual is shaped by their own history which, in turn, is shaped by the wider historical process to which they belong," thereby implying a "situated form of agency which emerges from and draws upon a collective history" (Crossley, 2013b: 295).

Moreover, habitus also develops and redevelops through experiences that reinforce and modify its structures (Bourdieu and Wacquant, 1992). Early experiences are particularly influential, as the schemata emerging from them form the basis through which new information is selected (Bourdieu, 1990). As experiences accumulate, there tends to be a relative closing of the open system of dispositions constituting the habitus (Bourdieu and Wacquant, 1992). In this sense, the habitus is "a present past that tends to perpetuate itself into the future by reactivation in similarly structured practices" (Bourdieu, 1990: 54).

4.2.2.3 REFORMED VIEW OF HABIT

In the work of Mauss (1973) and Bourdieu (1990), dissatisfaction with the more rigid notion of habit developed in psychology led to their use of habitus as a more complex, dynamic, and generative concept. Other scholars like Dewey (2002 [1922]) in psychology and Merleau-Ponty (1962) in phenomenology had similar concerns with the narrow and rigid view of habit, but rather than reject the concept, they chose to rehabilitate and extend it (Crossley, 2013a). Recent work in the organizational sciences by Cohen (2007) has also adopted this broader conceptualization of habit.

Concept of habit. While the dominant view in psychology conceptualizes habit with respect to automaticity (Wood and Neal, 2007), early work by Dewey (2002 [1922]) advocated for a broader conceptualization. At one extreme of a continuum, Dewey understood habit as consistent with the dominant view in psychology—that is, habit as automatically triggered by contextual cues without thought or feeling—which he described as "routine habit." But at the other extreme, Dewey (2002 [1922]) viewed habit as more flexible and lively, which he described as intelligent or artistic habit. In similar ways, phenomenologist Merleau-Ponty (1962) saw habit as an acquired ability to respond to situations of a particular form with certain ways of acting. This end of the continuum compares favorably with the notion of habitus used more recently in sociology (Mauss, 1973; Bourdieu, 1990).

Further, while the dominant view in psychology suggests that habits based in automaticity are pervasive (James, 1914 [1890]; Wood et al., 2002), Dewey suggested that this form of habit represents a pathological extreme that is not often reached. Specifically, he argued that all habit-forming activity begins down a path toward thoughtless/automated action. However, "nature which beckons us to this path of least resistance also puts obstacles in the way of our complete acceptance of its invitation," and through these obstacles, "a signal flag of distress recalls consciousness to the task of carrying on" (2002 [1922]: 173).

Habit development and performance. Dewey (2002 [1922]) emphasized that habit is a disposition to particular ways of action that is acquired through past experience. According to Dewey, though, habits could develop in different ways depending on their type; for example, "routine habits" would develop and be limited by repetition of past acts in past conditions, whereas a flexible habit would grow more varied and adaptable through experience. In similar ways, Merleau-Ponty (1962) viewed the process of habit formation as one in which an individual acquires the ability to respond with a certain type of action to situations that bear similar characteristics but are in no way identical; thus, there is flexibility of habit in that individuals are acquiring an ability for doing something, based on learning a relation of meaning between situational properties and responses. As an example, Merleau-Ponty (1962: 142) described "forming the habit of dancing" as "discovering, by analysis, the formula of the movement in question, and then reconstructing it on the basis of the ideal outline by the use of previously acquired movements, those of walking and running." Moreover, this work argues that habits form on the basis of ongoing interactions between the actor, other actors, and the broader environment, and re-form based on the continuing course of these interactions which include ongoing disturbances (Crossley, 2013a).

In general, Dewey (2002 [1922]) viewed habits as repertoires of potential behavior that can be triggered by an appropriate stimulus or context, and that a habit exhibits unexpected potentialities when performed in a different context from the one in which it was established. From this view, habit is a more generative notion in that habits can be drawn upon, adapted, and reorganized for different purposes in different conditions. In this way,

Cohen (2007, 2012) saw habits as flexible and as resources for improvising, although he also acknowledged the difficulty in efforts to reshape habit through conscious intervention.

4.2.2.4 SUMMARY

With increasing attention focused on strengthening the micro-foundations of routines (Felin et al., 2012), habit has been put forward as a central component (Cohen, 2007; Winter, 2013). The potential of habit to fulfill this role is, however, constrained by extant views of the concept among routines scholars. While many see habit similarly (i.e. based in automaticity), our review shows that this is a restrictive perspective. We observe that the reformed view of habit advanced by scholars like Merleau-Ponty and Dewey (on which Cohen, 2007 builds), and the notion of habitus as developed by Mauss and Bourdieu, have substantial overlap, with both characterizing habit more broadly than, and in many ways different from, the dominant view of habit as understood in psychology. These "alternative" views of habit see it as the ability to act competently in a prereflective but intentional and intelligent way, which contrasts markedly with the dominant view of habit in psychology which sees it as non-reflective, automatic response to known stimuli, which can be prone to misfire and only overcome through considerable willpower. The commonalities and divergences in the treatment of habit highlighted here point to a need for developing a more integrative and coherent understanding of habit. In the following section we explore the relationships among contextual features, deliberation, and mindfulness within our habit typology.

4.3 A Typology of Habit

At its core, habit represents an acquired tendency to engage in an activity in particular ways (Camic, 1986). But as evident from the related scholarship in psychology and sociology, there are different perspectives on habit that are based in differences in the extent of automaticity by the individual performing the activity, and the variability of the conditions in which he or she performs it. In this section, we develop a typology of habit that explores and accounts for these differences (Figure 4.1). We then use this typology as a basis to discuss the relationships between habit and mindfulness.

In our typology, we use activity to indicate the larger task that is being performed, such that its performance is reflected in a sequence of

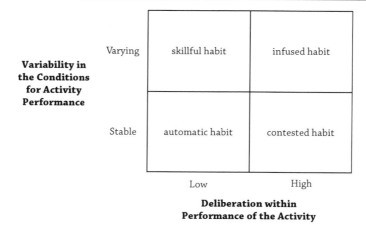

Figure 4.1 A typology of habit

underlying actions. An example of an activity would be driving from home to work. This activity is composed by the actions of entering the car, starting its engine, and so on.[3] Our typology focuses on habits that can be viewed as established, and does not consider the performance of an activity prior to habit formation.

The first dimension, variability in performance conditions, refers to the extent to which features of the context in which the activity is performed are different across its enactments. Scholars in psychology have argued that variability in performance conditions has important implications for habit, as habit formation involves the development of associations in memory between actions and stable contextual features (Verplanken and Wood, 2006). At a more aggregate level, organizational scholars suggest stability in the operating environment of organizations has important implications for routinization of activities (March and Simon, 1958). Similarly, researchers in sociology have argued that the stability of performance conditions plays a key role in the formation of habitus (Bourdieu, 1990; Crossley, 2013a). Scholars from this tradition, as well as those advocating for a reformed view of habit, have also underscored how variability in conditions can produce varied performances of the same habit (Bourdieu, 1990; Dewey, 2002 [1922]).

Our second dimension captures the extent to which deliberation enters into habitual behavior, either in supporting or disrupting it. The term deliberation is used widely in the debate on routines, but it is rarely explicitly defined. According to *Merriam Webster*, deliberation refers to "careful thought or discussion done in order to make a decision." Dewey (2002 [1922]: 190), on which much of the current attempts to revisit the notion of habit in routines are based, defines deliberation as "a dramatic rehearsal (in imagination) of various competing possible lines of action." Similarly, Winter (2013) highlights that deliberation aligns closely with System/Type 2 processes in dual processing accounts of individual behavior. System/Type 2 processes tend to be relatively slow, conscious, abstract, rule-based, and connected with consequential decision-making, while System/Type 1 processes tend to be relatively fast, automatic, non-conscious, associative, and involved in experience-based decision-making (Evans, 2007).

In our typology, the automatic habit, which often involves fairly simple activities, is habit as understood in modern psychology (Wood and Neal, 2007). Automatic habit is typically developed and performed in stable conditions, and for the individual actor, there is little deliberation within the performance of the activity. The latter is emphasized in neuroscience research (Jog et al., 1999) showing how, when a particular activity is performed, the underlying actions tend to become "chunked" together, with recordings of neuronal activity suggesting limited deliberation taking place within the sequence of actions (with greater signs of engagement at the beginning and end of the sequence). This corresponds with one extreme of the habit continuum from the reformed view of habit, which Cohen (2007: 780) describes as "dead" habit. Dewey (2002 [1922]: 172–3) suggested that for an individual, habit at this extreme is "a ditch out of which he cannot get, whose sides enclose him, directing his course so thoroughly that he no longer thinks of his path or his destination... stimulus and response are mechanically linked together in an unbroken chain." This corresponds to the idea of habit as rejected by Bourdieu (1990), in favor of habitus.

The contested habit reflects recent scholarly attention by psychologists (Neal et al., 2013). With contested habit, the focus is also on activities performed in stable conditions, but the process involves a greater level of deliberation by the individual. In particular, the contested habit is based on recent research that examines the juxtaposition of habit and willpower, examining the role of self-control/willpower in inhibiting the performance of particular patterns of action (Quinn et al., 2010). In contrast to traditional habit, with contested habit, high levels of deliberation work to inhibit a response, or to "will apart" an otherwise chunked sequence of actions. Bourdieu (1990: 108) also notes that "[habitus] may be superseded in certain circumstances... by other principles, such as rational and conscious computation." This also reflects the juxtaposition of will and "dead" habit described by Dewey (2002 [1922]), although habit can also be changed through prereflective improvisation.

For activities that are performed in varying/dynamic conditions, and involve relatively low deliberation, we enter the realm of skillful habit.[4] This refers, for instance, to the "feel for the game" of a footballer (Bourdieu, 1990). Here the individual is able to adapt her behavior to the changing conditions in which the activity is carried out (e.g. the spatial distribution and movement of players, the ball in motion) in a way that is largely prereflective, but still purposive and displaying intelligence and understanding of the situation (Crossley, 2013a).

Finally, when the performance conditions are varying and deliberation is high, habit can be viewed as infused with deliberation, i.e. infused habit. This recognizes the unexpected potentialities of "a flexible, sensitive habit" (Dewey, 2002 [1922]: 72) that can generate different action sequences based on different conditions (Bourdieu and Wacquant, 1992), and represents an ability that can be called upon when facing "new emergencies" (Dewey, 2002 [1922]: 66). While skillful habit represents a prereflective and almost instinctive adaptation of behavior given encountered conditions, infused habit involves greater deliberation and engagement in the behavior. This quadrant captures "the infusion of thought [into habit] that Dewey spoke of, which solves surmountable problems around the edges of existing skills and routines, thereby enhancing the scope and adaptability of existing habits" (Winter, 2013: 134).

4.3.1 Habit and Mindfulness

The typology developed in this chapter offers insights for the relationship between habitual behavior and mindfulness, which in turn, has implications for our understanding of the linkage between routinization and mindfulness. We begin by concentrating on the individual level of analysis, consistent with our focus in this section on the relationships between habit and individual behavior. In reviewing psychological research on mindfulness, Dane (2011) argues that most studies share a common core understanding of mindfulness as the self-regulation of attention so that it is (1) focused on immediate experience, both internal to the person (e.g. emotional states) and external (i.e. the environment), and (2) has wide breadth. Dane (2011) further argues that this differentiates mindfulness from other states of attention, such as absorption (when attention is narrowly concentrated on the task at hand), counterfactual thinking and prospection (when attention is concentrated on the past or on the future), and mind wandering (when attention is broad and not directed to the present). Some approaches, notably that of Langer (1989), see mindfulness as involving cognitive differentiation through the creation or refinement of distinctions and categories.[5]

When characterized as self-regulated, wide-breadth attention to one's experience (Dane, 2011; Glomb et al., 2011), mindfulness directs attention to a wider range of details in the context and how one is dealing with it, and in this way enriches the information that is selected into the deliberation process. For instance, Langer (1989: 153) argues that "mindfulness is a choice of contexts. The mindlessness-mindfulness distinction is concerned with how we create information or assign meaning to to-be-processed information." However, mindfulness, as a state of attention, does not necessarily imply deliberation. Heightened attention increases the input that we process, but that processing might not take place through the language-based, cognitive activities that we usually associate with deliberation. A skilled football player, to go back to Bourdieu's example, is certainly mindful of her surroundings as she adapts her actions to the speed of the ball, the disposition of other players, and her own physical situation, but we define her as skillful because in many circumstances she knows what to do without deliberating about it—as a novice and less skillful player would need to do.

Our typology suggests that all types of habit, with the exclusion of automatic habit, are mindful because they require attention and adaptation to the context. Skillful habit, as illustrated by the performance of a skilled football player, requires mindfulness primarily with an external focus. Contested habit requires mindfulness primarily with an internal focus, on the operation of the body or mind, while infused habit requires focus on both internal and external dimensions, as the actor consciously attempts to adapt habit in the face of variations in context.

These ideas have implications for understanding the link between routinization and mindfulness. While some authors emphasize trade-offs between routinization and mindfulness (Weick and Sutcliffe, 2006), others argue that they sustain each other at individual (Laureiro-Martinez, 2014) and organizational levels (Levinthal and Rerup, 2006; Rerup and Levinthal, 2014). From the perspective of our typology, whether or not routinization at an organizational level sustains mindfulness can depend on the type of habit that predominates for participants. When automatic habit dominates, routines are mindlessly executed on the basis of a few salient cues in the environment. An example of this may be the case, discussed in Cohen and Bacdayan (1994), of Soviet troops arriving in Cuba secretly and in civilian clothes, only to form into ranks and march away in formation. When other types of habits dominate, however, the performance of routines can be mindful. This appears to be the case, for instance, in the processes underlying both local/lower-level and global/higher-level variations in routines for new product development at Alessi (Salvato, 2009). In that case, mindful employees reacted to local problems by generating some variation, and mindful top managers picked up on successful variations and institutionalized them. In our view, the idea of "infused habit" might help to explain the micro-foundations of routine evolution in similar cases, including how bottom-up (operational) and top-down (strategic) processes are linked (Vogus and Sutcliffe, 2012) in ways that prevent organizational adaptation from being driven by sudden and dramatic "wake up calls" of serious crises (Rerup and Levinthal, 2014).

4.4 Discussion

In this study, we consider habit as a foundational concept for routines theory, building on the recent attention directed to habit by routines scholars (Cohen, 2012; Winter, 2013). While habit has traditionally been viewed through the lens of psychology, focusing on the automatic triggering of actions in stable conditions, our study offers a broader and more integrative look at the concept. Specifically, we develop a typology of habit, which is rooted in work on habit and habitus from psychology and sociology, and we explore the role of mindfulness in the different forms of habit. We believe that this perspective offers considerable potential to further understanding of the micro-level foundations of routines theory. This integrative view of habit offers important implications that extend understanding of two core perspectives in the routines literature: the capabilities perspective and the practice perspective (Parmigiani and Howard-Grenville, 2011).

4.4.1 Implications for Research on the Capabilities Perspective of Routines

The capabilities perspective typically examines routines as whole entities, and focuses on their role as building blocks of organizational capabilities

(Parmigiani and Howard-Grenville, 2011). Our study offers insight for the capabilities perspective in two primary areas: the role of individuals and the role of context.

4.4.1.1 THE ROLE OF INDIVIDUALS

Capabilities-based scholars have not historically focused closely on how individuals shape routine enactment, which in part has spurred recent calls for greater foundational understanding of routines (Salvato and Rerup, 2011; Felin et al., 2012). Yet this research does argue that routine participants are faced with competing tensions, often viewed as a trade-off, involving deliberation—its absence enables fluid performance of habits of limited scope in familiar conditions, while its presence broadens the scope of action across a wider range of conditions, but typically does so at the expense of disruptions in behavior (Nelson and Winter, 1982; Winter, 2013).[6] While viewing such tensions as a trade-off between fluidity/efficiency and adaptability/flexibility focuses on habit and deliberation as separate concepts, scholars have called for greater attention to understanding the interplay between habit and deliberation, and the corresponding implications for routines and capabilities (Winter, 2013). And there have been parallel calls to provide a clearer understanding of the relationships between mindful and "less-mindful" behavior in relation to routines (Levinthal and Rerup, 2006).

Our typology of habit, and consideration of mindfulness within it, helps us to better understand how the type of habit influences the balance among these competing tensions. First, we highlight that two habit types— automatic and contested—are quite consistent with how capabilities-based scholars tend to view the tension as a deliberation trade-off. For automatic habit, there is little, if any, deliberation among routine participants, which enables fluid performance of habits in stable conditions. With contested habit, there is deliberation on the part of participants with mindfulness directed internally, with the typical objective to inhibit an undesired performance of habit. Second, we highlight that skillful habit and infused habit—both present in varying conditions—are less consistent with extant views. For skillful habit, there is less of a trade-off present between fluidity/efficiency and adaptability/flexibility, as there is little deliberation involved for routine participants, but by being mindful of external conditions, they are able to attain both fluid and adaptive performance of habit. In the case of infused habit, we argue that there is not separation between habit and deliberation, as deliberation is actively enrolled in the performance of infused habit (with mindfulness directed both internally and externally).

These insights have important implications for research into the micro-foundations of routines and capabilities because they suggest that scholars need to look beyond a monolithic view of habit, and take into account multiple forms of habit that are present in different conditions (i.e. stable versus varying) and involve deliberation and mindfulness in different degrees and ways. Future research should include efforts to examine the performance implications of routines depending on which habits prevail (e.g. routines built primarily on automatic habit vs. infused habit), as well as the processes through which multiple types of habits intermesh in routines. Moreover, our study encourages future research to move beyond a bipolar view of the individual actor, moving like a pendulum between habit and deliberation, and instead to focus more closely on the varied relationships between habit and deliberation. As one example, deliberation itself may be a habit, as in the view of Dewey (2002 [1922]), particularly when it is recognized in the "learnt" way of professionals reasoning about their task. In addition, work on mindfulness has begun to shed light on the multiple ways in which automatic and mindful behavior support and co-constitute each other at both individual and organizational levels (Levinthal and Rerup, 2006; Laureiro-Martinez, 2014). As discussed earlier, our typology of habit can help to further unpack these processes.

4.4.1.2 THE CONTEXT OF ROUTINES

In the routines literature, the idea that routines are context-dependent is a fundamental one (Cohen et al., 1996). Consistent with this idea, scholars working from the capabilities perspective have tended to view the material context as external structures that trigger and channel the actions of parti-cipants performing a routine (Becker, 2004). At an individual level, this aligns with the "automatic habit" tradition of research arguing that stimuli from the environment automatically trigger the performance of habits (Wood and Neal, 2007). This connects with the idea that the affordances of objects (i.e. the possibility for action that an object offers) can be pro-cessed in automatic ways (Gibson, 1979; Cohen, 2012). But our study also points to other ways in which artifacts and context come into play in relatively automatic ways for individuals performing routines. For example, Merleau-Ponty's (1962) discussion of how a blind person uses a stick for perceiving suggests that some artifacts are in fact mediators of behavior, in the sense that they influence the nature of behavior rather than simply "trigger" it. This suggests that context is part of habit in a generative way, and that individuals can resourcefully use artifacts while performing habits. Building on work on the role of materiality in organizations (e.g. Cacciatori, 2012; Leonardi et al., 2012), and on research that examines how some artifacts (e.g. procedures) can stimulate and/or suppress deliberation, mindfulness, and ultimately agency (Adler and Borys, 1996), offers promise for advancing understanding of how different types of artifactual conditions affect the emergence and flexibility of routines.

Moreover, context dependence is based on the idea that routine effectiveness depends on the alignment between routines and their surrounding conditions (Nelson and Winter, 1982). But in recent work focusing on routine replication, capabilities-based scholars have argued that effectiveness depends less on fit with local conditions, and more on maintaining the internal coherence of the routine. Specifically, this research has found that as organizations seek to transfer routines to new locations, their performance improves with exact replication, as opposed to adapting the routine to fit the context (Szulanski and Jensen, 2006). This work raises important questions regarding the value of replication versus adaptation for organizational routines, and whether routines may be less dependent on context than previously thought.

Contributing to this debate, our study suggests that the value from exact replication versus contextual adaptation may depend upon the habits of routine participants. For example, when routines are based largely in automatic habits, organizations may benefit from pursuing a strategy of exact replication because the internal coherence of a routine is more salient with automatic habits at its foundation (i.e. greater chunking of behavior). By contrast, when the underlying habits for a routine are infused ones, organizations may benefit from greater adaptation to the local environment because there are fewer problems associated with disturbing the internal coherence of the routine. Future research can advance this debate through greater attention to how the habits of routine participants are (and are not) dependent upon different aspects of context; in these efforts, scholars may benefit from drawing upon psychological research on affordance (Gibson, 1979) and contextual influences on habit (Wood et al., 2005).

In addition, findings from the research on routine replication suggest that context is "layered." Maintaining internal coherence of routines requires replicating exactly the artifactual and organizational arrangements of a routine; that is, it focuses on the immediate context for participant actions. This immediate context might or might not fit with the larger context as reflected in the wider organizational and market conditions, such as cultural norms.

Our typology suggests that different forms of habit may be predominant at different contextual levels. While automatic habit may be predominant in relation to the immediate context in routines, "outer" layers of context seem to call more upon habit as practical knowledge (i.e. skillful and infused habit) to perform in particular classes of situation and cultural context. A "layered" view of context, together with the typology of habit that we propose, may help future research to explore how routines nest into other structures of the organization (Howard-Grenville, 2005).

4.4.2 Implications for Research on the Practice Perspective of Routines

The practice perspective focuses on the internal structure of routines. From this perspective, routines are viewed as comprising ostensive aspects (i.e. the abstract pattern of actions) and performative aspects (i.e. the enactment of the pattern of actions), and as effortful and ongoing accomplishments (Feldman and Pentland, 2003). Our study also offers insight for scholars working from the practice perspective in the areas of the role of individuals and context.

4.4.2.1 THE ROLE OF INDIVIDUALS

Routines scholars working from the practice perspective have emphasized the agency of routine participants, focusing on specific actions taken by specific individuals at specific times and in specific places (Parmigiani and Howard-Grenville, 2011). To this point, practice-based routines researchers have given relatively little attention to the potential role of habit in the micro-foundations of routines, which is not surprising given the level of attention directed to the concept of automatic habit in psychology (Wood and Neal, 2009), and its general inconsistency with the idea of routines as effortful accomplishments. In fact, the emphasis on agency—and the view of routines as practices that must be accomplished—is put forward in contrast to the idea that routines are simply based in the mindless, automatic habits of individuals. However, in work exploring the temporal orientation of actors, agency scholars have argued that when actors are primarily oriented to the past, there is a habitual aspect of agency (Emirbayer and Mische, 1998). Drawing on this research, Howard-Grenville (2005) argues that when participants are oriented to the past, there is little flexibility and change in routines.

While prior work has tended to equate the habitual aspect of agency with past temporal orientation, our typology suggests that different forms of habit may involve different forms of temporal orientation. Consistent with prior work, automatic habit aligns with past temporal orientation, and we would expect little flexibility and change in routines based in such habits. However, if routines are based in skillful habit, we would expect greater orientation to the present (i.e. adapting to the circumstances at hand), and greater flexibility in the routine. If routines involve contested habit, we would expect that participants are simultaneously oriented to the past and present, with present intentions and resources (i.e. willpower) seeking to inhibit tendencies for past iterations, and with the flexibility and change in routines dependent upon the balance among competing pressures. For routines based in infused habit, participants may be simultaneously orientated to the past, present, and future; for example, actors may draw on patterns of action established in the past as resources that can be modified and/or recombined to enable more effective functioning in the present or future; in these instances, we would expect greater flexibility and change in routines. Future research into the habitual aspect of agency—including the different forms that habit may take, and the different temporal orientations that may be at play—offers considerable potential for advancing understanding of the practice perspective of routines.

In addition, practice approaches to routines generally consider agency and structure to be co-constituted (Feldman and Pentland, 2003). However, practice-based studies of routines have tended to give primacy to agency and have provided a less developed account of the role of structure in the dynamics of routines—partly as a reaction to a view of routines as rigid and automatic. Unlike habit in the dominant psychology tradition, the work on habitus and related research on the reformed view of habit is more social in nature. Mauss and Bourdieu, for instance, both underscore that habitus is formed in and shaped by the social groups in which individuals live, forming a key mechanism through which social structure influences individual agency, which in turn reproduces structure. Scholars advocating the reformed view of habit, like Merleau-Ponty and Dewey, also recognize that habit emerges in interaction with others, and view individuals' capacity of perceiving, forming objectives, and acting (in short, agency) as constituted by habit (Dewey, 2002 [1922]; Crossley, 2013a). Therefore, habit offers the opportunity to explore the dispositional aspect of human agency (Crossley, 2013a) and appears as a promising avenue to further explore the dynamics of structure and agency, particularly in terms of investigating how various types of structures contribute to routine dynamics—an issue that has only recently begun to be addressed explicitly (Howard-Grenville, 2005). Our typology of habit, by differentiating between habits that are more or less rigid, and have reinforcing or contrasting relationships with deliberation and mindfulness, might offer a way to unpack the situations in which the duality of structure and agency is weighed more toward "structure" and replication, or "agency" and variation.

4.4.2.2 THE CONTEXT OF ROUTINES

Our study also responds to a call for extending understanding of the practice perspective of routines through greater attention to how context shapes the dynamics of organizational routines (Parmigiani and Howard-Grenville, 2011). In extant research, scholars have emphasized how routines are enacted simultaneously with other elements of the organizational context, which can inhibit flexibility and change in routines. For example, Howard-Grenville (2005) argued that there is less flexibility and change in routines when they are strongly embedded in structures of the organization, i.e. technological, coordination, and cultural.

While extant work has focused on how relatively stable features of the organizational context tend to constrain the dynamics of routines, our study offers some perhaps surprising insight into how the dynamics and variability of context can both inhibit and promote adaptability and change in routines through habit formation. We argue that stable contextual conditions tend to give rise to automatic and contested habits for individuals, and when organizational routines are based in those types of habits, we expect limited flexibility and change in the routines; moreover, for such routines, accomplishing change will likely require the investment of considerable willpower resources. By contrast, we argue that more variable conditions enable the formation of skillful and infused habits, which we expect to promote adaptability and change in routines. In order to better understand how context affects the dynamics of routines, we encourage future research to explore more closely how context affects stability and variability in the habits of participants.

4.5 Conclusion

In this chapter, we have developed a typology of habit that offers a more integrative look at the concept, drawing upon the different ways habit has been conceptualized in psychology and sociology. We also seek to clarify the relationships between habit, deliberation, and mindfulness, arguing that habit does not necessarily always preclude deliberation and, especially, mindfulness. As such, habit might offer a suitable micro-foundation for approaches that see organizational routines as compatible with mindful organizing. Our typology of habit offers productive directions for further research in both the practice and capabilities traditions. By showing areas of overlap and contrast between different approaches, and by highlighting related opportunities for future research for both capabilities- and practice-based scholars, we hope that habit might in the future become a "trading zone" (Kellogg et al., 2006: 22) in which productive dialogue between the capabilities and practice traditions can be established, while continuing to benefit from the richness afforded by their differences.[7]

Notes

1. In describing the receding of habit within sociology, Camic (1986) points to Durkheim and his view that as a developing field in search of scientific legitimacy, sociology needed to focus on subject matters that other sciences were not studying (i.e. habit belonged to psychology).
2. Bourdieu (in Bourdieu and Wacquant, 1992: 122) remarked that "I said habitus so as not to say habit."
3. What constitutes an action or an activity depends on the level of granularity of the analysis. For example, the action of starting the car engine could be considered an activity made up of various actions such as inserting the key into the ignition, turning the key, etc.
4. While routines research often uses "habit" and "skill" interchangeably, we view skill as a particular form of habit, with habit as a broader concept.
5. Weick et al. (1999) build on Langer (1989) in their treatment of organizational mindfulness, and emphasize interpretive work and cognitive differentiation. However, Weick and Sutcliffe (2006: 517) also argue that "when people enrich the distinctions they make, their efforts begin to resemble practices associated with mindfulness meditation (i.e. Eastern pathways to mindfulness). As a result, their experience becomes less mediated by concepts and more nonconceptual."
6. Competing tensions, such as seeking efficiency and needing flexibility, often surface in routines. Viewed through the lens of organizational paradox (Smith and Lewis, 2011), routines scholars have tended to focus on different responses for accommodating these tensions, with capabilities-based scholars emphasizing spatial and temporal separation (e.g. standard phases of efficiency-seeking functioning of operational routines vs. change phases in which operational routines are modified), while practice-based scholars emphasize a synthetic view in which routines are simultaneously stable and dynamic.

7. The authors would like to dedicate this chapter to the memory of Michael Cohen, who was a source of inspiration for both of us. We would also like to thank Jennifer Howard-Grenville and Claus Rerup for their thoughtful guidance.

References

Adler, P. S. and Borys, B. (1996). "Two Types of Bureaucracy: Enabling and Coercive." *Administrative Science Quarterly*, 41/1: 61–89.

Becker, M. C. (2004). "Organizational Routines: A Review of the Literature." *Industrial and Corporate Change*, 13/4: 643–77.

Bourdieu, P. (1990). *The Logic of Practice*. Stanford, CA: Stanford University Press.

Bourdieu, P. and Wacquant, L. J. D. (1992). *An Invitation to Reflexive Sociology*. Chicago, IL: University of Chicago Press.

Cacciatori, E. (2012). "Resolving Conflict in Problem-Solving: Systems of Artifacts in the Development of New Routines." *Journal of Management Studies*, 49/8: 1559–85.

Camic, C. (1986). "The Matter of Habit." *American Journal of Sociology*, 91/5: 1039–87.

Cohen, M. D. (1991). "Individual Learning and Organizational Routine." *Organization Science*, 2/1: 135–9.

Cohen, M. D. (2007). "Reading Dewey: Reflections on the Study of Routine." *Organization Studies*, 28/5: 773–86.

Cohen, M. D. (2012). "Perceiving and Remembering Routine Action: Fundamental Micro-Level Origins." *Journal of Management Studies*, 49/8: 1383–8.

Cohen, M. D. and Bacdayan, P. (1994). "Organizational Routines are Stored as Procedural Memory: Evidence from a Laboratory Study." *Organization Science*, 5/4: 554–68.

Cohen, M. D., Burkhart, R., Dosi, G., Egidi, M., Marengo, L., Warglien, M., and Winter, S. (1996). "Routines and Other Recurring Action Patterns of Organizations: Contemporary Research Issues." *Industrial and Corporate Change*, 5/3: 653–98.

Cohen, M. D., Levinthal, D. A., and Warglien, M. (2014). "Collective Performance: Modeling the Interaction of Habit-Based Actions." *Industrial and Corporate Change*, 23/2: 329–60.

Crossley, N. (2013a). "Habit and Habitus." *Body & Society*, 19: 136–61.

Crossley, N. (2013b). "Pierre Bourdieu's *Habitus*." In T. Sparrow and A. Hutchinson (eds.), *A History of Habit from Aristotle to Bourdieu*. Lanham, MD: Lexington Books, 291–308.

Dane, E. (2011). "Paying Attention to Mindfulness and Its Effects on Task Performance in the Workplace." *Journal of Management*, 37/4: 997–1018.

Dewey, J. (2002 [1922]). *Human Nature and Conduct*. Amherst, NY: Prometheus Books.

Dionysiou, D. D. and Tsoukas, H. (2013). "Understanding the (Re)Creation of Routines from Within: A Symbolic Interactionist Perspective." *Academy of Management Review*, 38/2: 181–205.

Emirbayer, M. and Mische, A. (1998). "What is Agency?" *American Journal of Sociology*, 103/4: 962–1023.

Evans, J. B. T. (2007). "Dual-Processing Accounts of Reasoning, Judgment, and Social Cognition." *Annual Review of Psychology*, 59: 255–78.

Feldman, M. S. and Pentland, B. T. (2003). "Reconceptualizing Organizational Routines as a Source of Flexibility and Change." *Administrative Science Quarterly*, 48/1: 94–118.

Felin, T., Foss, N. J., Heimeriks, K. H., and Madsen, T. L. (2012). "Microfoundations of Routines and Capabilities: Individuals, Processes, and Structure." *Journal of Management Studies*, 49/8: 1351–74.

Gibson, J. J. (1979). *The Ecological Approach to Visual Perception*. Boston, MA: Houghton Mifflin.

Glomb, T. M., Duffy, M. K., Bono, J. E., and Yang, T. (2011). "Mindfulness at Work." In A. Joshi, H. Liao, and J. J. Martocchio (eds.), *Research in Personnel and Human Resources Management*, vol. 30. Bingley, UK: Emerald Group Publishing Limited, 115–57.

Hodgson, G. M. (2003). "The Mystery of the Routine: The Darwinian Destiny of an Evolutionary Theory of Economic Change." *Revue Économique*, 54/2: 355–84.

Howard-Grenville, J. A. (2005). "The Persistence of Flexible Organizational Routines: The Role of Agency and Organizational Context." *Organization Science*, 16/6: 618–36.

James, W. (1914 [1890]). *Habit*. New York: Henry Holt and Company.

James, W. (1939). *Talks to Teachers on Psychology*. New York: Henry Holt and Company.

Jog, M. S., Kubota, Y., Connolly, C. I., Hillegaart, V., and Graybiel, A. M. (1999). "Building Neural Representations of Habits." *Science*, 286/5445: 1745–9.

Kellogg, K. C., Orlikowski, W. J., and Yates, J. (2006). "Life in the Trading Zone: Structuring Coordination across Boundaries in Postbureaucratic Organizations." *Organization Science*, 17/1: 22–44.

Knudsen, T. (2008). "Organizational Routines in Evolutionary Theory." In M. C. Becker (ed.), *Handbook of Organizational Routines*. Cheltenham: Edward Elgar, 125–51.

Langer, E. J. (1989). "Minding Matters: The Consequences of Mindlessness-Mindfulness." In L. Berkowitz (ed.), *Advances in Experimental Social Psychology*. San Diego, CA: Academic Press, 137–73.

Langley, A., Smallman, C., Tsoukas, H., and Van de Ven, A. H. (2013). "Process Studies of Change in Organizations and Management: Unveiling Temporality, Activity, and Flow." *Academy of Management Journal*, 56/1: 1–13.

Laureiro-Martinez, D. (2014). "Cognitive Control Capabilities, Routinization Propensity, and Decision-Making Performance." *Organization Science*, 25/4: 1111–33.

Leonardi, P., Nardi, B., and Kallinikos, J. (eds.) (2012). *Materiality and Organizing: Social Interaction in a Technological World*. Oxford: Oxford University Press.

Levinthal, D. and Rerup, C. (2006). "Crossing an Apparent Chasm: Bridging Mindful and Less-Mindful Perspectives on Organizational Learning." *Organization Science*, 17/4: 502–13.

March, J. and Simon, H. (1958). *Organizations*. New York: John Wiley.

Mauss, M. (1973). "Techniques of the Body." *Economy and Society*, 2/1: 70–88.

Merleau-Ponty, M. (1962). *Phenomenology of Perception*. New York: Humanities Press.

Narduzzo, A., Rocco, E., and Warglien, M. (2000). "Talking about Routines in the Field: The Emergence of Organizational Capabilities in a New Cellular Phone Network Company." In G. Dosi, R. R. Nelson, and S. G. Winter (eds.), *The Nature and Dynamics of Organizational Capabilities*. Oxford: Oxford University Press, 27–50.

Neal, D. T., Wood, W., and Drolet, A. (2013). "How Do People Adhere to Goals when Willpower is Low? The Profits (and Pitfalls) of Strong Habits." *Journal of Personality and Social Psychology*, 104/6: 959–75.

Neal, D. T., Wood, W., and Quinn, J. M. (2006). "Habits: A Repeat Performance." *Current Directions in Psychological Science*, 15/4: 198–202.

Nelson, R. R. and Winter, S. G. (1982). *An Evolutionary Theory of Economic Change*. Cambridge, MA: Harvard University Press.

Parmigiani, A. and Howard-Grenville, J. (2011). "Routines Revisited: Exploring the Capabilities and Practice Perspectives." *Academy of Management Annals*, 5/1: 413–53.

Quinn, R. E., Pascoe, A., Wood, W., and Neal, D. T. (2010). "Can't Control Yourself? Monitor Those Bad Habits." *Personality and Social Psychology Bulletin*, 36/4: 499–511.

Rerup, C. and Levinthal, D. (2014). "Situating the Concept of Organizational Mindfulness: The Multiple Dimensions of Organizational Learning." In G. Becke (ed.), *Mindful Change in Times of Permanent Reorganization*. Berlin: Springer, 33–48.

Salvato, C. (2009). "Capabilities Unveiled: The Role of Ordinary Activities in the Evolution of Product Development Processes." *Organization Science*, 20/2: 384–409.

Salvato, C. and Rerup, C. (2011). "Beyond Collective Entities: Multilevel Research on Organizational Routines and Capabilities." *Journal of Management*, 37/2: 468–90.

Smith, W. K. and Lewis, M. W. (2011). "Toward a Theory of Paradox: A Dynamic Equilibrium Model of Organizing." *Academy of Management Review*, 36/2: 381–403.

Szulanski, G. and Jensen, R. J. (2006). "Presumptive Adaptation and the Effectiveness of Knowledge Transfer." *Strategic Management Journal*, 27/10: 937–57.

Turner, S. F. (2014). "The Temporal Dimension of Routines and their Outcomes: Exploring the Role of Time in the Capabilities and Practice Perspectives." In A. J. Shipp and Y. Fried (eds.), *Time and Work*, vol. 2. New York: Psychology Press, 115–45.

Verplanken, B. and Wood, W. (2006). "Interventions to Break and Create Habits." *Journal of Public Policy & Marketing*, 25/1: 90–103.

Vogus, T. and Sutcliffe, K. (2012). "Organizational Mindfulness and Mindful Organizing: A Reconciliation and Path Forward." *Academy of Management Learning & Education*, 11/4: 722–35.

Weick, K. E. (1969). *The Social Psychology of Organizing*. Menlo Park, CA: Addison-Wesley.

Weick, K. E. and Sutcliffe, K. M. (2006). "Mindfulness and the Quality of Organizational Attention." *Organization Science*, 17/4: 514–24.

Weick, K. E., Sutcliffe, K. M., and Obstfeld, D. (1999). "Organizing for High Reliability: Processes of Collective Mindfulness." *Research in Organizational Behavior*, 21: 81–123.

Winter, S. G. (2013). "Habit, Deliberation, and Action: Strengthening the Microfoundations of Routines and Capabilities." *Academy of Management Perspectives*, 27/2: 120–37.

Wood, W. and Neal, D. T. (2007). "A New Look at Habits and the Habit–Goal Interface." *Psychological Review*, 114/4: 843–63.

Wood, W. and Neal, D. T. (2009). "The Habitual Consumer." *Journal of Consumer Psychology*, 19/4: 579–92.

Wood, W., Quinn, J. M., and Kashy, D. A. (2002). "Habits in Everyday Life: Thought, Emotion, and Action." *Journal of Personality and Social Psychology*, 83/6: 1281–97.

Wood, W., Tam, L., and Witt, M. G. (2005). "Changing Circumstances, Disrupting Habits." *Journal of Personality and Social Psychology*, 88/6: 918–33.

5

Evolutionary and Revolutionary Change in Path-Dependent Patterns of Action

Brian T. Pentland and Eun Ju Jung

Abstract: While routines are usually seen as a stabilizing aspect of the social world, recent history offers some examples of revolutionary change in areas where information and communication technologies are involved. Even when the technology stays the same, patterns of action can change and propagate very rapidly. This chapter builds on the evolutionary framework introduced by W. Brian Arthur (2009) to explain rapid, dramatic evolution of patterns of action. The framework emphasizes the importance of deliberate recombination, rather than random variation, as the primary engine of evolutionary change. The authors use this framework to help explain why some contexts may be subject to bursts of new routines, while others are relatively stable.

One does not need to spend much time on social media, such as YouTube, Twitter, or Instagram, to realize that novel combinations of ideas, activities, and technologies can spread quickly. From *selfies* to *flashmobs*, there are numerous examples. By "spread," we are not referring to sharing (re-posting, re-tweeting, etc.) of a particular image, message, or video; we are talking about the evolution and diffusion of a pattern of action, social practice, or routine. For example, one flashmob video, "Christmas Food Court Flash Mob" has over 43 million views as of January 2014 (<http://youtube/SXh7JR9oKVE>), but that is just one out of over 6.8 million distinct flashmob videos on YouTube. A flashmob requires coordinating the activities of an open-ended set of participants at a particular time and place. Further, the event needs to be recorded and posted. The question is, how can elaborate patterns of action, such as flashmobs, spread so rapidly?

While somewhat esoteric, this example is interesting because it sheds light on a central problem in the dynamics of organizational routines: when do routines stay the same and when do they change? Explaining stability and change is also a central problem in process theories of organizing (Hernes and Maitlis, 2010; Langley and Tsoukas, in press). Langley and Tsoukas (in press) argue that:

> The field of process organization studies is centrally concerned with time and with all important "how" questions. Process studies aim to capture the dynamic, continuous and endogenous nature of change and changing, whether intended or not.

In this chapter, we theorize about the mechanisms that can initiate and sustain a process of radical change in routines. Radical change is difficult to explain because routines are generally understood to be path-dependent phenomena (Schulz, 2008; Sydow et al., 2009; Vergne and Durand, 2011; Turner, 2014). Path dependence implies that past patterns of action predict future patterns, so there is an inherent tendency toward inertia and stability (Baum and Singh, 1994; Aldrich, 1999).

In this chapter, we draw on examples from social media to hypothesize about the conditions under which new routines might form, or existing routines might undergo rapid change. We are especially interested in the role of information and communication technologies (ICTs) in enabling these transformations. We adopt the definition of organizational routines as recognizable, repetitive patterns of interdependent actions (Feldman and Pentland, 2003), but we consider patterns of action that may occur outside the context of formal organizations. We focus on patterns of interdependent action; readers may think of these as descriptions of social practices, if they prefer.

We begin with a brief review of evolutionary processes in non-biological systems, a discussion that is heavily influenced by the work of W. Brian Arthur (2009) on the role of recombination in the evolution of technology. Following Turner (2014), we consider the role of time in the evolutionary process and also the mechanisms through which routines may spread. By putting these ideas together with the concept of narrative network (Pentland and Feldman, 2007; Goh et al., 2011), we propose a model of the process through which routines may evolve rather rapidly. We use the example of the telephone (and its technological descendants) as an example.

5.1 Evolutionary Processes

Evolutionary models involving random variation (V), selection (S), and retention (R) are widely used in explaining change in social and organizational systems (Van de Ven and Poole, 1995; Zollo and Winter, 2002; Bickhard and Campbell, 2003; Turner, 2014). However, Arthur (2009) contends that pure Darwinian evolution (VSR) is not an appropriate model for technological change because it understates the role of combination and recombination:

> In technology, by contrast, combinations are the norm. Every novel technology and novel solution is a combination, and every capturing of a phenomenon uses a combination. In technology, combinatorial evolution is foremost. Darwinian variation and selection are by no means absent, but they follow behind, working on structures already formed. (Arthur 2009: 188)

Arthur (2009) uses the phrase "combinatorial evolution" to describe the way that components like central processing unit (CPU), keyboard, and monitor can be recombined to create different kinds of computers. Recombination is especially applicable to digital artifacts (Pentland and Feldman, 2007; Yoo, 2012), where modularity and standardized interfaces make it easy. Digital technologies such as service oriented architecture (Huhns and Singh, 2005; Choi et al., 2010), APIs (application program interface), and mashups (Hartmann et al., 2008; Hwang et al., 2009; Yu and Woodard, 2009; Yoo, 2012) exemplify the idea of recombination. Social media platforms often provide a variety of APIs that can be recombined and "mashed up" in various ways, such as displaying search results on a map.

The biological model of random variation understates the role of recombination, and it also understates the role of agency, intentionality, and design. As Arthur (2009) points out, engineers recombine existing technology to solve problems. They do so very carefully and thoughtfully, not randomly. Thus, in contrast to the biological case, where random mutations are unlikely to be functional, intentional recombinations are very likely to be functional, at least for some purpose.

While Arthur (2009) is focused on technology as a collection of physical artifacts (e.g. jet engines), his argument transfers readily to sociomaterial practices, such as routines. First, Arthur defines technology very broadly, as *executable*: technology embodies a means to solve a problem. Routines generally emerge in response to problems or goals that need to be addressed (Cohen et al., 1996), so they would fit this definition. Second, routines clearly involve recombination, and they have decomposable parts (Becker, 2004). Routines are often broken into chunks or sub-routines (March and Simon, 1958). Finally, in the same way that engineers solve problems and create potentially reusable designs, practitioners of all kinds also solve problems and create potentially reusable patterns of action as a normal part of practice. For example, Goh et al. (2011) analyze the way that nurses and physicians evolve new patterns of action when new technology is introduced into a hospital. Barley (1986) offers a similar analysis for radiological technicians and physicians. In these examples, the new technology introduces a wave of incremental changes in the way work is done, but it does not determine the particular patterns of action that evolve. Barley's (1986) phrase "technology as an occasion for structuring" suggests that technology sets the stage, but does not dictate the players' lines.

Arthur (2009) argues that whenever engineers confront a new problem, they generate a new design by recombining pieces from existing designs. The more challenging the problem, the more likely they will generate a novel combination. When designers confront a new problem, the time scale for designing, building, and releasing a new technology to solve that problem is relatively slow (months or years). For example, a hospital might get new radiological equipment every few years.

When users confront problems, the time scale may be much faster (hours, minutes, or less). In principle, each new situation of use can potentially provide an occasion for users to innovate or improvise. Each patient, each scan, can pose special problems that may require an innovative solution. This difference in time scale mirrors the distinction in software development between "design-time" (which may occur once every few months, even for software) and "run-time" (which may occur once every few seconds, or faster) (Yu et al., 2008).

The distinction between design-time and run-time exemplifies one of the key challenges that Leonardi and Barley (2008) identify in theorizing about sociomaterial systems: how to include the role of design as well as the role of use? Here, we treat them as different aspects of the same evolutionary process, but we note that the time scale on which they occur is generally very different. Turner (2014: 132) noted that "agency and artifacts play central enabling and constraining roles in the evolution of routines." He provides an extensive review of the role of time in the literature on routines, and discusses the use of evolutionary models as a common explanatory mechanism. His review suggests that the current research literature has not focused on the possibility that artifacts and actions may evolve on different time scales, or through different mechanisms.

It is instructive to compare evolutionary processes in biological, technical, and action domains. The difference in time scale is particularly salient, but there are additional differences, as summarized in Table 5.1 and discussed in the paragraphs that follow.

Biology. In natural biological systems, evolution occurs quite slowly. It is limited by a number of factors. First, variations are random, so most of

Table 5.1 Comparison of evolutionary processes in biology, technology, and actions

	Biological	Technological (artifacts)	Action patterns (routines)
Mechanism	Reproduction	Designers solve problem	Users solve problem
Type of variation	Random	Intentional	Intentional
Time scale	Reproductive generation	Design time (product or process release cycle)	Run time (product or process use cycle)
Locus	Decentralized	Relatively centralized	Decentralized
Transmission	Genetic	Diffusion of artifacts	Diffusion of actions
Degree of recombination	Limited	High	Very high

them are not likely to be adaptive. In contrast, solutions to engineering problems are likely to be adaptive, almost by definition. Second, biological systems have limited ability to exploit the power of recombination. Even species that benefit from the recombinant effects of sexual reproduction cannot simply pick and choose characteristics to pass on to their offspring, and species that reproduce asexually do not have any mechanism for recombination. Third, biological systems are limited by the reproductive time scale of the organism. Organisms that reproduce quickly, like bacteria, evolve much faster than organisms that take months or years to reach reproductive maturity. Finally, even if a mutation is adaptive, it spreads only via reproduction—there is no mimesis or Larmarckian process to speed it along.

Technology. When applied to things (physical products or artifacts), evolution can only occur when the artifact is redesigned. For physical artifacts, this can be months or years. For digital artifacts, such as software programs, this can occur more quickly. But even software requires a cycle of design–build–test–release–install before a change becomes effective. On the temporal dimension, technology may be slower than some species (e.g. bacteria), but faster than others (e.g. humans). The big advantage in technological evolution arises from the intentional nature of the changes and the effect of recombination, as discussed earlier. Also, once it has been designed, it can be widely deployed, which sets the stage for further evolutionary adaptation and recombination.

Action patterns. When applied to action patterns, such as routines, the time scale is potentially much faster because changes can occur *each time the pattern is carried out*. Thus, changes can occur on a time scale of minutes or even seconds. Because there may be many people engaged in a similar practice, the locus of the process is highly decentralized; the change could occur anywhere. When spread and reproduced across a digital network, the evolutionary process can proceed very quickly (Yoo, 2012).

Of course, these three domains are not entirely independent. In particular, a great deal of attention has been focused on the relationship between technological and organizational change. The notion of technological determinism has been fairly well refuted in favor of constructivism (Leonardi and Barley, 2010). Changes in technology or managerial intention are neither necessary nor sufficient to change action patterns. Deliberate attempts to induce change are not always effective, and changes often occur in the absence of deliberation. Path dependence provides a reasonable explanatory mechanism for these observations, and it has become the standard explanation for both inertia and incremental change (Pentland et al., 2012). However, path dependence does not readily explain episodes of dramatic change in routines quite as readily. In the next section, we will work through a familiar example that we can use as a basis for theorizing about the phenomenon.

5.2 Example: The "Telephone"

To help theorize about revolutionary change, consider the "telephone." We put "telephone" in quotes because the device itself has changed dramatically in recent years, as have the activities we associate with our "phones." Mazmanian (2013) presents a detailed, longitudinal field study of the use of a particular kind of cellular phone in a particular organization. Like Barley (1986), she demonstrates that users can enact different patterns of action based on the same technology. So, with the important caveat in mind that this is not a deterministic process, we want to examine how this technology may interact with typical patterns of action.

We start from the familiar "plain old telephone service" (POTS, also known as a landline) and the typical patterns of action that accompanied that technology. From that baseline, we consider two kinds of changes: new technical functionality and new social activities. Roughly speaking, we can think of these as technical evolution and social evolution. These dimensions are obviously entangled and imbricated in many ways, but we want to focus on the simple situation where a new technology provides people with ability to perform old things as well as to do new things (Leonardi et al., 2012).

Figure 5.1 portrays three generic stages in the history of the telephone. It is intended to be illustrative, not comprehensive. The first stage (T=1) is the

	T=1	T=2	T=3
Technology	Land Line	Cell phone <-------- unchanged ------->	
Pattern of action	Making a phone call <-------- unchanged ------->		"Meet you at Disneyland..."

Figure 5.1 Stages of evolution in telephone technology and routines

familiar "land line." The land line facilitated a familiar pattern of action known as *making a call*: one person *dials the phone*, then waits, until *another person answers the phone*. With the POTS that we now refer to as a "land line" the location of the phone is tied to the phone number. If you called a friend at his or her home number, you never had to ask, "Are you home?"

The second stage (T=2) includes the introduction of new technology: the cell phone. This well-established technology has been studied in many contexts (e.g. Manning, 1996). Here, we want to focus on the fact that unlike calls made with land lines, the physical locations of the caller/callee were no longer specified. Nevertheless, the old pattern of action was still possible.

Finally, in stage three (T=3), we see that the cell phone can be used for new patterns of action that were not possible with a land line. This innovation facilitated new patterns of action, such as coordinating a meeting place without doing detailed planning in advance (e.g. "I'll meet you at Disneyland; call me when you get there"). Users capitalize on the mobility of the device to enact novel patterns of action that solve existing problems.

We could elaborate on this example in a number of different ways. Along the technological dimension, cell phones (and then so-called "smart phones") have incorporated a large number of specific innovations, such as texting, touch screens, built-in cameras, global positioning, increased network speed, and so forth. Each of these technological changes involves a recombination of prior technology, as described by Arthur, and a familiar cycle of design, production, diffusion, and competition. At the same time, there is a parallel story to be told about changes in social practice, from selfies to flashmobs and beyond.

Consider some other popular crowd practices such as wikis (Kane and Fichman, 2009), open source programming (Lerner and Tirole, 2002), and crowdsourcing (Howe, 2006). Web 2.0 technology provides users with real-time editing and interaction functions, which allows a wide set of participants to create and share new content (O'Reilly, 2007). These new features allow us to carry on existing practices (e.g. knowledge sharing) and to create new practices. For example, in the context of a transaction, there is a buyer and a seller. But the customer's role is no longer limited to a simple buyer in the classic economic sense. Customers can share their ideas on product and service innovation, discuss the ideas with online user groups, and the "seller" can directly adopt innovation ideas from customers. Instead of assigning a new product development task to a fixed group of employees, companies are incorporating a large crowd of customers. Procter & Gamble's open innovation platform, Dell's "Idea storm," and Starbucks' "My Starbucks Idea" are some current examples.

Technology-enabled collaboration creates new social practices such as crowdfunding, an Internet funding platform that allows project creators to raise funds from crowds in online websites. Entrepreneurs raised almost $2.7 billion from crowdfunding platforms in 2012. Technology suggests certain social practices are embedded in technologies by designers, but those features can be enacted by users in various ways (Orlikowski and Iacono, 2001). Moreover, a new feature (or affordance) creates a new set of structural constraints and opportunities. The question is, what makes it possible for new routines to form and spread rapidly?

5.3 A Theory of (R)Evolutionary Change in Routines

Consistent with current interest in the role of artifacts in routines (D'Adderio, 2011), our goal here is to theorize about the evolution of routines (practices) that are technologically enabled. We can then ask about the implications of this framework for routines in general. While we are skeptical about the possibility of predicting the rise or fall of particular practices, we theorize about the factors that may contribute to rapid, transformational change. To do so, we incorporate some vocabulary from Pentland and Feldman's (2007) idea of a narrative network.

5.3.1 Narrative Network: Concepts and Definitions

A narrative network can be defined as a method for representing and visualizing patterns of technology in use (Pentland and Feldman, 2007). It represents the possible ways of carrying out a routine or a practice. Each node in the network is a fragment that describes who does what. The network shows how the fragments can be recombined.

Actants are part of each narrative fragment. They are the *who* (people or machines) that are taking part in the story. In a typical phone call, there are several actants: two people, two phones, and a network/switching system that connects them. In a smart phone, one may also find additional actants (such as a contact list, a voice-activated assistant, and so on). Actions are the *what*. This could include dialing, answering, talking, typing, and so on. Narrative fragments are combinations of actants and actions. Fragments are recombined to create pathways through the network, which represent ways of doing the practice. For example, "Dialing a number" involves at least two actants (a person and a phone), and some combination of actions (touching, tapping, speaking, etc.). One can think of narrative fragments as subroutines or chunks of activity that advance an overall story.

As conceptualized by Pentland and Feldman (2007), the nodes in the network are narrative fragments. As one traverses the network from node to node, each particular pathway defines a particular story as a list of fragments. For example, the familiar routine of "phone tag" might consist of narrative fragments like this: "I dialed the number," "I left a message," "She called me back," and so on. The introduction of text messaging seems to have made the phone tag routine less common, if not actually obsolete. A given set of narrative fragments, and connections between those fragments, defines the possible ways to carry out a pattern of action.

The narrative network also provides a vocabulary for representing the ostensive and performative aspects of a routine (Feldman and Pentland, 2003). The ostensive aspects of a routine could be thought of as typical pathways ("how we do things around here"). Different organizational participants may be aware of different pathways, or different parts of the same pathway. The performative aspect of a routine is the set of actualized pathways; the specific sequences of action that occur as a routine is performed.

When the narrative network is small, and contains few pathways, there are only a few ways to carry out the pattern. As the network gets more nodes and more pathways that connect those nodes, there are exponentially more ways to perform the pattern (Haerem et al., 2015). Eventually, if the set of fragments or pathways begins to produce new and distinctive patterns of action, those patterns might be recognized as part of a different routine. The process for forming and recognizing a novel pattern can be thought of in mechanistic terms, such as search of a landscape (Levinthal, 1997), or in symbolic interactionist terms (Dionysiou and Tsoukas, 2013). They key point is that the search is deliberate: the people are *trying* to find a convenient, foolproof way to meet up at Disneyland.

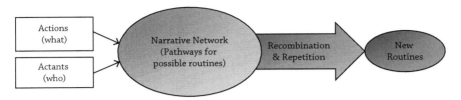

Figure 5.2 Recombination and repetition of pathways generates new routines

We can break down the overall effect of ICTs into a simple set of contributing factors, each of which is necessary but not sufficient to generate new routines. There are two necessary ingredients: (a) an increased set of possible action patterns, as captured in the network; and (b) increased recombination (exploration) and repetition (exploitation) of those patterns. ICTs influence both of these dimensions. First, ICTs increase the number of narrative fragments by influencing the set of potential actions and actants. Second, ICTs influence the potential recombination of narrative fragments, through the structure of the network, as suggested in Figure 5.2.

Growing the network. Increased numbers of actants and actors increase the size of the narrative network, thereby increasing the set of possible pathways. In the case of the telephone, the set of actions has grown from simply placing a call to include a much broader range of communicative actions, such as sending a text, sending a photo, or sending a video. When the feature set of a technological artifact expands, it directly increases the number of actions available to its users. In the case of smart phones, the increase has been particularly dramatic because of "apps"—software that extends the functionality of the basic device in countless ways.

Pentland and Feldman (2007) discussed the effect of ICTs on the repertoire of actions. But ICTs also influence the potential set of actants ("who"). Together, however, they create a larger space of possible narratives. As the "telephone" changes over time, there are new technological actants, such as the embedded camera, touch screen, and voice assistant. But there is also a much broader set of human actants that can be brought into the pattern of action (e.g. when we broadcast a text message).

We could refine this framework by identifying other phenomena that influence the size of the narrative network. We could identify factors that increase or decrease the number of feasible pathways, for example. Many such extensions and refinements seem feasible. At this point, we are simply

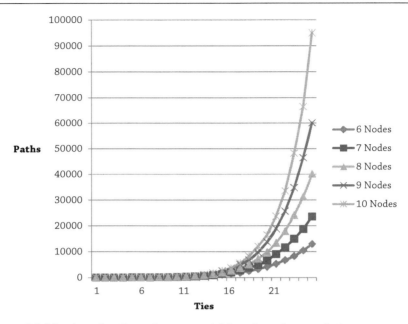

Figure 5.3 Number of paths and exponential function of network size

pointing out that increasing actions and actants should, all else being equal, increase the size of the network.

The key insight is that changes in the size of the network have an exponential effect on the number of pathways that can be followed to complete the task (Haerem et al., 2015). Figure 5.3 shows the results of an analysis of thousands of randomly generated networks; the vertical axis represents the number of pathways in the network. When there are a small number of nodes, there are only a few pathways, so there are only a few possible ways to complete a task. As the number of nodes increases (due to a larger set of actions/actants), the number of possible paths increases exponentially.

Increased recombination and repetition. Increasing the size of the narrative network is not sufficient to generate new routines. People must find useful new pathways and repeat them. It seems likely that ICTs may influence the rate of recombination and repetition, as well. This is because ICTs provide standards and platforms that allow narrative fragments to be more readily recombined and used together in a given situation.

Problem-solving entails exploring or searching through the network of possible paths to solve a particular problem (e.g. coordinating a trip to

Disneyland). In doing so, users can recombine various elements of the network to construct a solution. For example, they might start with a phone call and then send a text, or perhaps a text with a photo. Alternatively, they might simply share their location through a GPS-aware application of some sort. In doing so, they are solving the common problem of how to carry out a successful meeting when the time is uncertain and the location is unfamiliar to everyone involved. The rate of recombination is influenced by factors such as the number of users and the variety of problems they are solving. Each time users solve a problem, they are navigating a pathway in the narrative network.

We can think of the recombination process as a form of search or exploration. It is a form of path-making in a relatively open field. Depending on problems people confront, the required work and range of organizing (e.g. what, who, why, how) are different. We can think of the repetition as analogous to exploitation; it is like path following. As pathways (narrative patterns) are discovered, they can be repeated. In so doing, they become more recognizable as patterns, and they become routines.

The cycle time on each of these processes is an important aspect of the phenomenon. The availability of new actions and classes of actants is connected to the release of new technology. Thus, changes in the narrative network are connected to technological evolution, where users have to wait for designers to conceive, test, manufacture, and distribute new tools to solve their problems. This is the framework that Arthur (2009) relies on, more or less explicitly, in theorizing about the evolution of artifacts.

But recombination and repetition are run-time processes carried out by end-users. When people can create their own solutions (e.g. adapting and appropriating their tools at "run-time," instead of only at "design-time"), the number of possible solutions will increase. Each such solution is a chunk of executable capability, potentially available for recombination with other chunks. The expanded repertoire can be applied toward different problems, such as assembling a flashmob at Disneyland, or novel forms of crowdsourcing.

In general, more participants, solving more problems, will tend to increase the number of available solutions. Social learning (including observation and mimicry) provides a variety of mechanisms for the transfer of ideas and practices (Bandura, 2001; Pentland, 2014). Not all solutions will diffuse equally far or equally fast, but all else being equal, broader distribution should tend to enable further (re)combination. Furthermore, some ICTs provide mechanisms through which solutions (and (re)combinations of solutions) can be intentionally promoted (e.g. the "share" button). They become recipes for action that can be reproduced and subsequently revised or recombined to create new patterns.

5.4 Extending the Argument to Other Patterns of Action

To summarize, Figure 5.2 suggests a two-step process that creates the possibility of very rapid evolution of new routines. First, factors that tend to increase the size of the narrative network can create an exponential increase in the number of possible pathways. Technological innovations such as the smartphone are particularly effective in this regard, but in principle, anything that contributes to the size of the network is relevant. Second, if more end-users are exploring and then exploiting (creating and then following) these pathways, there is a greater chance that useful new patterns will be discovered and become recognizable as routines.

If we apply this framework to more traditional settings, it may shed some light on why revolutionary change is less common in settings such as formal organizations. First, there are a number of factors that will tend to limit substantial changes to an action set—the feasible, allowable actions— in any part of a formal organization. First, consider the division of labor, which may be implemented through formal roles and job descriptions that define what actions are appropriate (Miner, 1990, 1991). In addition, there is often a formal control environment that includes accounting controls, process controls, and quality controls, and these may be enforced though the technical infrastructure (e.g. a set of computerized systems where these controls are embedded). For the same reasons, there are likely to be relatively minor changes to the set of actants (human or non-human), since each actant engaged in a process is expected to conform to a defined role. Thus, in a formal environment, changes to the narrative network are likely to be relatively small.

At the same time, for many of the same reasons, there may be less opportunity for exploration (recombination) of new pathways if they do become available. Quality and process management frameworks tend to minimize recombination. Also, the set of problems that users confront may be relatively uniform, minimizing the need for exploration and recombination. Other factors, such as internal controls, performance appraisals, and other systems for measurement and reward may tend to reinforce existing action pathways. To the extent that discovering new action pathways (exploration) is inconsistent with repeating familiar pathways (exploitation), it helps explain why organizations find it difficult to be "ambidextrous"—exploring and exploiting at the same time (He and Wong, 2004).

When changes are intended, they are often deliberately small and targeted on particular actions or actors, in an effort to minimize issues of organizational change. They may also be targeted at specific pathways. A classic case is the addition of action steps for fraud prevention, which is often implemented by requiring an additional level of approval or signature. There are always opportunities for path-making, but in the context of formal organization, it seems likely that feasible new paths are harder to find.

5.5 Conclusion

Time is a central issue in theories of process and a central issue in the dynamics of routines, as well. Turner (2014) notes that evolutionary theories based on variation, selection, and retention have been used to conceptualize change in routines, but current research has not emphasized the role of recombination, nor has it unpacked the different time scales on which evolution might occur. Here, we emphasize the importance of recombination in action patterns and its potential to occur on a much faster time scale than purely technological change (as described by Arthur 2009). The theory we outline here is somewhat speculative, but it does provide a process through which path-dependent patterns of action (a.k.a. organizational routines) can rapidly change: namely, through the availability of a lot more paths and a lot more people recombining those paths to solve problems. While these conditions are rare inside formal organizations, which generally seek to control and prevent change, they can be observed in less formal settings, such as social media platforms.

By combining structure (the pathways) and agency (the choice of pathways), this framework may offer the beginnings of a process-based theory of organizational change, where dynamic networks of events would be the basic unit of observation. This would provide an alternative to current theory about technology and change, which is often framed as a contest between determinism and constructivism (Leonardi and Barley, 2010). On the deterministic side, one might argue that technology tends to limit changes in practice, because it constrains actions and introduces interdependence between actions, which limits the ways they can be recombined. On the constructivist side, one might argue that technology can create occasions for changes to the ways people do things by creating an available repertoire of potential actions. However, the repertoire of actions is created at "design-time." From an evolutionary perspective, the possibility of revolutionary change arises from rapid recombination by users, at "run-time." This potential for rapid change should increase when the number of users is increased, and when they are able to communicate and copy the revised action pattern, and (re)combine it into their own action patterns.

We have proposed an evolutionary theory of routine dynamics that focuses on the action patterns. The theory has two stages, each of which is necessary but not sufficient: changes in the narrative network and the rate of recombination/repetition. We have offered some ideas about what might drive or limit these factors (such as technological change, formal division of labor, and so on). Clearly, a great deal more refinement is possible, but the logical structure here is parsimonious, consistent with existing theory, and seems like a promising framework for future research.

Acknowledgment

This material is based upon work supported by the National Science Foundation under Grant No. SES-1026932. Any opinions, findings, and conclusions or recommendations expressed in this material are those of the authors and do not necessarily reflect the views of the National Science Foundation.

References

Aldrich, H. (1999). *Organizations Evolving*. Beverly Hills, CA: Sage Publications.

Arthur, W. B. (2009). *The Nature of Technology: What It Is and How It Evolves*. New York: Free Press.

Bandura, A. (2001). "Social Cognitive Theory of Mass Communication." *Media Psychology*, 3/3: 265–99.

Barley, S. R. (1986). "Technology as an Occasion for Structuring: Evidence from Observations of CT Scanners and the Social Order of Radiology Departments." *Administrative Science Quarterly*, 31/1: 78–108.

Baum, J. A. and Singh, J. V. (1994). "Organizational Niches and the Dynamics of Organizational Mortality." *American Journal of Sociology*, 100/2: 346–80.

Becker, M. C. (2004). "Organizational Routines: A Review of the Literature." *Industrial and Corporate Change*, 13/4: 643–78.

Bickhard, M. H. and Campbell, D. T. (2003). "Variations in Variation and Selection: The Ubiquity of the Variation-and-Selective Retention Ratchet in Emergent Organizational Complexity." *Foundations of Science*, 8/3: 215–82.

Choi, J., Nazareth, D. L., and Jain, H. K. (2010). "Implementing Service-Oriented Architecture in Organizations." *Journal of Management Information Systems*, 26/4: 253–86.

Cohen, M. D., Burkhart, R., Dosi, G., Egidi, M., Marengo, L., Warglien, M., and Winter, S. (1996). "Routines and other Recurring Action Patterns of Organizations: Contemporary Research Issues." *Industrial and Corporate Change*, 5/3: 653–98.

D'Adderio, L. (2011). "Artifacts at the Centre of Routines: Performing the Material Turn in Routines Theory." *Journal of Institutional Economics*, 7/2: 197–230.

Dionysiou, D. D. and Tsoukas, H. (2013). "Understanding the (Re)Creation of Routines from Within: A Symbolic Interactionist Perspective." *Academy of Management Review*, 38/2: 181–205.

Feldman, M. S. and Pentland, B. T. (2003). "Reconceptualizing Organizational Routines as a Source of Flexibility and Change." *Administrative Science Quarterly*, 48/1: 94–118.

Goh, J. M., Gao, G., and Agarwal, R. (2011). "Evolving Work Routines: Adaptive Routinization of Information Technology in Healthcare." *Information Systems Research*, 22/3: 565–85.

Haerem, T., Pentland, B. T., and Miller, K. (2015). "Task Complexity: Extending a Core Concept." *Academy of Management Review*, 40/3: 446–60.

Hartmann, B., Doorley, S., and Klemmer, S. R. (2008). "Hacking, Mashing, Gluing: Understanding Opportunistic Design." *IEEE Pervasive Computing*, 7/3: 46–54.

He, Z. L. and Wong, P. K. (2004). "Exploration vs. Exploitation: An Empirical Test of the Ambidexterity Hypothesis." *Organization Science*, 15/4: 481–94.

Hernes, T. and Maitlis, S. (2010). *Process, Sensemaking, and Organizing.* Oxford: Oxford University Press.

Howe, J. (2006). "The Rise of Crowdsourcing." *Wired Magazine*, 14/6: 1–4.

Huhns, M. N. and Singh, M. P. (2005). "Service-Oriented Computing: Key Concepts and Principles." *IEEE Internet Computing*, 9/1: 75–81.

Hwang, J., Altmann, J., and Kim, K. (2009). "The Structural Evolution of the Web 2.0 Service Network." *Online Information Review*, 33/6: 1040–57.

Kane, G. C. and Fichman, R. G. (2009). "The Shoemaker's Children: Using Wikis for Information Systems Teaching, Research, and Publication." *Management Information Systems Quarterly*, 33/1: 1–17.

Langley, A. and Tsoukas, H. (2010). "Introducing Perspectives on Process Organization Studies." *Process, Sensemaking, and Organizing*, 1/9: 1–27.

Langley, A. and Tsoukas, H. (eds.) (In press). The *Sage Handbook of Process Organization Studies*. Beverly Hills, CA: Sage Publications.

Leonardi, P. M. and Barley, S. R. (2008). "Materiality and Change: Challenges to Building Better Theory about Technology and Organizing." *Information and Organization*, 18/3: 159–76.

Leonardi, P. M. and Barley, S. R. (2010). "What's under Construction Here? Social Action, Materiality, and Power in Constructivist Studies of Technology and Organizing." *Academy of Management Annals*, 4/1: 1–51.

Leonardi, P. M., Nardi, B. A., and Kallinikos, J. (2012). *Materiality and Organizing: Social Interaction in a Technological World*. New York: Oxford University Press.

Lerner, J. and Tirole, J. (2002). "Some Simple Economics of Open Source." *Journal of Industrial Economics*, 50/2: 197–234.

Levinthal, D. A. (1997). "Adaptation on Rugged Landscapes." *Management Science*, 43/7: 934–50.

Manning, P. K. (1996). "Information Technology in the Police Context: The 'Sailor' Phone." *Information Systems Research*, 7/1: 52–62.

March, J. G. and Simon, H. A. (1958). *Organizations*. New York: John Wiley.

Mazmanian, M. (2013). "Avoiding the Trap of Constant Connectivity: When Congruent Frames Allow for Heterogeneous Practices." *Academy of Management Journal*, 56/5: 1225–50.

Miner, A. S. (1990). "Structural Evolution through Idiosyncratic Jobs: The Potential for Unplanned Learning." *Organization Science*,1/2: 195–210.

Miner, A. S. (1991). "Organizational Evolution and the Social Ecology of Jobs." *American Sociological Review*, 56/6: 772–85.

O'Reilly, T. (2007). "What is Web 2.0. Design Patterns and Business Models for the Next Generation of Software." *Communications and Strategies*, 65/1: 17–37.

Orlikowski, W. J. and Iacono, C. S. (2001). "Research Commentary: Desperately Seeking the "IT" in IT Research—A Call to Theorizing the IT Artifact." *Information Systems Research*, 12/2: 121–34.

Pentland, A. (2014). *Social Physics: How Good Ideas Spread—The Lessons from a New Science*. New York: Penguin.

Pentland, B. T. and Feldman, M. (2007). "Narrative Networks: Patterns of Technology and Organization." *Organization Science*, 18/5: 781–95.

Pentland, B. T., Feldman, M. S., Becker, M. C., and Liu, P. (2012). "Dynamics of Organizational Routines: A Generative Model." *Journal of Management Studies*, 49/8: 1484–508.

Schulz, M. (2008). "Staying on Track: A Voyage to the Internal Mechanisms of Routine Reproduction." In M. C. Becker (ed.), *Handbook of Organizational Routines*. Cheltenham: Edward Elgar, 228–55.

Sydow, J., Schreyögg, G., and Koch, J. (2009). "Organizational Path Dependence: Opening the Black Box." *Academy of Management Review*, 34/4: 689–709.

Turner, S. (2014). "The Temporal Dimension of Routines and their Outcomes: Exploring the Role of Time in the Capabilities and Practice Perspectives." In A. J. Shipp and Y. Fried (eds.), *Time and Work: How Time Impacts Groups, Organizations and Methodological Choices*, vol. 2. Hove: Psychology Press, 115–45.

Van de Ven, A. and Poole, M. (1995). "Explaining Development and Change in Organizations." *Academy of Management Review*, 20/3: 510–40.

Vergne, J. P. and Durand, R. (2011). "The Path of Most Persistence: An Evolutionary Perspective on Path Dependence and Dynamic Capabilities." *Organization Studies*, 32/3: 365–82.

Yoo, Y. (2012). "Digital Materiality and the Emergence of an Evolutionary Science of the Artificial." In P. M. Leonardi, B. A. Nardi, and J. Kallinikos (eds.), *Materiality and Organizing: Social Interaction in a Technological World*. New York: Oxford University Press, 134–54.

Yu, J., Benatallah, B., Casati, F., and Daniel, F. (2008). "Understanding Mashup Development." *IEEE Internet Computing*, 12/5: 44–52.

Yu, S. and Woodard, C. (2009). "Innovation in the Programmable Web: Characterizing the Mashup Ecosystem." In G. Feuerlicht and W. Lamersdorf (eds.), *Service-Oriented Computing—ICSOC 2008 Workshops*. Berlin: Springer, 136–47.

Zollo, M. and Winter, S. G. (2002). "Deliberate Learning and the Evolution of Dynamic Capabilities." *Organization Science*, 13/3: 339–51.

Section B
Empirical Explorations of Routines from a Process Perspective

6

The Role of Artifacts in Establishing Connectivity Within Professional Routines

A Question of Entanglement

Paula Jarzabkowski, Rebecca Bednarek, and Paul Spee

Abstract: This chapter focuses on the critical role of artifacts within the cycles of action through which routines are performed. Conceptualizing actors and artifact as entangled in action, it offers a multi-layered approach to the study of routines. The chapter also advances the theorizing of professional routines that stretch across organizations. Drawing on a global ethnography of the reinsurance industry, the authors demonstrate how professional knowledge is performed in such routines. They develop a processual framework that shows how the professional routine unfolds within three connected layers of entangled actions, actors, and artifacts: connecting with the profession; connecting with individual work; and connecting with collective work. The authors address the context of reinsurance, specifically examining the role of the rating sheet in the entanglement of action, actor, and artifact in performing the "deal appraisal routine" that is central to the profession of underwriting.

6.1 Introduction

This chapter is situated in the growing body of work that has raised new questions and avenues of research about the generative potential of routines (Feldman, 2000; Feldman and Pentland, 2003; Parmigiani and Howard-Grenville, 2011). In particular, recent studies have highlighted the role of artifacts and brought them to the foreground in the performance of routines. For example, a towel changing routine (Bapuji et al., 2012) involves not only actors and the actions involved with the disposal of used towels, but the towels themselves and issues such as how the routine is shaped by their position in the bathroom. Hence, recently scholars suggest that routines be thought of as sociomaterial ensembles, comprising bundles of action (social) and artifact (material) that, together, produce the routine (Pentland et al., 2012). We adopt this sociomaterial understanding of routines, which we define as one of "entanglement" whereby *entanglement* of actor and artifact is constitutive of action within the routine, rather than primacy being given to either (Howard-Grenville, 2005; Lazaric and Denis, 2005; D'Adderio, 2008; Cacciatori, 2012).

We examine entanglement at multiple layers within the context of a *professional* routine. Such routines stretch across organizational boundaries because they are grounded in the expertise and knowledge of the profession and, so, add to our understanding of routines as supra-organizational. In particular, professional routines raise two main theoretical and empirical puzzles for routine theory. First, professionals, such as consultants, doctors, and lawyers, are autonomous actors who have considerable jurisdiction to deploy their skills and knowledge to make individual decisions about their work (Greenwood et al., 1990; Empson, 2001). The nature of that work is typically highly customized, requiring a tailored approach or specific diagnosis that meets the needs of the particular client or situation (Larsson and Bowen, 1989; Sharma, 1997; Bednarek et al., 2015) so marginalizing the possibility of routinized solutions. Yet, increasingly the flows of often quantitative information underpinning that work, accompanied by technological tools that enable its codification, lend themselves to routinizing some aspects of such professional work (Abbott, 1988). For example, accountants use similar technical tools to perform relatively routinized accounting processes that are, at the same time, tailored to the specific accounting demands of particular clients. Hence, in a professional routine standardized technical tools or artifacts might be integral to the varied enactment of that routine by individual professional actors (Abbott, 1981; Maister, 1993). Second, professional actors' affiliation can be more to the profession than to a specific organization (Denis et al., 1996), so challenging assumptions about the extent to which their routines can be considered organizational. A professional routine might better be conceptualized as supra-organizational, generating coherence between the routine work performed inside organizations and the way that work is embedded in the profession. Given that routines are performed within the everyday work of actors in situ (Feldman and Pentland, 2003), these two points lead us, as scholars, to consider how professional routines connect to both the profession and also the everyday work of individual actors, often through the artifacts that constitute the technical tools of the profession. We seek to illuminate these puzzles about connectivity in professional routines through the concept of entanglement.

6.2 Theorizing Entanglement of Action, Actor, and Artifact

While artifacts are integral to the perpetuation of routines (Nelson and Winter, 1982), debates remain over their role in the coordination and performance of routines. Initially, the role of artifacts was seen at the level of operating procedures. While providing the basis for repetition of a routine, such research pointed to the lack of flexibility in artifacts, which constrains the adaptability of a routine to changes in the environment (Nelson and Winter, 1982). More recently, studies have examined the implication of artifacts in the coordination of a routine's performance, including a focus on artifacts as a source of variation and/or persistence in creating and recreating the performative aspect of routines. These studies examined how the knowledge properties inscribed in artifacts, such as rules, procedures, and power relations, become stabilized as abstract representations of some aspect of performance (Carlile, 2002; Bechky, 2003b; D'Adderio, 2003). These abstract representations inscribe knowledge of how the patterns of action should be coordinated (e.g. Howard-Grenville, 2005; Turner and Rindova, 2012). For example, in her study of a product development process in a high-tech manufacturing setting, D'Adderio (2008) illustrated how a software program stored procedures and rules that influenced when and where certain tasks were accomplished, and these design features of the software both enabled and constrained individual performances of the process. Further studies illuminated the way an artifact both enables and constrains performances as a routine unfolds (Howard-Grenville, 2005; Leonardi, 2011) or how artifacts enable routines to be aligned toward different organizational goals (D'Adderio, 2014). While some studies highlighted the way occupation-specific artifacts, such as product specifications, constrain coordination of interdependent actions across occupations (Bechky, 2003a, 2003b), others demonstrated the facilitative role of occupation-specific artifacts as these make differences in knowledge accessible to other occupations, thus enabling actors to integrate and transcend occupation-specific knowledge in subsequent actions (Kellogg et al., 2006; Majchrzak et al., 2012). Artifacts are thus shown to be critical to the performance of routines because of the knowledge that they inscribe; yet we need to understand more about how that knowledge is enacted within a routine, as actors work with artifacts (Leonardi, 2011).

While previous studies of routines tended to foreground, and give analytical primacy to, either the human actors (e.g. Feldman, 2000; Zbaracki and Bergen, 2010), or placed great emphasis on the artifact or technology (e.g. D'Adderio, 2003), recent work suggests a focus on *actions* rather than actors or artifacts as the unit through which to study routines (D'Adderio, 2011; Pentland, 2011). Actions are defined as a bundle of actor and artifact (Pentland et al., 2012) as their distinction is often blurred in practice. This approach enables us to focus on the interdependence of actors and artifacts within the actions through which routine tasks are accomplished (Leonardi, Orlikowski and Scott, 2008; 2011). It focuses attention on how action coordinates the performative-ostensive cycle, through the entanglement of actor and artifact, instead of giving primacy to one or the other (D'Adderio, 2003, 2008; Howard-Grenville, 2005; Lazaric and Denis, 2005; Bapuji et al., 2012; Cacciatori, 2012). More recently, D'Adderio (2014) illustrated how a routine is enacted variably through the adaptation of artifacts. Specifically, her study showed that, while artifacts provided the basis to replicate a routine initially, their malleable properties also enabled actors to adapt the enactment of the routine to the new circumstances they encountered in transferring routines across an organization. Artifacts are thus integral to the way actors enact routines.

This chapter takes action, which comprises the *entanglement* of actor and artifact, as the core unit of analysis. The notion of entanglement rests on the assumption that the social and the material are inextricably entwined (Leonardi, 2011). Rather than seeing artifacts as "things" with particular functionality—for example, seeing shovels as objects with which to dig holes, which relegates the materiality of the shovel to its functional purpose—the focus is on the socially situated action of doing digging in which the actor, the shovel, and the action of digging are inextricably bound in a sociomaterial relation. The artifact and the social are thus not separate, but are fused and generative of actions. This approach moves away from over-privileging either the actor or the artifact by examining the two as entangled in actions (e.g. Leonardi, 2011) examines how engineers attempt to reconcile human agency with a technology's material agency. His study shows complex imbrications, or arrangements, of human and material agency that provide different affordances to the unfolding activity. However, this study still gives sequential primacy to either actor or artifact in order to study how they shape each other. By contrast, we build on such work to explain how both actor and artifact are entangled in actions.

Our study focuses on the entanglement of actor and artifact within the actions that constitute professional routines, which we propose are connected across multiple layers from the mores of the profession to individual actors' everyday work, to the way that these sustain the profession over time. Extant work on the role of artifacts in routines is generally focused more on the *organizational* rather than the *inter-organizational* processes that might span a profession (e.g. Feldman, 2000; Feldman and Pentland, 2003; Parmigiani and Howard-Grenville, 2011). For example, studies examine the accomplishment of organizational tasks (D'Adderio, 2003), goals (D'Adderio, 2014), or new processes (Cacciatori, 2012), but have yet to study how artifacts are integral to performing professional routines across organizational boundaries. Nonetheless, other studies focused on work more generally have shown the central role of artifacts in establishing professional "jurisdictions" (Bechky, 2003a). In particular, Nelson and Irwin (2014) show how librarians re-crafted their professional identities in the face of the introduction of search engine technologies (also see Fiol and O'Connor, 2005). There is thus much scope to increase our understanding of professional routines by examining the concept of entanglement in instantiating routines across organizational boundaries.

6.3 Empirical Context: Appraising Deals in the Reinsurance Industry

This chapter draws from an ethnographic program of research into the reinsurance industry spanning 25 firms globally (see Jarzabkowski et al., 2015a, 2015b), in which we observed financial deal appraisal as a consistent professional routine. Reinsurance is the insurance of insurance companies; insurance firms pay reinsurers a premium ("price") to cover a percentage of their potential losses. A reinsurance deal sets out the specific parameters of the insurance firm's portfolio that reinsurance will cover. For instance, a firm that insures properties in New Zealand may purchase a reinsurance deal to cover potential losses and enable it to pay its policyholders in the event of a catastrophe that would damage or destroy many properties simultaneously, such as happened in 2010 with the Christchurch earthquakes. The insurer will buy cover from a reinsurer for damages that exceed a specified amount—for example $250 million—arising from a specified event, such as an earthquake. These deals are also segmented into what the industry calls "layers." For instance, one deal might have two layers; one providing cover from $250–$450 million, and another from $450–$750 million. Each such reinsurance deal is unique, reflecting the specific portfolio of underlying risks, such as damages to residential or commercial properties or marine vessels and cargo, requiring a bespoke appraisal for each deal. The routines to appraise such deals provide the empirical focus of this chapter.

Reinsurance underwriting is a long-standing financial profession, originating some 150 years ago (Borscheid et al., 2013). Underwriters are the professionals in charge of allocating "pots of capital" to those deals that they have appraised as generating the highest return for their firms (Bednarek et al., 2015). As typical with professional actors, they have strong affiliations to their profession and its specific professional qualifications and norms (Von Nordenflycht, 2010), as well as considerable autonomy to make important decisions for their firms (Abbott, 1988; Kunreuther et al., 1995).

The deal appraisal routine (DAR) is the essential work of reinsurance underwriting and what it means to be an underwriter. It establishes the price a reinsurance firm will charge for the capital it holds to cover an insurance firm against large-scale losses. To appraise a deal, underwriters have a professional understanding of the tasks necessary to convert information about the risk involved (Abbott, 1988) into a tradable financial object. To accomplish such an appraisal, an underwriter moves in a series of not strictly linear but nonetheless sequential steps as they work with the raw data received from a broker to establish a quote (price) for that deal. Receiving the information from the client or broker signals the start of the DAR and it is completed when the underwriter releases the final quoted rate to the client. The performance of the DAR will be further described here through our empirical illustration.

To accomplish the DAR, an underwriter draws upon professional expertise and knowledge including the use of routine-specific artifacts. In this chapter, we focus on the rating sheet, a specific type of spreadsheet incorporating particular functions that are tailored to accomplishing the DAR (see Figure 6.1). We examine how underwriters, as professional actors, and the rating sheet are entangled in performing the actions of the DAR. While underwriters draw on various artifacts to appraise deals (Jarzabkowski et al., 2013, 2015b), these have more or less prevalence in different routine tasks, whereas the rating sheet is used throughout the DAR. Furthermore, it is a common artifact throughout the profession, consistently used globally regardless of the deal being analyzed. We thus conceptualize it as a key

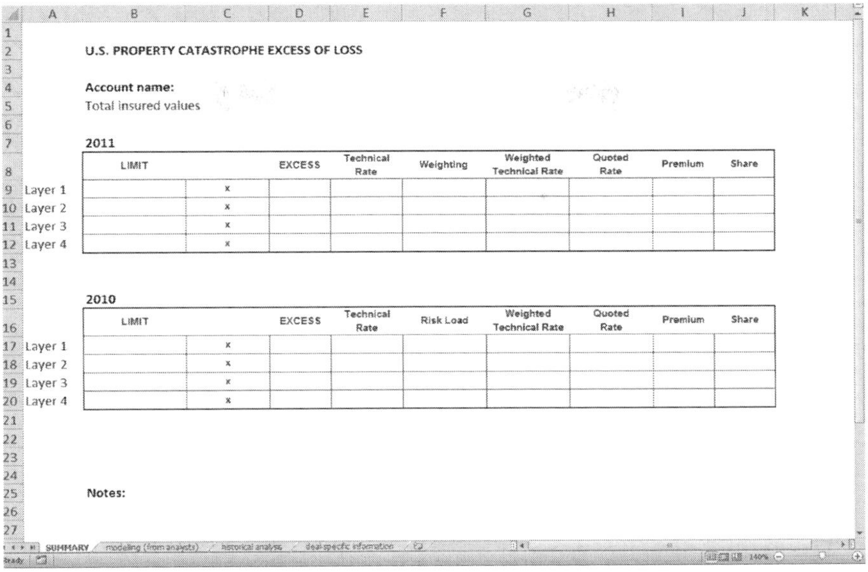

U.S. PROPERTY CATASTROPHE EXCESS OF LOSS

Account name:
Total insured values

2011

	LIMIT		EXCESS	Technical Rate	Weighting	Weighted Technical Rate	Quoted Rate	Premium	Share
Layer 1		x							
Layer 2		x							
Layer 3		x							
Layer 4		x							

2010

	LIMIT		EXCESS	Technical Rate	Risk Load	Weighted Technical Rate	Quoted Rate	Premium	Share
Layer 1		x							
Layer 2		x							
Layer 3		x							
Layer 4		x							

Notes:

Figure 6.1 Simplified sample rating sheet for deals

professional artifact or "tool of the trade." As we will show in due course, it is *the* means through which underwriters relate to and understand reinsurance deals, and its knowledgeable use is entangled with the nature of the profession and its routine actions.

6.4 Empirical Illustration: Three Layers of Entanglement Within a Professional Routine

We offer a multi-layered approach to understanding connectivity between the performance of routine tasks and their embeddedness within professional work. We do so through studying the way action comprises entanglement of actor and artifact. Each layer is introduced independently, before demonstrating the conceptual process relationship through which they are connected across organizational boundaries, and within which professional routines are performed.

6.4.1 Layer 1: Connecting with Profession

Any routine is situated within a body of knowledge constituting the profession (Schön, 1983; Abbott, 1988; Lave and Wenger, 1991; Knorr Cetina,

1999). Underwriters are professionals who perform the DAR knowledgably in consistent ways that would be recognizable by their underwriter peers, just as professionals such as surgeons, scientists, or lawyers perform routines that are largely recognizable and consistent to their peers. Professions often have particular artifacts that situate actors within their profession. Their identity and belonging to a particular profession is entangled with knowledge about how to use that artifact in ways that are simultaneously recognizable across actors but also individually applied to the specifics of each local enactment (Schatzki, 2002). For example, high-energy physicists are knowledgeable in the routinized use of a "detector" even as each specific use varies according to the local experiment at hand (Knorr Cetina, 1999). Similarly, in underwriting, the rating sheet is an artifact used by any underwriter to appraise each specific deal.

First, the use of the artifact (the rating sheet) within the routine (DAR) identifies an actor as belonging to a particular profession (reinsurance underwriter). As an underwriter described, "we use a rating sheet for every decision" (fieldnote) as a core tool of the trade for performing the DAR. While different types of reinsurance deals might require an array of additional different tools (Borscheid et al., 2013), all underwriters no matter where they are in the world or what type of deal they are appraising use a rating sheet. Indeed, such "spreadsheets are at the very heart of the insurance world" (Baxter, 2012: 1). We therefore came to see the artifact, actor, and their professional actions as entwined; only underwriters do deal appraisal and, so, own and use the ratings sheet.

Second, artifacts embed some of the knowledgeable practice at the heart of professions. Not only do professional actors know how to use the central artifacts of their profession and to tailor them to the localized context or, in our case, deal at hand, but those artifacts also have embedded within them particular ways of working (Knorr Cetina, 1999). In our case, the ratings sheet has particular formulas and ways of structuring numeric information (see Abbott, 1988) that are integral to, and shape the work of the underwriter; leading them to appraise deals in the particular ways outlined in layer 2, rather than in other ways. Indeed, this deep connection between "being an underwriter" (member of a profession) and engaging with the practice that is embedded within its core artifact is central to training and the process of joining the profession (Lave and Wenger, 1991). We frequently observed trainee underwriters sitting alongside an experienced underwriter, "watching what they did in the rating sheet" (interview), helping them to do parts of the analysis, and becoming socialized into the routinized ways of working that are embedded within the rating sheet. Indeed, this was the central way we observed learning and mentor/mentee relationships unfold in our fieldwork.

Third, the use of an artifact indicates the type of profession and the nature of the knowledge that is valued (Abbott, 1988). Underwriters construct the legitimacy or basis for their truth claims about deals through their skilled use of the rating sheet. Specifically, through the rating sheet underwriters construct themselves as financial professionals, engaged in the business of calculation. As one underwriter explains, the rating sheet helps "generate a price and then we can tweak that price up or down [within the rating sheet]...so it's soft information which I want to make hard" (interview). That is, their professional role is turning both quantitative and also "soft" or judgment-based information, into numbers and "hard facts." Hence, the use of the rating sheet is tied to assumptions and expectations about the tools that a finance professional should use. Indeed, the centrality of rating sheets in defining reinsurance professionals can be put into the context of the rise of quantitative information and associated tools (Abbott, 1988), such as spreadsheets that are at the heart of being a financial trader (Benninga, 2006; Beunza et al., 2006). However, the rating sheet both connects and differentiates underwriters from this broader world of finance as they have deep knowledge of a particular *type* of spreadsheet; the rating sheet that is specifically designed to enable the DAR. Knowledgeable use of the rating sheet thus identifies their particular professional jurisdiction (Bechky, 2003a).

In summary, this illustration of layer 1 makes the following conceptual points about connectivity in professional routines. First, professional actors are entangled with specific artifacts. Knowing how to use these tools-of-the-trade identifies an individual as a professional actor and establishes a connection to others of that profession. That is, the artifact—the rating sheet in our case or the surgical equipment in medicine—is not organization-specific but rather supra-organizational. Second, the artifact enables this connectivity because it embeds professional knowledge of how to do the work that defines the profession (Abbott, 1988; Bechky, 2003b). In our case the artifact is entangled with the work of calculating, so defining underwriters as belonging to a "quantitative" profession (Abbott, 1988). Similarly professional knowledge might be entangled with the routinized use of the Black-Scholes-Merton model in the case of financial traders (MacKenzie and Millo, 2003) or with detectors for high-particle physicists (Knorr Cetina, 1999). To demonstrate this further, we now introduce another layer of connectivity that moves from the notion of *being an underwriter* to doing the actual *work* of underwriting.

6.4.2 Layer 2: Connecting with the Work of the Routine

This section demonstrates the way that actors and artifacts are not analytically separate but entangled (Orlikowski, 2007) in producing the work of a routine. Current studies in routine theory suggest that artifacts structure when and how actions are accomplished (e.g. Cacciatori 2012; D'Adderio, 2014). We show that in a professional routine, where the performance of the routine involves considerable autonomy by the actor to use their knowledge and skill, such artifacts do not determine the actions undertaken. Rather, they connect the actor and the work of the routine. Our approach extends the empirical focus of artifacts in routine theory, which often examines technologies that structure the workflow process (e.g. D'Adderio 2008; Leonardi 2011), by showing how action comprises an artifact's functionality and a person's skills and knowledge, as these are brought to bear in performing a routine.

The DAR is the central *work* of underwriters. Each underwriter appraises many deals each year as part of their everyday routine work. The rating sheet is the accepted artifact for this work, commonly used across the profession; yet, there remains variation in the way the DAR is performed, grounded in the underwriter's professional skills and knowledge, and the unique nature of each deal and its underpinning risks. Hence, the functions and features within the rating sheet are adapted to the specifics of each deal. Importantly, the rating sheet is not automated, or a type of model that can run calculations independently. Hence, it does not perform the DAR. Rather, the DAR is performed through the entanglement of actor and artifact. For illustrative purposes, we will explain the DAR within a specific type of risk, US property catastrophe ("cat"), the largest segment of the reinsurance market by volume.[1]

The DAR is a critical professional routine through which several gigabytes of data on the various characteristics of the underlying risk for each deal (number of houses, value of houses, type of building materials, proximity to flood zone or fault line, and so forth) are converted into a numerical value that the underwriter will offer as the quoted rate, meaning the price at which they are willing to sell their capital to underwrite the deal. As a deal is not readily accessible or analyzable, the DAR unfolds as a locally accomplished and frequently repeated process involving a set of steps—Technical Analysis, Weighted Technical Analysis, Market Analysis—which transforms the mass data into a tradable price. The rating sheet is structured to support this routine; for example, with particular functions that require a technical rate to be developed in one column that is maintained separately from the weighted technical rate in another column. We now explain the entanglement of actor and artifact in the actions involved in these three steps in the DAR.

Technical Analysis is the first step in the DAR, commencing when the underwriter receives an information pack about the specific deal from a broker. At this stage, the underwriter inserts data from the information pack into the rating sheet, and arranges it according to the relevant tabs. Iterating between the information pack and the rating sheet's specific tabs, such as a "historical" tab which outlines all the historical losses a deal has suffered in the past, the underwriter establishes the basic premises of the deal (see Figure 6.1). Once the spreadsheet has been populated, often by manually transferring data from the information pack into the rating sheet, an underwriter requires information from analysts to progress the DAR. To support the underwriter's work, analysts run probability models that provide forecasts on the severity of losses for any particular deal. Based on the information pack, an underwriter provides the analysts with details on which of two to three models to use and how to run them.[2] This advice and process varies depending on the specific characteristics of a deal, for example whether the quality of building is considered standard or sub-par and which models are appropriate to the parameters of this deal. Selecting which models to run, and instructing on which parameters to use, is a skilled professional action, showing an understanding of the relative strengths of each type of model in analyzing specific features of each type of deal.

After receiving the various modeled outputs from the analyst by email, typically within 24 to 48 hours, an underwriter adds these into the rating sheet under "Modeled output 1" and "Modeled output 2," and, potentially, "Modeled output 3." Again, this transfer may involve either manual or automatic copying from the analyst's email into the rating sheet:

> We now have a new pricing tool . . . the valuable thing is you will be able to directly integrate the results coming out from the models. Before you had to take it separately and then to put it in the machine, and from there you had to be careful that all was correct and so on, and now it will be taken right from the models. (Fieldnote)

After populating the modeled output columns, underwriters combine their various outputs. Using functions within the ratings sheet, they can give primacy to one model or another for different layers of the deal; for example giving 40 percent primacy to Model 1 and 60 percent to Model 2 at the threshold layer because of professional judgment that Model 1 better captures the specific characteristics of this particular deal, while considering the second layer of risk best captured by only Model 2, and so on. As each deal is unique, combining the models involves considerable knowledge in both the characteristics of the deal and the analytic features of the models. As each modeled output is combined in the rating sheet, the outcomes populate a new column that is for the "Technical Rate" (see Figure 6.1). This Technical Rate completes the Technical Analysis step in the routine, presenting a modeled view of the deal, which incorporates within it the underwriter's professional judgment about both the deal and the models. Typically, underwriters document the judgments underpinning the Technical Rate in a dedicated section within the rating sheet labeled "notes." This allows the underwriter's professional skill to be revisited by others if necessary in the future, so showing how the rating sheet also provides a critical financial audit trail of this otherwise quite autonomous set of judgments about a unique deal.

Weighted Technical Analysis. The Technical Rate now becomes the reference point for the second step of the DAR. To accomplish the Weighted Technical Analysis, an underwriter usually performs multiple analyses that bring in deeper knowledge of the particular features of this deal, such as a client analysis and historical analysis, drawing on various supporting information, such as maps, notes, and the rates in previous rating sheets. In the process, specific weightings are applied that adjust the technical rate based on the professional and specific knowledge of the underwriter, building on rather than overruling the probabilities and parameters contained in the technical rate. As one underwriter explained, while adjusting some parameters in the rating sheet: "The rating sheet is an excel sheet that has modeling built into it, so that I can enter the technical prices derived from AIR or RMS models, then do all my own assumptions and pricing on top of that" (fieldnote).

These "assumptions" and "pricing" are incorporated through the functionality of the rating sheet, as the Weighted Technical Rate is generated in a separate column next to the Technical Rate. The cell showing a deal's "Weighted Technical Rate" (see Figure 6.1) is linked to another tab called "Weighting." As part of each analysis, the underwriter establishes and tweaks the weightings in this tab, which manipulates the "Weighted Technical Rate" upwards or downwards, including factoring in the firm's profit margin as the underwriter runs through a series of possibilities weightings. An underwriter might "increase" the modeled results based on knowledge about the specific features of the client's portfolio, such as that they only insure buildings with state-of-the-art fire systems. For example, in one instance an underwriter remembered that one client had much higher claims from a particular hurricane due to the high net worth of those properties they insured, which meant there were more pools and therefore pool screens that had blown about causing more damage. He therefore manually increased their loss ratio accordingly, explaining "these factors [like pool screens] you can't put into the model" (fieldnote). By performing such analyses, an underwriter brings specific professional knowledge and skill into the DAR to balance the technical assumptions reflected in the pure Technical Rate. While performing the Weighted Technical Analysis, an underwriter again adds notes into the rating sheet, providing a trail of the rationale for adjustments to the purely Technical Rate. This second step culminates in the Weighted Technical Rate, which remains fixed within that column in the rating sheet, although, like the Technical Rate from the previous step, the underwriter can alter it to incorporate further information at a later stage.

Market Analysis. In the final step of the DAR, the underwriter conducts a market analysis that situates the deal's Weighted Technical Rate in the dynamics of the market. Drawing on tacit knowledge, such as whether prices in the market generally are up or down this year, gleaned through rumors, gossip, and information from professional networks, the underwriter conducts a sensecheck on price relative to his/her assessment of current market dynamics. This ultimately results in the final "Quoted Rate" for each layer of the deal which builds on previous analyses and is captured in a separate column (see Figure 6.1). This step may mean the underwriter further adjusts the Weighted Technical Rate from the prior step based on additional analysis and judgment (highlighting the iterative movement between steps in the routine) or may result in a Quoted Rate that differs from the Weighted Technical Rate because of the addition of a market loading.

During this step, an underwriter usually performs comparisons with a selection of deals that have already been appraised and have Quoted Rates. For instance, underwriters often export the current deal's Quoted Rate from the rating sheet into a new spreadsheet that represents each deal's rates as plotted graphs, displayed as colored curves. Such representation offers a relative comparison of rates across deals. Across the two worksheets, an underwriter is able to compare deals according to their Quoted Rates, manipulating different comparators to gain a sense of the validity of the Quoted Rate on the current deal in the current market. For example, one afternoon an underwriter and his assistant were sitting together looking at the multiple different colored curved lines of such a graph, appraising whether Deal-A was priced consistently with other deals in that territory. Pointing to the screen the underwriter noted that the price "seems to be about the average; what we can expect from this region this year" (fieldnote). Based on this comparison, the underwriter might also go back to the rating sheet and make further adjustments to better reflect his/her view of the correct quoted rate for this deal, again documenting the rationale in the notes section on the sheet. At this point, the final step in the DAR is completed, as a quoted rate has been achieved. The underwriter then decides whether to offer a quote for this deal and, if so, copies the figures from the rating sheet into an email that will be sent as a formal offer to the broker/client.

In summary, this illustration of layer 2 makes the following conceptual points about connectivity in professional routines. First, it explains standardization within the customized performance of a routine by an individual professional actor, as that actor performs the routine across multiple situations (Larsson and Bowen, 1989; Sharma, 1997). The work of any professional, whether an underwriter appraising yet another deal or an orthopedic surgeon operating on yet another broken bone, requires professional knowledge and skill to perform the routine within the specificities of that particular situation. Nonetheless, alongside these customizations, a common artifact enables each performance to be standardized as a recognizable and legitimate process. For example, a specific surgical instrument, a "rongeur," in orthopedic back surgery will be used slightly differently by an orthopedic surgeon each time, but still always entails chipping away at a small bone. Second, this entanglement of actor and artifact also enables consistency across multiple professional actors. While each professional actor applies their own specific knowledge, their individual performance is entangled with a common tool-of-the-trade through which these dispersed professionals are able to perform professional work in a largely similar, routine way. For example, knowledgeable use of the rongeur by orthopedic surgeons helps standardize the practice of back surgery amongst such professionals. Our conceptualization of the entanglement of actor and artifact in action thus addresses the puzzle of variation and standardization in professional routines (Turner and Rindova, 2012). The artifacts neither perform professional routines, nor determine how an action is performed. Rather, as we illustrated, the artifact is entangled with the actor's actions in bringing professional knowledge to bear upon the work, so enabling knowledgeable differentiation in each individual performance of the routine. The artifact both enables consistency in the routine across its multiple performances, and also variation in the application of professional knowledge in each individual performance of the routine.

6.4.3 Layer 3: Connecting with Collective Work

The final layer of our framework explaining the process of connectivity in professional routines involves connecting to the collective work of the profession. We first define collective work. We then show that professional artifacts are integral to its accomplishment (layer 3) and, in doing so, reinforce the validity of the routine work performed by the professional actor (layer 2), forming a feedback loop that instantiates that actor's position as a credible member of that professional community (layer 1).

The collective work of the profession. Each individual and specific enactment of a professional routine by an actor has a micro outcome that is germane to that profession. In the case of reinsurance underwriting this is providing a Quoted Rate on a deal, while in the legal profession it might be finalizing a contract (see layer 2). This micro-accomplishment is connected to a broader outcome that sustains the collective work of the profession. In underwriting this collective work involves a market for exchange, not only on this deal but the market for trading such deals more broadly, while in law, the generation of legal contracts sustains the contractual nature of the legal system. Namely, the collective work of a profession is a wider system within which the work of the individual routine gains meaning and to which it contributes. In particular, no single performance of the routine accomplishes this work. Rather multiple actors performing the routine multiple times collectively accomplish it; each working with sufficient consistency in their own specific context for their outputs to be recognizable by others in the profession and to constitute inputs that sustain their collective work. Hence, the individual routine is connected to the collective work of the profession and the actors, artifacts, and actions that make up that profession; whether that be buyers and suppliers and the trading tools and technologies that enable their exchange, as in a reinsurance market, or a legal system comprising other law firms, judges, and clients with their contracts, courts, and legal procedures.

The artifact and enabling collective work. Artifacts are critical to, and entangled with, sustaining the collective work of professions. We illustrate this in three ways, drawing from our observations of the rating sheet in reinsurance. First, the rating sheet enabled a deal to be appraised and, hence, for a quoted price to be offered into the market, so enabling the collective work of trading. In a financial profession it is unthinkable to trade risks without engaging in some calculative practice (Abbott, 1988; Callon and Muniesa, 2005). In reinsurance the rating sheet is the core artifact enabling this calculation, and thus the collective practice of trading. As one underwriter stated, you always need to "find something technical to hang your hat on" (interview) in order to participate in the collective work of trading and it is the rating sheet that enables this.

Second, the use of the common artifact resulted in a collectively recognizable output, and this was integral to moving from the work in the individual routine to the collective work of the profession. For example, regardless of the variation in information on bushfires in California compared with the information on hurricanes in Florida, through the rating sheet both are made commensurate as a price (Espeland and Stevens, 1998). They are expressed in similar ways as a quote that meets professional industry expectations. Specifically, in the language of our profession, the quote is expressed in specific terminology as a "rate-on-line," which are the various market rates for each layer of the deal. This then enables the trading of multiple reinsurance deals by multiple actors on a comparable basis, despite the different types of judgment and analysis that might underlie their respective quotes. Hence, the common artifact enables the outcomes of the individual work routine to be collectively understood and used to further the collective work.

Third, collective understanding of the artifact underpinning outputs of the DAR is important in building confidence in the individual enactments that form the collective work of the profession. It is central to the collective work of underwriters that a quote is familiar to and understood by all those involved. This meaningfulness is not just because it is in the same format, as a number expressed as a rate-on-line. Rather, professional peers consider the output of the individual routine a meaningful contribution because they *know* where it comes from and how it is enabled—through a rating sheet that follows largely similar steps and constitutes an auditable trail of the rationale for the quote. Other market participants (buyers and competitors) know the quotes generated are founded in the rigorous analytic procedure of the DAR, which incorporates each stage of analysis within the rating sheet. Collective confidence in the prices at which deals trade is thus established through knowing that everyone uses a common artifact.

Finally, accomplishing this collective work through a common artifact also instantiates individual actors and their work within the profession. More than the connectivity of layer 1, which involves identification with a profession through the use of its common artifacts, in this layer, connectivity involves being part of the actual work that is accomplished by the profession. In reinsurance, the ubiquity of the rating sheet helps build confidence—or not—in the work of individuals and their capacity to participate in, and so sustain, the collective work. For example, one way to ridicule others in the profession is to suggest that they are not competent in using the technical procedures enabled by the rating sheet: "well he's seat of the pants; he's not technical, it's rubbish" (interview). Only those whose work is seen as appropriately constructed within the common artifacts and actions of the profession has that work appreciated as part of the collective. Connecting individual routines to the collective work of a profession through a common artifact thus instantiates the position of a professional in a community, forming a processual feedback loop to "Connecting with profession" in layer 1.

In summary, this illustration of layer 3 makes the following conceptual points about connectivity in professional routines. The term "professions" contains some notion of the collective work or project that professional actors should be achieving (Abbott, 1988). In our case, it was trading in a market for reinsurance risk, whereas in other cases, such as an educational or healthcare system, it might be a particular standard of service provision. Any individual work, when released into the collective, is therefore perpetuating both the quality and distinctiveness of the collective work done by this profession. For example, individual underwriters perform the DAR and their output—a quoted evaluation of price—is then included into the wider system of trading on reinsurance risk. The entanglement of actor and artifact is critical to understanding this connection to the collective work of the profession as use of the tools-of-the-trade generates confidence that any individual work has been done "correctly" in a way that pertains to the standards accepted or promoted by the profession. For example, high-particle physicists use detectors, and this use of a common artifact enables their work to be recognizable as valid contributions to collective knowledge in their scientific community (Knorr Cetina, 1999). Indeed, scientists who do not draw upon the legitimated scientific tools to contribute to knowledge will be considered incompetent, or the scientific basis of their contributions will be questioned, so restricting their membership within that community or ability to contribute to its collective work (Knorr Cetina, 1999; Hilgartner, 2012). Our illustration of how entanglement generates connectivity with collective work, also, therefore, completes the loop back to connectivity with layer 1. The identity of the actor as a professional is, in part, constituted by their ability to competently contribute to the work of the collective, through the skilled use of its common artifacts.

6.5 A Framework for Understanding the Multi-Layered Connectivity of Professional Routines

This chapter has drawn on a specific empirical example to theorize the notion of professional routines and, through illustrating our concept of entanglement, the role of artifacts in explaining the connectivity of routines across organizational boundaries.

Building on the conceptualization of routines as sociomaterial ensembles (Pentland et al., 2012), we offer a nuanced approach to study routines through the concept of entanglement which allows us to move away from a separation of actor and artifact—or the privileging of one over the other—to a consideration of their integral involvement in action (Leonardi, 2011; Pentland et al., 2012; D'Adderio, 2014). For example, we have shown how the DAR is performed neither by the actor nor the artifact in isolation, but is enabled through an entanglement of both as professional actors bring their expert knowledge to bear *through* the artifact in a way that is both consistent across the profession and yet varied with each localized enactment of the routine.

Further, we developed a framework that provides a basis to theorize about connectivity, particularly within professional routines. Our framework explains layers of "connectivity" between the profession, individual professional work, and the collective work of the profession (see Figure 6.2). Our framework demonstrates the way professional knowledge is embedded in a specific artifact (tool-of-the-trade), which gives structure to the

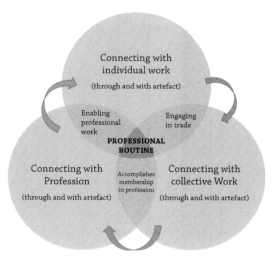

Figure 6.2 The layers of a professional routine

performance of a routine. In addition, it illustrates the way professionals, in performing routines with these artifacts, help to sustain the collective work of, and also (re)instantiate their membership in, the profession. Building on the entanglement of actor and artifact, it explains how the individual work of professionals (layer 2) connects with the collective work of a community (layer 3) and how this in turn instantiates individual actors as members of a profession (layer 1). This framework furthers a dynamic view of how a routine is accomplished in context (Howard-Grenville, 2005; D'Adderio, 2014), which can include the context of profession. In particular, the work of professional actors (layer 2) is a recognizable micro-process involving the local accomplishment of recognizable tasks, which is itself part of a larger process that enacts the wider professional routine across multiple actors (layer 1 and layer 3).

Our framework helps to address puzzles to advance routine theory in the context of professional routines, a novel analytical focus in the routines literature. First, it furthers understanding of the puzzle of how variation in professional work can also be standardized within routine processes (Maister, 1993). In particular, we show that the common nature of an artifact provides an important structuring device that adds consistency to the immense variation in the ways autonomous professionals do routine work (Greenwood et al., 1990; Empson, 2001; Von Nordenflycht, 2010). Second, through our focus on enacting a common professional routine across organizations we address the supra-organizational nature of routines. In particular, we show how the strong connectivity of professionals to their profession can be enacted within the specific requirements of their various organizations. In advancing our understanding of connectivity within professional routines, we extend routine theory from its dominant focus on the intra-organizational to the supra-organizational aspects of routines. Our study thus contributes to understanding of how routines unfold across the boundaries of multiple organizations and in particular how they adhere not only to organizations but to professions. More specifically, we show how the entanglement of artifact and actor are central to coordinating the actions of dispersed inter-organizational actors within a profession.

Future research may further develop the supra-organizational nature of professional routines, for instance, with regards to the collective knowledge and associated identity of a profession (layer 1) or how the collective work of a profession is sustained, legitimated, and even updated through multiple individual routine performances by individual professional actors (layer 3). Additionally, studies might wish to better understand the way variation in everyday professional work can be standardized and coordinated (layer 2). Alternatively, scholars might focus on how each layer is interdependent and connects with the others. Finally, future research could explore how the entanglement of artifact and actor is central to establishing the "claims of jurisdiction" amongst different professions (e.g. Abbott, 1988; Nelson and Irwin, 2014) and the struggles that may arise through collaborations involving different professionals (e.g. Bechky, 2003a). In particular, our findings have established the centrality of the rating sheet, as a particular type of spreadsheet, in defining the professional claims of underwriters over the DAR. Future research may explore the role of spreadsheets as a particular artifact that enables the balancing of quantitative and qualitative information, within the routine processes of professions that are increasingly subject to quantification (Abbott, 1988).

Acknowledgments

We would like to thank Jennifer Howard-Grenville and Claus Rerup for their helpful feedback and insight, which helped us further refine and improve this chapter.

Notes

1. Property is the largest segment of the reinsurance market (38.7%), and the US is the dominant geographic market for reinsurance (51.3%) (MarketLine, 2012).
2. In (re)insurance there are a number of vendor models that reinsurers, insurers, and reinsurance brokers use to calculate probabilities of catastrophes. In addition, large reinsurers will also run their own internally developed models.

References

Abbott, A. (1981). "Status and Status Strain in the Professions." *American Journal of Sociology*, 86/4: 819–35.
Abbott, A. (1988). *The System of Professions: An Essay on the Division of Expert Labor.* Chicago, IL: Chicago University Press.
Bapuji, H., Hora, M., and Saeed, A. M. (2012). "Intentions, Intermediaries, and Interaction: Examining the Emergence of Routines." *Journal of Management Studies*, 49/8: 1586–607.
Baxter, R. (2012). "Spreadsheets Light Up on the Insurance Risk Radar." *Actuarial Post.* <http://www.actuarialpost.co.uk>, accessed October 2, 2014.

Bechky, B. A. (2003a). "Object Lessons: Workplace Artifacts as Representations of Occupational Jurisdiction." *American Journal of Sociology*, 109/3: 720–52.

Bechky, B. A. (2003b). "Sharing Meaning Across Occupational Communities: The Transformation of Understanding on a Production Floor." *Organization Science*, 14/3: 312–30.

Bednarek, R., Burke, G., Jarzabkowski, P., and Smets, M. (2015). "Dynamic Client Portfolios as Sources of Ambidexterity: Exploration and Exploitation Within and Across Client Relationships." *Long Range Planning*, forthcoming.

Benninga, S. (2006). *Principles of Finance with Excel*. Oxford: Oxford University Press.

Beunza, D., Hardie, I., and MacKenzie, D. (2006). "A Price is a Social Thing: Towards a Material Sociology of Arbitrage." *Organization Studies*, 27/5: 721–45.

Borscheid, P., Gugerli, D., and Straumann, T. (2013). *The Value of Risk: Swiss Re and the History of Reinsurance*. Oxford: Oxford University Press.

Cacciatori, E. (2012). "Resolving Conflict in Problem-Solving: Systems of Artifacts in the Development of New Routines." *Journal of Management Studies*, 49/8: 1559–85.

Callon, M. and Muniesa, F. (2005). "Economic Markets as Calculative Collective Devices." *Organization Studies*, 26/8: 1229–50.

Carlile, P. R. (2002). "A Pragmatic View of Knowledge and Boundaries: Boundary Objects in New Product Development." *Organization Science*, 13/4: 442–55.

D'Adderio, L. (2003). "Configuring Software, Reconfiguring Memories: The Influence of Integrated Systems on the Reproduction of Knowledge and Routines." *Industrial and Corporate Change*, 12/2: 321–50.

D'Adderio, L. (2008). "The Performativity of Routines: Theorizing the Influence of Artefacts and Distributed Agencies on Routines Dynamics." *Research Policy*, 37/5: 769–89.

D'Adderio, L. (2011). "Artifacts at the Center of Routines: Performing the Material Turn in Routines Theory." *Journal of Institutional Economics*, 7/2: 197–230.

D'Adderio, L. (2014). "The Replication Dilemma Unravelled: How Organizations Enact Multiple Goals in Routine Transfer." *Organization Science*, 25/5: 1325–50.

Denis, J. L., Langley, A., and Cazale, L. (1996). "Leadership and Strategic Change Under Ambiguity." *Organization Studies*, 17/4: 672–99.

Empson, L. (2001). "Fear of Exploitation and Fear of Contamination: Impediments to Knowledge Transfer in Mergers between Professional Service Firms." *Human Relations*, 54/7: 839–62.

Espeland, W. N. and Stevens, M. L. (1998). "Commensuration as a Social Process." *Annual Review of Sociology*, 24/1: 313–43.

Feldman, M. S. (2000). "Organizational Routines as a Source of Continuous Change." *Organization Science*, 11/6: 611–29.

Feldman, M. S. and Pentland, B. T. (2003). "Reconceptualizing Organizational Routines as a Source of Flexibility and Change." *Administrative Science Quarterly*, 48/1: 94–118.

Fiol, C. M. and O'Connor, E. J. (2005). "Stuff Matters: Artifacts, Identity, and Legitimacy in the U.S. Medical Profession." In A. Rafaeli and M. G. Pratt (eds.),

Artifacts and Organizations: Beyond Mere Symbolism. London and New York: Routledge, 241–58.

Greenwood, R., Hinings, C., and Brown, J. (1990). "'P2-form' Strategic Management: Corporate Practices in Professional Partnerships." *Academy of Management Journal*, 33/4: 725–55.

Hilgartner, S. (2012). "Selective Flows of Knowledge in Technoscientific Interaction: Information Control in Genome Research." *British Journal for the History of Science*, 45/2: 267–80.

Howard-Grenville, J. A. (2005). "The Persistence of Flexible Organizational Routines: The Role of Agency and Organizational Context." *Organization Science*, 16/6: 618–36.

Jarzabkowski, P., Bednarek, R., and Cabantous, L. (2015a). "Conducting Global Team-Based Ethnography: Methodological Challenges and Practical Methods." *Human Relations*, 68/1: 3–33.

Jarzabkowski, P., Bednarek, R., and Spee, A. P. (2015b). *Making a Market for Acts of God: The Practice of Risk Trading in the Global Reinsurance Industry.* Oxford: Oxford University Press.

Jarzabkowski, P., Spee, A. P., and Smets, M. (2013). "Material Artifacts: Practices for Doing Strategy with 'Stuff.'" *European Management Journal*, 31/1: 41–54.

Kellogg, K. C., Orlikowski, W. J., and Yates, J. (2006). "Life in the Trading Zone: Structuring Coordination across Boundaries in Postbureaucratic Organizations." *Organization Science*, 17/1: 22–44.

Knorr Cetina, K. (1999). *Epistemic Cultures: How the Sciences Make Knowledge.* Cambridge, MA: Harvard University Press.

Kunreuther, H., Meszaros, J., Hogarth, R., and Spranca, M. (1995). "Ambiguity and Underwriter Decision Processes." *Journal of Economic Behavior & Organization*, 26/3: 337–52.

Larsson, R. and Bowen, D. E. (1989). "Organization and Customer: Managing Design and Coordination of Services." *Academy of Management Review*, 14/2: 213–33.

Lave, J. and Wenger, E. (1991). *Situated Learning: Legitimate Peripheral Participation.* Cambridge: Cambridge University Press.

Lazaric, N. and Denis, B. (2005). "Routinization and Memorization of Tasks in a Workshop: The Case of the Introduction of ISO Norms." *Industrial and Corporate Change*, 14/5: 873–96.

Leonardi, P. (2011). "When Flexible Routines Meet Flexible Technologies: Affordance, Constraint, and the Imbrications of Human and Material Agencies." *Management Information Systems Quarterly*, 35/1: 147–67.

MacKenzie, D. and Millo, M. (2003). "Constructing a Market, Performing Theory: The Historical Sociology of a Financial Derivatives Exchange." *American Journal of Sociology*, 109/1: 107–45.

Maister, D. (1993). *Managing the Professional Service Firm.* New York: Free Press.

Majchrzak, A., More, P. H., and Faraj, S. (2012). "Transcending Knowledge Differences in Cross-Functional Teams." *Organization Science*, 23/4: 951–70.

MarketLine. (2012). "Global Reinsurance" (May). London: MarketLine Industry Profile.

Nelson, A. J. and Irwin, J. (2014). "'Defining What We Do—All Over Again': Occupational Identity, Technological Change, and the Librarian/Internet-Search Relationship." *Academy of Management Journal*, 57/3: 892–928.

Nelson, R. R. and Winter, S. G. (1982). *An Evolutionary Theory of Economic Change.* Cambridge, MA: Harvard Business School Press.

Orlikowski, W. J. (2007). "Sociomaterial Practices: Exploring Technology at Work." *Organization Studies*, 28/9: 1435–48.

Orlikowski, W. J. and Scott, S. (2008). "Sociomateriality: Challenging the Separation of Technology, Work, and Organization." *Academy of Management Annals*, 2/1: 433–74.

Parmigiani, A. and Howard-Grenville, J. (2011). "Routines Revisited: Exploring the Capabilities and Practice Perspectives." *Academy of Management Annals*, 5/1: 413–53.

Pentland, B. T. (2011). "The Foundation is Solid, if you Know Where to Look: Comment on Felin and Foss." *Journal of Institutional Economics*, 7/2: 279–93.

Pentland, B. T., Feldman, M. S., Becker, M. C., and Liu, P. (2012). "Dynamics of Organizational Routines: A Generative Model." *Journal of Management Studies*, 49/8: 1484–508.

Schatzki, T. (2002). *The Site of the Social: A Philosophical Account of the Constitution of Social Life and Change.* Pennsylvania, PA: Penn State University Press.

Schön, D. A. (1983). *The Reflective Practitioner: How Professionals Think in Action.* New York: Temple Smith.

Sharma, A. (1997). "Professional as Agent: Knowledge Asymmetry in Agency Exchange." *Academy of Management Review*, 22/3: 758–98.

Turner, S. F. and Rindova, V. (2012). "A Balancing Act: How Organizations Pursue Consistency in Routine Functioning in the Face of Ongoing Change." *Organization Science*, 23/1: 24–46.

Von Nordenflycht, A. (2010). "What is a Professional Service Firm? Toward a Theory and Taxonomy of Knowledge Intensive Firms." *Academy of Management Review*, 35/1: 155–74.

Zbaracki, M. J. and Bergen, M. (2010). "When Truces Collapse: A Longitudinal Study of Price Adjustment Routines." *Organization Science*, 21/5: 955–72.

7

When "Good" is Not Good Enough

Power Dynamics and Performative Aspects of Organizational Routines

Helle Kryger Aggerholm and Birte Asmuß

Abstract: The chapter explores some of the performative resources available to individual actors when discursively creating and sustaining a certain organizational routine, namely performance appraisal interviews (PAIs). By looking at one substantial and recurrent micro-level activity in PAIs, namely the evaluation of employee performance, this chapter pursues a better understanding of the relationship between social interaction and the negotiation of power in micro-level routines on the one hand and the performance of larger organizational routines on the other. The study indicates that interactional micro-level routines are not power neutral. Due to the internal power dynamics of organizational routines, performative and ostensive aspects cannot be separated, given that both elements function as interactional resources for the participants in accomplishing the actions at stake. Although language and its effects have been acknowledged as important objects of study in organizational routines, the study highlights the constitutive role of language and interaction for organizational routines.

7.1 Introduction

The concept of organizational routines is commonly defined as repetitive, recognizable patterns of interdependent action, carried out by multiple actors (Feldman and Pentland, 2003: 95; Parmigiani and Howard-Grenville,

2011: 414; Dionysiou and Tsoukas, 2013: 181). Early work on routines, which adopted a capability perspective, mainly focused on what routines accomplish in terms of organizational goals, for instance performance, learning, and capabilities (Parmigiani and Howard-Grenville, 2011:417). Viewing routines as a "black box" and thereby adopting a relatively static image of routines, this perspective largely neglected the microprocesses through which routines are accomplished (Becker, 2008; Dionysiou and Tsoukas, 2013). Such criticism has given rise to a practice or performative perspective focusing on how routines are enacted on a day-to-day basis and with what consequences (Parmigiani and Howard-Grenville, 2011: 417). The performative perspective successfully captures the relational, action-driven, micro-oriented, and generative elements of routines (Feldman, 2000; Feldman and Pentland, 2003; Parmigiani and Howard-Grenville, 2011; Rerup and Feldman, 2011). However, insight into how individual participants on a micro-level interrelate their individual courses of action in order to form these repetitive, recognizable patterns of action is still limited (Dionysiou and Tsoukas, 2013).

This to contribute to filling the gap by exploring—at a micro-level—the role that individual agents play in discursively creating and sustaining a certain organizational routine, namely performance appraisal interviews (PAIs). Viewing PAIs from a capability perspective (Feldman, 2000; Parmigianiand Howard-Grenville, 2011), one of PAIs' main functions is to manage and integrate organizational and employee performance (Fletcher, 2001: 473). In addition, understanding PAIs from a performative perspective emphasizing the enactment and process elements of the routine shows that PAIs are organizational interactions where superior–subordinate relations are shaped, (re)confirmed, and re-evaluated and where various aspects of power are at stake. This chapter pursues a better understanding of this dynamic relationship by investigating one substantial and recurrent activity in PAIs, namely, the evaluation of employee performance. This activity is defined as a micro-level routine, i.e. a discursive, interactionally accomplished routine within a higher-level organizational routine.

The present study specifically aims to investigate the effects of discursive actions on the internal dynamics of the PAI, which involves participants' reactions to the outcome of previous iterations of the routine. In doing so, the concepts of power and power asymmetries and how they come into play by means of discursive actions will be addressed as central. Based on a constitutive understanding of the relationship between communication and organization (Putnam and Nicotera, 2009; Schoeneborn et al., 2014), the study methodologically applies a micro-ethnographic approach in order to show how employees discursively accept or dismiss the evaluation performed by their manager—the evaluation of employee performance being a micro-level (Pentland et al., 2012) interactional routine as part of the larger organizational routine of the PAI. The study revolves around the following research question: How does social interaction and the negotiation of power in micro-level routines relate to the performance of larger organizational routines?

The study contributes to an empirically grounded understanding of how aspects of power come into play in the moment-by-moment unfolding of a real-time discursive constitution of an organizational routine. It is proposed that power is emergent in the organizational routine interaction, and that it serves as an interactional resource available to the co-participants in the accomplishment and negotiation of micro-level routines. The intention of this chapter is to study the micro-level interaction between manager and employee in performing an organizational routine (in this case a PAI) in order to better understand the relation between the routine practice and the enactment of power.

In the following, a review is provided of the field of organizational routines in general and performative aspects of organizational routines in particular and the role of power for organizational routines is discussed. This is followed by an account of PAIs as organizational routines. After that, the organizational context of the routines, the PAI and the micro-ethnographic method of study, are presented. This is followed by three micro-level analyses of a recurrent interactional routine within the PAI, namely performance evaluation. The final section discusses the insights of the empirical findings in the specific organizational routine of a PAI; how power comes into play in the accomplishment of a micro-level routine such as employee evaluation; how the use of different types of assessment plays an important role in the participants' micro-management of different social actions performed in the routine; and finally how the use of video-based micro-ethnography can move the study of organizational routines even further.

7.2 Organizational Routines and the Influence of Power

Several scholars argue that organizational routines are sociomaterial accomplishments (D'Adderio, 2011; Leonardi, 2011) containing both ostensive (ideal or schematic form) and performative (actual production) aspects (Kuhn, 2012). As such organizational routines are constituted by a set of patterns that are enabled and constrained by a variety of organizational, social, physical, and cognitive structures based on which organizational members enact a particular performance (Pentland and Rueter, 1994: 491). Hence, in between the ostensive and the performative lies human agency. "Human agents interpret, ignore, or adapt rules, and give a particular stamp to the recurrent behaviour patterns to be observed. They also contribute to transforming organizational routines slowly by adapting the performative to the ostensive and vice versa" (Becker and Zirpoli, 2008: 130). By not separating the people who carry out the routine from the routine itself, it is possible to study routines as a richer phenomenon (Feldman, 2000). In that sense, organizational routines are dynamic processes, involving inter-dependent actors whose agency makes a difference in how the routines are enacted (Dionysiou and Tsoukas, 2013: 183). Thus, scholars such as Pentland and Rueter (1994) and Feldman (2000) suggest that participants have a repertoire of action paths to choose from, and "the choice from among the repertoire varies according to preceding actions and is guided, though not determined, by the grammar or 'rules' about what actions go together" (Feldman, 2000: 613). Although actors are constrained by rules and their existing understandings of routines, researchers, however, acknowledge that actors still have significant degrees of freedom in how they interpret given situations and perform routines in specific practice (Feldman, 2000; Essén, 2008; Bruns, 2009). Thus, situation-specific enact-ments of routines might result in deviations from formal rules (Bruns, 2009; Desai, 2010), as well as eventual readjustment of the actors' understanding of those routines (Feldman and Pentland, 2003). Consequently, actors possess significant reflexive capacities and degrees of freedom in how they perform routines in practice (Emirbayer and Mische, 1998; Kozica et al., 2014), and the routines can change endogenously through the very performance of those routines (Feldman and Pentland, 2003; D'Adderio, 2009; Parmigiani and Howard-Grenville, 2011). Therefore, current research acknowledges the social character of organizational routines and focuses on understanding the significance of the micro-level aspects of how routines are enacted in practice (Parmigiani and Howard-Grenville, 2011).

These interdependent activities among the actors inevitably involve "relations of power" (Giddens, 1993: 128; Dionysiou and Tsoukas, 2013: 194). Literature on the subject distinguishes between structural power and relational power. Structural power refers to potential power that comes from possessing valued resources acquired from the positions occupied by individuals within a larger organizational structure, e.g. education, occupa-tional status, or gender (Thomas, 1972; Cast, 2003). Relational power, on the other hand, refers to power that is based on feelings about and relationships with others, reflecting the individual's relative investment in the relationship (Cast, 2003). Thomas (1972) refers to this type of power as "influence," as the individual holds "potential for control based on one's interpersonal skill, independent of his social position" (1972: 606). Hence, some actors may be less powerful in terms of their position in the organizational structure, but their ability to influence others, including those in more powerful positions, can be viewed as a "social skill" (Fligstein, 2001; Dionysiou and Tsoukas, 2013). Thus, individuals may bring different resources to the relationship and have multiple bases of power (Huston, 1983). Consequently, each resource offers a distinctive source of power to the actors, and may potentially exert a unique effect on their ability to control meanings in the performance of the situation (Stolte, 1994; Cast, 2003).

It is acknowledged that some actors in organizational routines "are usually more empowered than other participants to create and impose rules and artifacts on others, to monitor performance and enforce compliance, to legitimate specific actions over others" (Dionysiou and Tsoukas, 2013: 195). Feldman and Pentland (2003) state that more powerful actors in general are able to "turn expectations into rules, and thus, to enact the organization in ways they think appropriate" (2003: 110). Powerful individuals will be more able than others "to alter the situation so that meanings in the situation are consistent with their own definition of the situation, including definition of self and others" (Cast, 2003: 188).

Reconsidering Nelson and Winter's (1982) characterization of routines as a "truce," Zbaracki and Bergen (2010) have conducted an empirical study of a pricing routine by analyzing the micro-foundations of a price-adjustment routine at a manufacturing company. Here, they show how major price changes put truces at risk, as latent conflict over information and interests becomes overt. A study like this shows that routines are not just stable entities, but adaptive performances that include communication, negotiation, and potential conflict filtered through the power dynamics between actors. Hence, as stated by Parmigiani and Howard-Grenville (2011: 441) the power of actors "affects the degree to which they can or will enact the routine as it is ostensively interpreted and understood," and in particular, an individual's structural power in terms of organizational role, hierarchical position, and incentives may affect how a routine is enacted (Zbaracki and Bergen, 2010).

Drawing on symbolic interactionism, Dionysiou and Tsoukas (2013) propose a conceptual process model for creation and recreation of routines in which they extend the performative aspect of routines by exploring how routines as collective accomplishments are (re)created through interaction from within. Even though their model generally assumes participants to engage in "consensually validated" role-taking within the performative perspective of the routine, and hence to some extent ignores the potential power asymmetries, Dionysiou and Tsoukas discuss the notion of power and its potential influence on the process. As stated by Fiske and Depret (1996: 43), "power allows people to ignore the most informative cues about others" whereas people with less power are more likely to be attentive to the interpretations, expectations, and actions of powerful others (Edmondson et al., 2001; Metiu, 2006). Hence, Dionysiou and Tsoukas state that "those routine participants in lower power positions may rely on role taking in order to seek accurate information about the perceptions, interpretations, and intentions of those in higher power positions, not just to conform to the latters' expectations but to skillfully identify ways to increase their influence and get their own interests through" (2013: 195).

Based on a review of existing literature on organizational routines it can be inferred that the aspect of power and power relations is pivotal to understanding the performative perspective of routines. While previous research on organizational routines has generated very useful insight into the role of power, actor, and agency (Feldman, 2000; Howard-Grenville, 2005; Lazaric and Denis, 2005; Zbaracki and Bergen, 2010; Dionysiou and Tsoukas, 2013), relatively limited attention has been given specifically to the influence of power and power dynamics in the performance of specific routines. Thus, there seems to be a need for further studies focusing specifically on power within an interactional, micro-level perspective.

In light of this apparent gap, the intention of the present chapter is to study the micro-level interaction between manager and employee when performing an organizational routine (in this case a performance appraisal interview) in order to better understand the relation between the routine practice and the enactment of power. In addition to contributing to the understanding of power in a routine context, this study contributes to the burgeoning research on the micro-foundations of routines. This responds to recent calls for studying the micro-level aspects of routines by bringing the individual actors into focus (Felin and Foss, 2005, 2009, 2011; Abell et al., 2008).

7.3 Performance Appraisal Interviews as Organizational Routine

Performance appraisal interviews have since the 1990s been a widely used management tool (Asmuß, 2008, 2013). They are strongly acknowledged for being an important tool for performance management (Beardwell and Claydon, 2010)and for their central role in implementing corporate strategy (Caruth and Humphreys, 2008), as they are one of the most common managerial practices for strategically aligning organizational behavior (Van Riel et al., 2009; Sorsa et al., 2014). For example, Sorsa et al. (2014) demonstrate in their study how strategy discourse and specific strategy texts are made visible through the linguistic and non-verbal discursive resources used by both agents in PAIs.

PAIs have been defined as "once-a-year reviews on employees' motivation, performance, satisfaction, attitudes toward their companies" (Nathan et al., 1991: 353). Thus, evaluating employee performance is one of the central tasks taking place in this organizational activity. Here, the superior is entitled to express his/her opinion and pass a judgment about a subordinate's work performance based on a number of strategic goals predefined by the organization.

Hence, an organizational routine is created through the reciprocal, interactional relationship between the performative and ostensive aspects; the performative aspects are essential for creation and recreation of the ostensive aspects, while the ostensive aspects constrain and enable the performative ones (Feldman and Pentland, 2003: 105–9). Based on the work of Dionysiou and Tsoukas (2013), Figure 7.1 shows what the ostensive and performative aspects of the PAI entail and how they are interrelated.

In terms of PAIs the ostensive parts of the routine can be understood as the shared schemata or cognitive understandings guiding the setting, procedural rules, content, context, outcome, etc., of the superior–subordinate interaction as well as a set of mutually coherent action dispositions, i.e. habits and skills. The ostensive elements of the PAI are beneficial to both PAI participants (superior and subordinate) in that they can organize their conduct in accordance with mutually consistent behavioral expectations related to this type of routinized interaction (Blumer, 1969). Such expectations facilitate and guide adjustment of individual courses of action in future instances of PAIs, as well as increase the efficiency of communication between superior and subordinate before, during, and after the PAI (Gersick and Hackman, 1990; Labianca et al., 2000; Dionysiou and Tsoukas, 2013). The level of shared understanding (schemata) of the PAI as a joint activity enables both parties to anticipate each other's behavior and meet basic requirements for coordinating joint activities. In other words, the ostensive aspects set the scene for the performative elements of the PAI and vice versa. In the study at hand, specific focus is put on the questionnaire guiding the PAI as an ostensive element, which plays a

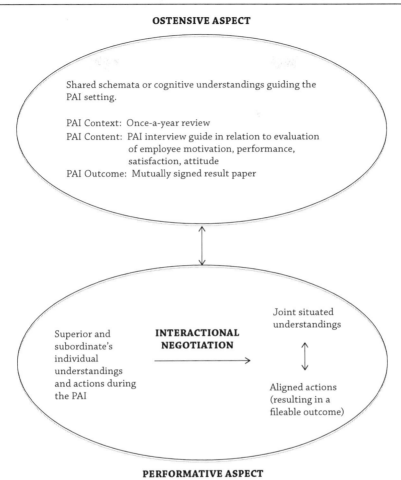

Figure 7.1 The ostensive and performative aspect of PAI as an organizational routine (inspired by Dionysiou and Tsoukas, 2013: 190)

crucial role when performing employee evaluations. As the analysis will show, the PAI questionnaire both sets the scene for and legitimizes specific actions that serve as resources for the PAI participants when conducting employee evaluations.

The performative aspects of the PAI include the actual interaction between superior and subordinate. Having a thorough understanding of the ostensive, contextual aspects of the PAI, the participants have a predefined repertoire of discursive action paths to choose from (Pentland and

Rueter, 1994; Feldman, 2000). They engage in interaction with respect to the PAI in order to develop a joint, situated understanding of the concrete evaluative situation at hand, identify appropriate discursive actions, and align these individual courses of action accordingly. In line with Dionysiou and Tsoukas' (2013) understanding of the performative aspect of an organizational routine, the PAI is understood as "'joint' as it is an outcome of interaction, and it is 'situated' insofar as it is inseparable from the context in which interaction occurs" (2013: 191).

Hence, in PAIs participants need to balance between, on the one hand, ostensive aspects of PAIs in form of specific elements that guide, influence, or in any other way impact on the organizational routine and, on the other hand, performative aspects dealing with what is relevant to the interaction and possible to do at this specific point of time in the interaction. For instance, if one of the main aims of PAIs is to evaluate an employee's performance, then in situ interactional constraints can impede the actual production of an assessing verbal action, despite the fact that ostensive aspects of the PAI would make such an action relevant.

7.4 Methodology

Since the evolvement of the CCO paradigm (communication constitutes organization) (McPhee and Zaug, 2000; Putnam and Nicotera, 2009) communication has been considered to be an important aspect when investigating organizational phenomena. Placed within the broader discursive turn of organization studies (Cooren, 2007), focus has been on the distinction between conversation on the one hand and text on the other, conversation being conceptualized as the place where organizing takes place and texts as both the outcome of these conversations and the contextual features that in turn shape the conversations (Taylor and Robichaud, 2004). Following a Montreal School tradition by understanding organizational routines as sociomaterial accomplishments, it is possible to frame routines "as dialectics of text and conversation, where texts are organizationally embedded rules and vocabularies for interpretation and construction, while conversation refers to the ongoing (re)enactment of the routine" (Kuhn, 2012: 554).

The current chapter pursues a micro-analytical perspective (Streeck and Mehus, 2005; LeBaron, 2008) on the matter at hand by focusing on conversations as interaction, i.e. turns-at-talk that shape and are recurrently shaped locally in the ongoing conversation between the participants (Heritage, 1984: 242). In line with recent trends within Conversation Analysis (CA) the study applies a multi-modal perspective to interaction (Stivers and Sidnell, 2005; Mondada, 2007; LeBaron, 2008; Mortensen, 2013; Asmuß, 2015), which enables an investigation of performative aspects of routines not only as accomplished by means of verbal actions but also by means of embodied and artifactual resources.

An interactional perspective on organizational routines allows us to investigate how the manager and the employee mutually accomplish the organizational practice of evaluating an employee performance in a PAI. The strength of this approach is that it can shed light on organizational routines as situated in real life and as outcomes of authentic micro-practices in the form of interactional routines that are socially accomplished and negotiable. It thus enables a focus on interactional practices as both context-shaped and context-renewing (Heritage, 1984). This corresponds with the existing understanding of organizational routines as both emergent and generative (Parmigiani and Howard-Grenville, 2011: 421f.), and opens up the potential for an understanding of how interactional micro-practices like evaluations help to constitute the performative aspects of an organizational routine.

When trying to understand the situatedness of organizational routines, the notion of intersubjectivity as developed within CA (Hutchby and Wooffitt, 1998) becomes central in that it accounts for how joint sense-making—a central element of performative aspects of organizational routines (Dionysiou and Tsoukas, 2013)—takes place in organizational encounters. Intersubjectivity can be dealt with analytically, as access to the sense-making process can be gained by closely investigating the sequential organization of talk. Sidnell (2010: 136) points out that "[i]ntersubjectivity is maintained, incarnately, in the sequential organization of turns-at-talk, each subsequent turn necessarily displaying its speaker's understanding of a previous one." This in turn, relates to the concept of projectability (Sidnell, 2010: 170) in that the orderliness of conversations leads to certain actions being interactionally "projectable" as possible next actions. Thus, access to participants' joint understandings can be gained by investigating the micro-level activities that take place in organizational routines through the perspective of their being aligned or misaligned with the projected next relevant move. The current study makes use of this analytical resource in that the analysis centers on a close investigation of the sequential order of the manager's and employee's respective conversational moves. This enables us to see how joint understandings about the evaluating activity are interactionally negotiated and accomplished.

One recurrent interactional resource through which evaluations are accomplished is assessments (Pomerantz, 1984; Goodwin and Goodwin, 1987, 1992; Lindström and Mondada, 2009). Assessments are lexical or turn-sequential items that respond to some prior assessable item. In separating an evaluating action in an assessable, e.g. something that is to be assessed, and an assessment segment, e.g. the lexical item actually accomplishing the assessing action, a focus on the interactive nature of employee evaluations in PAIs is made relevant. This is of importance for the current study in relation to how the performative aspects of organizational routines are accomplished through the negotiable micro-practices of the participants.

7.5 Data

The data for the current study come from a corpus of video-recorded, authentic face-to-face performance appraisal interviews. The data have been collected over a four year-period in two private organizations that both use PAIs as a formalized tool for performance management. One of the companies is a large, privately owned market leader within its particular B2B (business-to-business) industry, whereas the other company is a private limited SME (small/medium enterprise) selling to the B2C (business-to-consumer) market. All the involved participants were either middle managers or employees covering a variety of different professional and organizational backgrounds (white-collar or blue-collar professions or management). In total, thirteen PAIs were video-recorded involving six different managers and thirteen different employees resulting in twenty-two hours of PAI recordings.

In line with central micro-ethnographic research procedures (LeBaron, 2008),video-recordings took place with the researcher present in the organization during the recording, but non-present in the actual PAI situation except for cases when the recording equipment had to be serviced. After having collected the data, the researcher conducted individual non-standardized interviews with the involved participants in order to get feedback on any issues that the manager or employee found relevant. This feedback was subsequently used to identify potentially relevant topics. Once the video-recording was completed, it was logged in regard to central aspects of the PAI such as evaluation, employee development, and dis/agreement (as derived from the interviews). For the sake of gaining insight into the overall activity of PAIs, two PAIs were roughly transcribed in their entire length, while the remaining eleven PAIs were transcribed in detail according to standard CA transcription conventions (Atkinson and Heritage, 1984: ix–xvi; Hepburn and Bolden, 2013) focusing specifically on sequences, where either the manager or the employee, or both, was orienting to employee evaluation.

In order to be able to tell what was meaningful (and not) for the participants, the method of Conversation Analysis was chosen. CA proved to be an adequate method for studying PAI interaction, as it is based on the premise of intersubjectivity. By means of the next-turn proof procedure it is the participants' orientation toward the ongoing communicative actions that functions as a measurement for identifying what is of importance to the participants and how they make sense of the ongoing conversational activities. Hence, the method of CA made it possible for us to meticulously study how for instance routine participants in lower power positions might rely on role-taking in order to seek accurate information about the perceptions, interpretations, and intentions of those in higher power positions, and thus, skillfully identify ways to increase their influence and push their own interests through (cf. Dionysiou and Tsoukas, 2013: 195).

Based on a recurrent pattern of conversational actions in regard to employee evaluations, a collection of relevant instances was built (Sidnell, 2013) consisting of a total of thirty-five instances of employee assessments conducted by a manager and responded to by an employee. This collection was divided into instances where the assessment was treated by the employee as fulfilling the task of evaluating employee performance and instances where the employee rejected the evaluation put forward by the manager and/or the employee pursued further evaluating actions by the manager. The three sequences presented in the current chapter were selected based on the criteria of clarity, shortness, and variety of dataset.

Taking ethical considerations into account, all data presented in this chapter are anonymized, e.g. photos of the interaction are stylized (see Figure 7.2) and in the transcripts all references to names, places, and other aspects that may decrease the anonymity of the companies and the persons involved have been altered.

As mentioned previously, the data stem from different PAIs including different managers and employees from different companies. However, the overall setting is consistent and resembles the one presented in Figure 7.2.

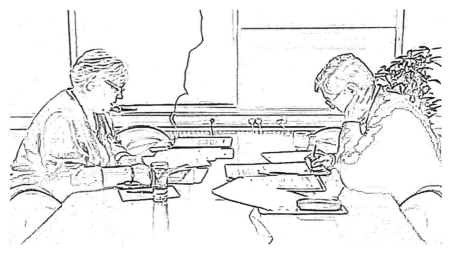

Figure 7.2 Performance appraisal interview setting

In Figure 7.2 an employee (here: left) and a manager (here: right) are facing each other at a meeting table. They have a number of material objects at their disposal: paper documents, especially the questionnaire guide, pens, coffee cups, and water glasses. Some of these material objects (e.g. the interview guide) are part of the ostensive aspects of organizational routines in that they guide the PAI by ordering the topics on the agenda and by functioning as a filing device when employee answers are oriented so as to be considered fileable. In that way, the interview guide frames the procedural rules, the conversational content, and (to some extent) the outcome (cf. Figure 7.1).

7.6 Data Analysis and Findings

As mentioned in the previous section, in the current study we chose to focus on one important aspect of PAIs, namely the activity of employee evaluation. As evaluating actions are recurrently performed via assessments (Goodwin and Goodwin, 1987, 1992), all assessment sequences in the data have been identified. Based on an extensive and meticulous analysis of the assessment sequences identified in the data, the following analysis presents three assessment sequences stemming from three different PAIs (three different managers and three different employees). The sequences are analyzed in order to demonstrate the recurrent interactional practices found in the data.

The overall aim of the analytical section is to show how aspects of power come into play in the micro-level practice of an interactional routine in order to better understand the relation between the routine practice and the enactment of power. Focusing on evaluations as micro-level interactional routines within the larger context of a specific organizational routine the analysis will focus on how the nature and quality of an evaluation is interactively negotiated by the co-participants in PAIs. All three excerpts will show how organizational routines are not power neutral, as the participants make use of and orient to both structural and relational aspects of power when negotiating the assessable nature of employee performance evaluation sequences. The analysis will focus on how this negotiation is interactively accomplished. We start out showing excerpt (1), where the manager makes use of his structural power in order to ensure the progression of the PAI more than to orient to an authentic performance evaluation. In excerpt (2), we show an example of how the employee makes use of her relational power in order to increase her influence on the outcome of the evaluation routine. Finally, we show in excerpt (3) how the manager draws on both her structural and relational power in the accomplishment of a successful evaluation routine.

7.6.1 When "Good" is Good Enough: Acceptance of an Interactional Routine

We will start the analysis by illustrating that an assessment segment like "good," depending on its sequential context, can perform other actions than an evaluation. This is of importance for the performative aspect of a PAI, as it shows that evaluating actions are liable to interactive negotiations by the routines actors, and that the PAI participants make use of power aspects as resources to accomplish relevant next actions. In the first excerpt, the co-participants interactively negotiate the evaluating quality of the evaluation performed and they reach the joint situated understanding that rather than actually evaluating an employee's performance it functions as an interactional device to move into closing of the current topic. Hence, this first excerpt is an example of how power dynamics play an important role in the performance of the routine in that the manager uses his structural power to ensure the progression of the PAI by forcing through a quasi-joint situated understanding leading to action alignment, which in this example indicates moving to the next topic.

In this case, which represents a frequent use of the assessment segment "good," "good" is used to initiate a topic closing, i.e. it is used as a resource for PAI participants to negotiate when to move from one agenda item to another rather than functioning as assessing employee performance. This is of relevance for the analysis of the subsequent excerpts (2) and (3), where we will show instances where the participants negotiate the social actions actually performed by the assessments produced. These negotiations about the assessing actions reveal insights into the role of interactional micro routines in the constitution of organizational routines like the PAI.

Throughout all transcripts, M refers to the manager and E to the employee, and all excerpts consist of a three lines: (1) an original line in Danish, (2) a word-by-word gloss in English, and (3) an intelligible version in English (in bold). In cases where lines 2 and 3 are identical, only line 3 is provided (see also the Transcription Glossary at the end of this chapter for an explanation of the symbols used in the transcripts).

In the following excerpt (1) the employee E reports about one of her current work tasks, a project, she is currently engaged in.

Excerpt (1a)
```
1  E: og derfor     vil   vi  gerne have de her dokumenter ( . ) og
       and therefore want we much  have these  documents        and
       and therefore we world like to have these documents and

2  E: sådan no*get*.
       such   thing
       something like that.
```

In lines 1–2, the employee points out that in order to work on the project, she needs more documentation materials, which is what she is now about to collect from other departments in the organization.

Excerpt (1b)
```
3  (0.2)

4  E: .hhh så det går vi i gang    med.=
         so this get we started   with
         so this is what we get started with now.
```

After a short pause (0.2), where the manager does not take any action to acknowledge the information provided, the employee continues the turn. She does so by using a formulation (Drew, 2003) that sums up the gist of the prior talk, namely what it is she is about to do now.

Excerpt (1c)
```
5  M:  =[GOdt.
           good
6          [((M opens r. hand and moves it towards table in
7           complete synchrony with " GOdt "))
```

In immediate response to the employee's summing up of her current work, the manager takes over. He does so by using a token that according to Goodwin and Goodwin (1987: 6) is an "assessment segment" ("good," l. 5). Yet, even though assigning a positive quality to the prior, the item at hand here also does what Schegloff and Sacks (1973) describe as a possible pre-closing, namely indicating that the topic or conversation is to be ended. This is underlined by the manager's hand gesture: he opens his hand flatly and makes a short, but decisive movement toward the table in close synchrony with the production of the term "good" (l. 7). The sequential position of the assessment segment (after a formulation) and the production of the term in close synchrony with a closing implicative hand gesture result in this excerpt in the assessing term "good" functioning as a pre-topic closer rather than an assessment of employee performance. The manager, by use of an embodied gesture, displays that he is entitled to perform this closing action, thus drawing upon his occupational status as the one formally in charge of the PAI and the one to decide when to close a topic and to move on with the interview. Hence, he uses his structural power in the interactional negotiation to move the performance of the routine in a certain, desired direction, which for him is closing the topic. Now, it is up to the employee in her next turn to align or disalign with the prior move by the manager.

Excerpt (1d)
```
8    (1.8)

9  M: Hh- S::.:=[der  har  jeg stående,  n- nu   kommer jeg her ud og
          S::    there have I   standing    now  come    I   here uot and
               here I have written down, now I turn to this here and
10         [ ((M points w.  r. hand to his paper documents))

11 M: så  ka' du så supplere med det   du  har, så  har  jeg skrevet at
      so can you so add      with this you have, so have I    written that
      than you can add what you have, so I  have written that

12 M: .hh at  noget  af det  vi  ser=er noget    vigtigt    det  er
          that something of this we  see=is something important that is
          that something that we see as  important is
```

In the subsequent pause, the employee does not initiate any verbal or embodied uptake in response. Hence, the employee refrains from any role-taking and, as a result, does not apply her (potential) relational power to influence the outcome of the sequence and push her own interests through. Instead, a 1.8 second long pause occurs, after which the manager orients in a verbal and embodied manner to his questionnaire guide, thus relating to the ostensive aspects of a PAI and opens up a new topic on the agenda. By doing so, he draws upon and makes sequentially relevant his formal occupational role in the interview as the one responsible for the progression of the PAI.

The analysis shows that whether a specific lexical item performs an evaluative or different action (here: a pre-topic closing) is decided upon interactively by the involved participants. By their way of orienting to the ostensive aspects (here: interview guide), they negotiate their respective organizational roles, rights, and obligations to perform specific actions. By doing so, the co-participants reach an agreement that the lexical item *good* was good enough: not in terms of performing a positive evaluative utterance, but instead in terms of initiating a topic closure at a place in the PAI where this is a relevant next action to perform.

7.6.2 When "Good" is Not Good Enough: Negotiation of an Interactional Routine

The second and third excerpts show examples where the co-participants agree that the action performed actually is an evaluating action. Yet, the participants orient differently to whether the quality of the assessment is adequate or not.

The following excerpt (2) shows an example of the co-participants disagreeing about the adequacy of the assessment (whether "good" actually is good enough), and through the micro-level analysis it is demonstrated how the relational power of the employee makes her capable of defusing the manager's structural power. Specifically, the analysis shows that the employee does not accept the performance evaluation offered by the manager. Instead, the employee pursues a different version of an employee performance evaluation. She does so despite the manager's structural power to decide upon the progression of the PAI. As will become clear, the ostensive aspects of the organizational routine in the form of the PAI interview guide represent an important resource for the PAI participants when negotiating the ability to assess employee performance.

In excerpt (2), the employee E is reporting about her past work tasks. The one she lists in this excerpt is ordering office equipment.

Excerpt (2a)
```
6  E:  =.hh HRr  så    har   jeg skrevet der,  <bestille varer>,
              then have I    written here order    products
          HRr  then I have written here ordering products
7      (1.0)
```

The employee presents her work task in a neutral way, focusing on the task proper. A relevant next action would be to acknowledge the information given, but the manager does not do so. Consequently, the employee continues. She does not do so by reporting about another work task, thus moving to the next item on her list, but instead continues to report on the same work task.

Excerpt (2b)
```
8  E:  >billigst   muligt  har  jeg bare   skrevet for  lige  at
          chespest possible have I   simply written for just  to
          as cheap as possible have I just written in order simply to

9  E:  have et  eller  andet.<
          have one or   the=other
          have something

10 M:  æh du  tænker på  kontorartikler.
          uh you think of office=supplies.
          uh are you thinking of office supplies
```

The way the employee now reports about her work task is by adding an assessable aspect to it "as cheap as possible" (l. 8). She thereby highlights that not only has she performed the task she was given, but she has even done it in a way that added to the overall company performance. This assessable aspect makes relevant a subsequent assessment by the manager, but this action is not performed. Instead he produces a request for clarification "are you thinking of office supplies" (l. 10), thus postponing the acknowledgment of the employee's performance that the employee has made relevant.

Excerpt (2c)
```
11 E:  ja, gener- [Ja; ( . ) hvad der  nu  ellers    er i stedet for
          yes gener- yes     what there now otherwise is instead of
          yes gener- yes whatever there may be instead of

12 E:  bare      bevidstløs  o' ( . ) bestil=dem  hvor  vi plejer.
          simply    unconscious to     order  them where we usually=do
          simply without reflection    ordering the ones we usually get

13 M:  jha;
          yes

14     (0.2)

15 M:  og gå  ud (o' få=øh)  som  [Svend skriv [er i := (œ::)
          and go out to uh  as  Svend writes in uh
```

157

The employee continues by adding yet another assessable aspect to her work report. This time she upgrades the assessable from "as cheap as possible" to "instead of simply without reflection ordering the ones we usually get" (ll. 11, 12), which reflects upon herself as being an employee who makes a tremendous effort to improve organizational processes. Yet, once again the manager does not address the assessable nature of her report. Instead, he minimizes the individual effort of the employee by referring to this as a standard organizational procedure "to go out as Svend writes" (l. 15). In terminal overlap with this, the employee takes over and voices a rejection of the manager's stance on her work task by claiming that this is what she has been doing all the time. Hence, by use of role-taking she is trying to identify ways to increase her relational power in the discursive negotiation and evaluation of the job performance and through this pushes her own interests through.

Excerpt (2d)
```
15  M:  og gå ud (o' få=øh) som [Svend skriv[er i:=(œ::)
        and go out to uh as Svend writes in uh
                                [((E looks at M))
16  E:                                       [Jamn det-
                                             yes but this

17  E:  det gør jeg [har jeg [altså gjort hele
        this do I   have I   PRT  done  all
        this i do, I have actually done all
18  M:               [ja
                      yes
                     [(( M retracts gaze from E, M starts
                         writing))
19  E:  ti[den  vil   jeg] så  sige.
        time=the will I    then say
        the time I would say
```

While the employee produces this rejection and gazes at the manager, the manager starts engaging in filing (l. 18). What we see here is an asymmetry in orientation to what task is to be fulfilled. By orienting toward the ostensive aspects of the organizational routine, i.e. the interview guide and the tentative final PAI result paper (the routine outcome), the manager intends to draw on his structural power as a resource to bring the negotiation in—for him—a desired direction. While the manager makes use of the filing activity to underline his occupational status as the one in charge, the employee does not simply give in; instead she makes use of discursive moves that place specific interactional obligations on the manager to which he has to respond.

Excerpt (2e) shows what happens when the manager, in overlap with the employee, takes over and produces the first clear assessment segment. What we see here is a clear example of role-taking on behalf of the employee in order to gain more influence in the negotiation and convey strong relational power in the interaction.

Excerpt (2e)
```
19  E:  ti [den      vil       jeg ]  så  sige.
        time=the     will      I      then say
        the time I would say
20  M:      [De:t     godt  Mette.]
            this=is   good  Mette.
            this is   good Mette

21  M:  de:       godt.
        this=is good.
        this is  good
```

The manager uses an assessment segment that is individualized by also using the employee's first name "This is good, Mette" (l. 20, anonymized first name of employee), and in the pause after the employee has ended her turn, he produces a repetition but this time in a more generic form by not using her first name.

Excerpt (2f)
```
22  (0.8)

23  E:  det    er  jeg  nok  lige  (lidt    en)  for  nærig;
        there  am  I    PRT  just  little   one  too  stingy
        in  this   respect  I am  probably  a  bit too  stingy.
```

After a significant pause of 0.8 seconds (l. 22), the employee takes over. She does not do so by acknowledging the assessment segment produced by the manager. Instead she pursues the topic of the work task reported on before by adding yet another assessable "in this respect I am probably a bit too stingy." Apart from this being an upgrade of the prior assessment by the employee using a strong assessment segment "stingy," it also constitutes an upgrade in that the employee now clearly relates the assessment to herself as a personal trait, rather than relating it directly to her work task. By doing so, she increases her relational power even more, in that she reflects her personal investment in the relationship, i.e. her job employment at the company. Hence, the employee indirectly rejects the evaluation proposed by the manager, as she with the upgraded report of her work performance, makes relevant yet another assessment from the manager. The manager responds accordingly by use of a new assessment segment.

Excerpt (2g)
```
24  M:  j [amen, det     ski [d- det- det er [kan] on.
            PRT    this=is blood- this   this is canon
        yes but this is blood this  this is awesome.
                        [(((M lifts up pen))
                                    [((M moves up and down
                                        in chair))
25  E:  [tihhl ahht skhhu betahhle fulhhd prihhs.]
            for   to   shall  pay     full   price
        to pay full  price

26  M:  Ja.
        yes

27  M:  [det   er [rigtig      go]dt.
        this is   really      good
        [(((M tilts pen))
                    [((M draws a line))]

28      (0.4)
```

Instead of using a generic assessment segment like "good," which as seen in excerpt (1) is closing implicative, the manager chooses this time an assessment segment that has a more authentic quality in that it does not represent a standard version of an assessment. He initially does so by beginning with a rather colloquial version "bloody good" (Danish "skid-" is most likely the beginning of something supposed to be very good, corresponding to English "bloody good"), which, even though it is cut-off under production, is still recognizable as this item. He then restarts using another strong, positive, non-standardized assessment token "this is awesome" (l. 24, Danish "kanon" is a very strong, colloquial positive assessment token). While doing so, he suspends the activity of filing, lifts up his pen (l. 24) and orients by means of body posture to the employee. By acting this way, the manager displays that he no longer orients to the ostensive aspects of the PAI (the PAI file); instead, by producing a non-standardized assessment, the manager clearly focuses on the interpersonal relationship with the employee in accordance with what the employee had pursued. In that sense, the employee wins the "power struggle," so to speak.

In response, the employee in line 26 indicates acceptance of the evaluation of her past work performance by producing a minimal acknowledgment "yes." The manager displays his understanding of the prior as an acceptance of the assessment by moving into closing. He does so in an embodied manner by tilting the pen and drawing a line in the questionnaire while at the same time producing a generic, standardized, and downgraded assessment, "this is really good" (l.27). Directly after this, the employee begins to report about another of her work tasks.

In excerpt (2), it is shown that not every assessment segment performs assessing work. As part of an interactional routine of evaluating work performance which is part of a larger organizational routine (PAI), the employee shows that a standardized, generic assessment combined with embodied behavior that does not display attention toward the employee, is not performing the kind of assessing work which the employee pursues. Instead the employee continues the pursuit of non-standardized, individualized assessments that are supported by embodied actions indicating clear attention toward the employee. Not until these are produced in full alignment with embodied orientation, is the evaluation sequence ready to move into closing.

In relation to the aspect of power and power dynamics within organizational routines, the excerpt shows that structural power granted through occupational status, i.e. the role of management, is not necessarily equivalent to performative influence. Instead, in excerpt (2) it becomes clear that the interactional moves initiated by the employee put constraints on the moves made by the manager limiting his ability to close the agenda item at a point in the PAI where the employee evaluation is not deemed adequate by the employee.

As mentioned previously, it is acknowledged that there is an asymmetric power distribution between actors in organizational routines (Dionysiou and Tsoukas, 2013: 195). Hence, at first glance, we think of a manager as a more powerful PAI actor than an employee when it comes to steering the performative aspects of a PAI in alignment with ostensive aspects (Parmigiani and Howard-Grenville, 2011: 441). However, as can be seen from excerpt (2) and in line with Fligstein's notion of power (2001), the employee may be less powerful in terms of structural power due to her position in the organizational structure, but her ability to influence the manager seems to be a result of her "social skill" and hence her possession of relational power. This analysis demonstrates empirically how actors in routines bring different resources to the relationship and draw on multiple bases of power, each of which, in correspondence with Cast (2003) and Stolte (1994), offers a distinctive source of power to the actors, and exerts a unique effect on actors' ability to control meanings in the performance of the PAI as an organizational routine. As a result, what might appear to be a less powerful employee actor in the beginning of the interaction turns out to be a rather powerful individual capable of altering the assessment situation through interaction so that meanings in the performance evaluation become consistent with her own definition of the situation.

7.6.3 Performing Employee Evaluations: Maintenance of an Interactional Routine

The last excerpt (3) shows an example of an employee performance evaluation being accomplished and agreed upon by both participants, resulting in joint situated understanding and aligned action (i.e. a prototypical example of the performative aspect outlined in Figure 7.1).

In the analysis in this section, we will show how a non-standardized, authentic evaluation of work performance does not necessarily need to be the result of the employee's relational power in terms of pursuing role-taking in order to increase their influence and push their own interests through. Instead, we will show an orientation by the manager indicating that this is the kind of action that is relevant in order to perform successful employee evaluation.

In the example, the interactional routine of performing employee performance evaluations is maintained as the manager produces non-standardized, authentic assessments, which the employee immediately aligns with because the meanings in the positive performance evaluation presumably are consistent with her own definition of the situation, including definition of self. The ostensive parts of organizational routines (in the form of the PA interview guide) again serve as a mutual resource for the PAI participants in that the interplay between, on the one hand, orienting to the ostensive aspects of the PAI and, on the other hand, pursuing and producing non-standardized versions of an employee evaluation are closely coordinated and oriented to by both participants.

The following extract comes from a point in the PAI that according to the PAI guide, deals with the employee's social competences and how these promote organizational performance. The manager starts by referring to the interview guide in order to legitimize the up-coming topic of discussion.

Excerpt (3a)
```
1  M:  .Hhh når   man så kigger på det her  med hvordan (0.3)
            when  one  so looks  at  this here  with how
            if one  looks at how

2  M:  [<involverer berørte parter til,
          involve    affected parties to
          to involve affected parties in order to
          [((M moves body towards questionnaire))

3         (0.8)

4  M:  til mål>  og  aftaler for at sikre  kvalitet,
          to goal  and deals   for to ensure quality
          in order to achieve goals and deals to ensure quality

5  P:  ( . )
```

In lines 1 to 4, the manager introduces a new discussion topic. She creates the topic shift discursively by noticeably reading aloud what is written in the interview guide, and in an embodied manner by physically turning her body toward the interview document that is placed on the table in front of her. After presenting the question to be talked about, the manager moves on by recognizably providing an answer to the question.

Excerpt (3b)

```
6  M:  œ::m  (0.2)  jeg  havde  noteret         [her  a´   du  er  god  ti´
       uhm          I    have   written=down  here  that  you  are  good  to
       uhm I have written down here that you are good at
7                                                [((M  points  to  her  questionnaire))

8  M:  at  samarbejde    med  lederteamet            o:g  med  enkeltpersoner.
       at  collabrate    with  managementteam=the and  with  individuals
       at collaborating with the management team and with individuals
```

The manager noticeably orients to the interview guide by physically pointing to it (l. 7) and verbally referring to the fact that this is something she has written down. By doing so, she creates a greater sense of authenticity around her individual assessment since—by having written it down beforehand—both parties are aware that it is something she has thought about independently, rather than a result of the interaction or negotiation between the two. Thereafter, she continues to produce a first positive assessment of the employee. She does so by first highlighting that this is going to be a positive assessment "you are good at" and then specifying that the positive assessment relates to "collaborating with the management team and with individuals." Thus, the manager sets the scene for the evaluation sequence and does not leave any doubt about the employee performing well.

In addition, by physically and verbally referring to the ostensive aspects of the PAI, in the form of the interview guide, she implicitly positions herself as a more powerful actor, due to her occupational status and subsequent organizational position, putting her in charge of the interview and responsible for further progression and enactment of the performance evaluation routine in the way she finds appropriate.

Excerpt (3c)

```
9      (0.8)

10     (0.3)  ((E  raises  eyebrows))

11 E:  J:a[?
       yes
```

The employee aligns with what the manager has made relevant, namely that the manager is to continue her turn. The employee does not take over immediately but indicates that she aligns with the assessment by raising her eyebrows (l. 10) and producing a continuer (l. 11).

Excerpt (3d)

```
12  M:  [de:t    ik´ kun-,   œ: altså helt klart lederteament          det har
         this=is not just  uh PRT  very clear  management team=the that has
         this is not just uh  right it is   obvious that the management team

13  M:  fungeret (0.2)   r : igtig fint.=de  er helt    vildt glad     for dig.
         functioned       very    fine. they are much  wild  pleased with you.
         has functioned   very well. They are extremely pleased with you.

14  E:  Ja.
         yes
```

The manager elaborates thereafter on the two items that are the focus in her first assessment: the management team and its individual members. She starts out by talking about the management team and assesses on behalf of a third party "they are extremely pleased with you" (l. 13). By doing so, she does not only claim knowledge about the employee's specific work performance; she actually displays authentic knowledge about the appreciation of the employee among the management team members. Thus, the manager orients to an interactional routine of producing non-standardized, authentic assessments in order to evaluate employee performance. The employee responds with yet another minimal response, thus displaying that she is aligned with the utterance and that she is going to take over. By doing so, she contributes to the interactional routine of authentic assessments as the basis for employee evaluation, leaving room for the manager to elaborate further.

Excerpt (3e)

```
15  M:  altså de:r      slet       ingen tvivl om.  Det  har Peter også
         PRT this=is  absolutely no    doubt about. That has Peter also
         well there is  absolutely no  doubt about this. This is also what

16  M:  fortalt o´ det det har   flere  af produktionslederne
         told and this this have several of productionmanagers=the
         told and this have several of the production managers

17  M:  også fortalt  at   de:r      jam- de er  jo helt vildt
         also told    that there=is  PRT they are PRT very wild
         also said that there-  they are actually extraordinarily

18  M:  glad     for  dig.
         pleased with you.
         pleased with you.

19       (0.2)

20  E:  Ja-.=
         yes
```

The manager continues to elaborate by first highlighting that there is no doubt about the positive assessment, and then by further accounting for the positive assessment by referring to two other third parties "Peter" and the group of production managers. She ends her account by producing an upgraded assessment from "they are extremely pleased with you" (l. 13) to "they are actually extraordinarily pleased with you" (l. 18). This high grade assessment is again minimally acknowledged by the employee (l. 20). In response the manager moves on to the other aspect that was positively assessed in the beginning, namely that the employee is doing well in collaborating on an individual level. During the whole sequence, the employee and manager have eye contact, which highlights their orientation to the ongoing evaluation as not being a fileable activity, but exclusively devoted to the activity of assessing the employee.

Excerpt (3f)
```
21  M:  =.hh så œ:: o´ det- det  er jo  tegn på a´   du: god ti´
            so u:: and this this is PRT token for that you good to
        so and this is a signal that you are good at

22  M:  o´::agere i  team.= altså [du fle-    jo: fitter ind, (.)
            at act  in team. PRT     you mer-  PRT fit   in
        at acting in a team. right you fit

23  E:                              [hm
                                    hm

24  M:  passer ind.
        fit in.
```

This issue of collaboration is introduced stepwise allowing the employee to interject and take over. First, the manager sums up the prior by using a formulation (Drew, 2003) "so and this is a signal that you are good at acting in a team" (ll. 21, 22) followed by a specification in the form of what good team work entails. Without the employee taking over, the manager continues by focusing on the second item on her list of assessables, the employee's ability to collaborate with individuals.

Excerpt (3g)
```
25  M:  .hh men jeg synes ogsa du er god til (.) .hh inden i
            but I  think also you are good at within
        but I also think you are good within

26  M:  et team o´ arbejde  med enkeltpersoner.
        a  team to work    with individuals.
        a team at working with  individuals.

27  M:  ((M continues for 12 seconds elaborating on why the employee
        performs well))
```

Similarly to the first item assessed, the manager starts out by using a positive, yet rather standardized assessment: "you are good [. . .] at working with individuals" (ll. 25, 26), which is subsequently elaborated on. The sequence ends, similarly to the prior assessment sequence (ll. 17, 18), with the manager producing a high grade assessment.

Excerpt (3h)

```
28  M:  fordi    du  er  sådan- glad     og (.) udadvendt  og  frisk  ikkos?.
        because you are such  cheerful and      extroverted and fresh  PRT
        because you are so cheerful and extroverted and perky
```

```
29      De:::t (.) jamen det  f: det funker    bare.
        This        PRT  this w: this works=well PRT
        This        PRT this simply works perfectly well.
```

After having accounted for why the employee is being assessed in such a positive way "you are so cheerful and extroverted and perky" (l. 28), the manager ends with a non-standardized, high grade assessment. After this, the sequence moves into closing.

The analysis of excerpt (3) shows that the interactional routine of assessing employee performance is mutually oriented to by both PAI participants: the manager orients to it by producing non-standardized positive assessments, and the employee orients to it by merely acknowledging the assessments produced by the manager. Here, the participants are fully aligned in the activity of maintaining an interactional routine that forms a substantial part of the overall organizational routine, the PAI.

In terms of power dynamics, it becomes apparent that the manager not only draws on her structural power to enact the performance of the evaluation routine in the way she sees fit. One of the reasons why the performance of the evaluation unfolds without problems appears to be the use of non-standardized, authentic assessments. These types of assessments are somewhat linked to the aspects of relational power in that they are based on feelings about others and the relationship and reflect the individual's relative investment in the relationship (Cast, 2003). By applying non-standardized, authentic assessments, the manager displays increased attention to the superior–subordinate relationship. Hence, independent of her organizational position, but based on her interpersonal skills, the manager succeeds in creating a joint situated understanding of the evaluation routine leading to aligned actions.

In response to our research question on the relationship between social interaction and the negotiation of power in micro-level routines on the one hand and the performance of larger organizational routines on the other, the analyses of the three excerpts have shown that interactional micro-level routines are definitely not power neutral; they are points in the PAI where power aspects recurrently come into play in the interaction serving as a resource for the co-participants to engage in joint sense-making regarding the nature and quality of the employee evaluation produced. Moreover, the analyses show that the ostensive aspects of organizational routines play a crucial role when the performative aspects are played out: the orientation to or suspension of orientation to the PAI questionnaire allows the manager to display either his/her full attention in the form of authentic assessments, or to display that the action in focus serves a different purpose than assessing employee performance. Thus, it is important to acknowledge that performative and ostensive aspects cannot be separated in relation to interactional routines, given that both elements function as interactional resources for the participants in the accomplishment of the actions at stake.

7.7 Discussion and Conclusion

Organizational routines have been studied by many from a practice or performative perspective focusing on how routines are enacted day-to-day and with what consequences (Feldman, 2000; Feldman and Pentland, 2003; Parmigiani and Howard-Grenville, 2011; Rerup and Feldman, 2011), but the way in which individual participants interrelate and negotiate their individual courses of action on a micro-level has remained an under-explored topic. In light of this apparent gap, the aim of the present study has been to explore the video-recorded data of PAIs in which practitioners in organizations negotiate the issue of performance evaluation focusing specifically on power in an interactional, micro-level perspective. In the following we will discuss our contributions, which will center on power dynamics in organizational routines, the sequencing of micro routines within an overall organizational routine, and the methodological implications of the study.

First and foremost, the study reveals the power dynamics that are inherently at stake in the routine performance. The study shows that traditional understandings of manager and employee relations can be reverted and changed by means of the ongoing interactional negotiations within organizational routines. It is an acknowledged fact that some participants in organizational routines "are usually more empowered than other participants" (Dionysiou and Tsoukas, 2013: 195) and in relation to PAIs, it is often assumed that the manager is overall more empowered than the employee in that it is the manager who is in charge of the interview guide and therefore "sets the scene" by controlling the content of the conversation. Thus, the manager becomes more empowered by using the ostensive routine elements to impose rules and legitimate specific actions. For example, by turning to the interview guide, it is the manager who decides when to turn to a new topic and at which point during the PAI the evaluation should take place.

Yet, the study reveals that empowerment is not a manager's issue alone. Instead, also the employee can draw upon aspects of power in order to negotiate his/her position of influence in the PAI. Here, the study made use of Thomas' (1972) understanding of structural power and relational power within the organizational routine context. The study shows how the actors through their possession of structural and/ or relational power bring different negotiation resources into the routine interaction.

In Figure 7.3 we illustrate our findings with regard to the power dynamics present in the PAI routine. As can be seen in the figure the superior/ manager and the subordinate/employee constitute the actors who mutually accomplish the performance of the routine. Due to his/her occupational position (among other things), the superior inherently possesses structural power, which can be applied as an additional resource in the interactional negotiation of meaning (illustrated by the striped circle). Hence, the superior has an exclusive power base, which can be brought into play in order to reach a joint situated understanding and subsequently an aligned action, which can be filed in the interview guide. Thus, by default the structural power makes the superior a more empowered PAI actor than the subordinate in relation to creating and imposing rules, monitoring performance and enforcing compliance, and legitimating specific actions over others (Dionysiou and Tsoukas, 2013: 195), which affect "the degree to which they can . . . enact the [PAI] routine as it is ostensively interpreted and understood" (Parmigiani and Howard-Grenville, 2011: 441). Consequently, as Figure 7.3 illustrates, there is an asymmetric division of structural power in regard to managers on the one hand and employees on the other. The ostensive aspect in the form of the interview guide and the responsibility for filing serves as a resource for the manager to perform specific actions (e.g. topic progression, assessment) that correlate with roles associated with superior–subordinate relations in PAIs. Hence, the study implies that specific resources within the ostensive aspect, related to PAI context, content, and outcome (see Figure 7.1), are available for the manager due to his/her structural power, while the same resources are not available to the employee.

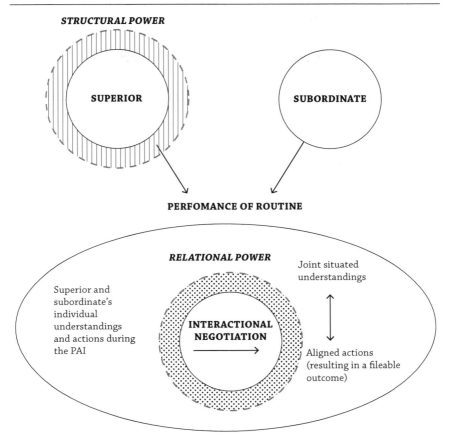

Figure 7.3 Power dynamics and performative aspects of PAIs

However, as can be seen from the analyses, structural power is not the only power base present in the performance of the routine. Illustrated in Figure 7.3 by the dotted circle, both the superior and the subordinate have the potential to make skillful use of his/her relational power and "social skills" in the interactional negotiation of meaning, thereby influencing the perceptions and interpretations of the other actor, and ultimately increasing his/her influence on the outcome, i.e. in this case the joint situated understanding of the evaluation routine.

Whereas managers can make use of both structural power and relational power in the negotiation of a performance evaluation, employees can "only" make use of their relational power. Nevertheless, this power asymmetry does not imply that the employee necessarily is less empowered than the manager. Instead, the study reveals that it is how and when power aspects are made relevant in the negotiation over employee performance that are central when the PAI participants try to accomplish a joint agreement about performance evaluation.

Secondly, our study contributes to the sequencing of micro-routines within an overall organizational routine, and shows how power dynamics are contributory factors in the actors "moving" from one micro-routine to the next. In our data we have focused on evaluation as a micro-level routine within a larger organizational routine such as a PAI. As shown, PAI participants have different orientations to "standardized" and "non-standardized" assessments (Maynard, 2003). In our data analysis we can see that "non-standardized" assessments are frequently oriented to as doing the work of "real" evaluations, whereas "standardized" assessments are oriented to as topic closure implicative. Accordingly, employees often pursue non-standardized assessments from their managers, while managers use standardized assessments for balancing the task of filing relevant information and that of performing assessing work. The analysis allows insight into the participants' respective expectations toward the organizational routine of a PAI, and highlights the role of different types of assessment in the participants' micro-management of different social actions performed in PAIs. Our analysis also indicates the contours of an evaluation continuum available to the manager responsible for the evaluation. The continuum ranges from standardized to non-standardized assessment work, the non-standardized assessments being applied in order to discursively create an evaluation that is jointly accepted by both parties, i.e. manager and employee, as authentic and legitimate. As we can see from our data, this continuum of assessment work is influenced by the structural power of the manager as well as the relational power of both actors who play an influential role in deciding when and if a standardized or non-standardized assessment performs the relevant next action.

Through the study of the power dynamics at stake in the PAI routine proper, it becomes apparent that the manager is unable to entirely control the outcome and progression of the PAI by use of merely structural power. The manager is not alone in control of the performative routine aspects; they rather seem to depend upon mutual co-creation. In the current study we show how subordinates try to negotiate and resolve disputes related to meanings, rules, and procedures in relation to the evaluative element of the PAI through the give-and-take of interpersonal communication (Stolte et al., 2001: 395). The employee tries to alter the evaluative situation through negotiation, and thus relational power, until the actual assessment is seen to be satisfactory and consistent with his or her own cognitive understanding of an appropriate, authentic, non-standardized evaluation. At the micro-level interactional routine of performance evaluation, our analysis shows that in order for an evaluation to be good enough it is necessary to deviate from the standardized, ordinary version and deliver a non-standardized assessment in order to achieve alignment and create a joint situated understanding of what a "true" employee evaluation is. Thus, the ostensive aspects indirectly guide and influence the performative aspects of the PAI just as the performative aspects guide and influence the ostensive aspects.

In addition, the study indicates that there is a close relation between the use of standardized and non-standardized assessments on the one hand and an orientation to ostensive and performative aspects of the routine on the other. The use of a standardized assessment is closely related to the ostensive aspects of the evaluation routine, in that it recurrently aligns with the manager's and at times, the employee's orientation to the question-naire and/or the activity of filing information, such as the outcome of the PAI. Non-standardized assessments are, in contrast, part of a clear orienta-tion by the manager and employee not to relate to larger organizational aspects of the PAI in the form of the ostensive aspects, but rather focus on the relational aspects of the PAI in the form of an authentic acknowledg-ment of the employee's work performance. Hence, specific linguistic forms of evaluation can be more closely related to the ostensive than the per-formative aspects of organizational routines and vice versa. This highlights the importance of close linguistic investigations of how PAIs unfold moment-by-moment in order to fully explore how performative and osten-sive aspects of an organizational routine are built from within.

Thirdly, our study contributes methodologically to the growing research on micro-foundations of routines responding to recent calls for studying the micro-level aspects of routines by bringing the individual actors into focus (Felin and Foss, 2005, 2009, 2011; Abell et al., 2008). The study implies that it is possible by use of video-based micro-ethnography to take the study of the relationship between organizational routines and micro-level interactional routines on the one hand, and performative and ostensive aspects on the other, a step further. As made possible by means of video-ethnographic work, the close study of moment-by-moment unfold-ing of an organizational routine facilitates important insights into the complex and dynamic relations of various discursive actions and thus helps to challenge assumptions about the stability of organizational routines. As the current study shows, it is the ongoing discursive actions carried out by the actors that shape and re-shape the moves that constitute the performative aspects of the overall organizational routine.

For the purpose of the current study, the method of Conversation Analysis has been applied. As a method relying on authentic interactions, CA has proven to have great potential in capturing the dynamics and sequential organization of real-time interaction. The use of video-observations makes it possible to detect how meaning moment-by-moment is negotiated by both verbal and embodied means. Getting such detailed insights into the constitutive micro-moves of routine dynamics would not have been possible by, for example, the use of retrospective data like interview or survey data.

However, such an in-depth study of routine dynamics also involves some limitations in regard to data collection and the representativity of analytical results. Authentic, video-based organizational data are difficult to get access to and being allowed to video-record intra-organizational data is often a question of trust. When studying organizational data in this way, we therefore depend on the willingness and acceptance of a great number of individual organizational actors (both superiors and subordinates) to be video-recorded in situations that in case of PAIs can entail delicate issues and sensitive information. Therefore, the researcher might not be granted access to PAIs where either the superior or the subordinate or both foresee a problematic conversation. Despite these limitations, we see the strength in the chosen approach in showing in depth how recurrent interactional micro-level linguistic actions like standardized and non-standardized assessments, play a crucial role in the emergence of larger organizational routines.

Language and its effects have long been acknowledged as important objects of study when trying to open and understand the black boxes of organizational routines. However, it is apparent that the ways in which people bring objects and their bodies into place during organizational routines in general—and PAI and evaluating work in particular—need further study and theorizing in order to reach a better understanding of the complex interrelation between the ostensive and performative aspects of organizational routines. For future research, we see the need to study power dynamics in organizational routines across various organizational settings, for example recruitment or strategy work, in order to increase our understanding of how power and organizational routines are interrelated. The current study suggests that the sequencing of micro-level routines is to some extent organized by power dynamics, and thus further studies on how micro-level routines are sequentially organized within larger organizational routines and how organizational actors can move from one routine to another are needed. Finally, the study demonstrates that it is highly relevant to investigate organizational routines in their natural environment, and the study calls for more video-ethnographic in-depth work on the emergence and constitution of organizational routines.[1]

Transcription Glossary

Based on the Jefferson transcription conventions as described in Atkinson and Heritage (1984: ix–xvi).

right	speaker emphasis
YES	noticeably louder than surrounding talk
u:	stretched sound
ka-	sharp cut-off of the prior sound
?	rising intonation
,	continuing intonation
;	small falling intonation
.	falling intonation
=	latching between utterances and words
><	noticeably quicker than surrounding talk
<>	noticeably slower than surrounding talk
↑	rising intonational shift
↓	falling intonational shift
.hh	audible in-breath
hh	audible out-breath
yehhs	laughter in word
(.)	micropause (less than 0.2 seconds)
(0.5)	time gap in tenths of a second
[yes]/[no]	overlapping talk
()	unintelligible talk
(())	information about embodied actions
PRT	particle

Note

1. We would like to thank our reviewers for extremely helpful and supportive feedback, which helped us in focusing our contribution to an extent that we undoubtedly would not have reached without them. The authors of course still

remain fully responsible for the content of this chapter. We would also like to thank the members of the organizations, whom we generously were allowed to observe. A study like this one would never have been possible without their willingness to participate.

References

Abell, P., Felin, T., and Foss, N. J. (2008). "Building Micro-Foundations for the Routines, Capabilities, and Performance Links." *Managerial and Decision Economics*, 29/6: 489–502.

Asmuß, B. (2008). "Performance Appraisal Interviews: Preference Organization in Assessment Sequences." *Journal of Business Communication*, 45/4: 408–29.

Asmuß, B. (2013). "The Emergence of Symmetries and Asymmetries in Performance Appraisal Interviews: An Interactional Perspective." *Economic and Industrial Democracy*, 34/3: 553–70.

Asmuß, B. (2015). "Multimodal Perspectives on Meeting Interaction: Recent Trends in Conversation Analysis." In S. Rogelberg, J. Allen, and N. Lehmann-Willenbrock (eds.), *The Cambridge Handbook of Work Meetings*. Cambridge: Cambridge University Press, 277–304.

Atkinson, J. M. and Heritage, J. (1984). *Structures of Social Action: Studies in Conversation Analysis*. Cambridge: Cambridge University Press.

Beardwell, J. and Claydon, T. (2010). *Human Ressource Management: A Contemporary Approach* (6th edn.). Harlow: Pearson.

Becker, M. C. (2008). "The Past, the Present and Future of Organizational Routines." In M. C. Becker (ed.), *Handbook of Organizational Routines*. Cheltenham: Edward Elgar, 3–14.

Becker, M. C. and Zirpoli, F. (2008). "Applying Organizational Routines in Analysing the Behaviour of Organizations." *Journal of Economic Behavior & Organization*, 66/1: 128–48.

Blumer, H. (1969). *Symbolic Interactionism: Perspective and Method*. Englewood Cliffs, NJ: Prentice Hall.

Bruns, H. C. (2009). "Leveraging Functionality in Safety Routines: Examining the Divergence of Rules and Performance." *Human Relations*, 629: 1399–426.

Caruth, D. and Humphreys, J. (2008). "Performance Appraisal: Essential Characteristics for Strategic Control." *Measuring Business Excellence*, 12/3: 24–32.

Cast, A. D. (2003). "Power and the Ability to Define the Situation." *Social Psychology Quarterly*, 66/3: 185–201.

Cooren, F. (2007). *Interacting and Organizing: Analyses of a Management Meeting*. Mahwah, NJ: Lawrence Erlbaum.

D'Adderio, L. (2009). "The Influence of Artefacts and Distributed Agencies on Routines' Dynamics: From Representation to Performation," in M. C. Becker (ed.),

Organizational Routines: Advancing Empirical Research. Cheltenham: Edward Elgar, 185–222.

D'Adderio, L. (2011). "Artifacts at the Centre of Routines: Performing the Material Turn in Routines Theory." *Journal of Institutional Economics*, 7/2: 197–230.

Desai, V. M. (2010). "Rule Violations and Organizational Search: A Review and Extension." *International Journal of Management Reviews*, 12/2:184–200.

Dionysiou, D. D. and Tsoukas, H. (2013). "Understanding the (Re)Creation of Routines from Within: A Symbolic Interactionist Perspective." *Academy of Management Review*, 38/2: 181–205.

Drew, P. (2003). "Comparative Analysis of Talk-in-Interaction in Different Institutional Settings: A Sketch." In P. Glenn, C. D. LeBaron, and J. Mandelbaum (eds.), *Studies in Language and Social Interaction: In Honor of Robert Hopper*. Mahwah, NJ: Lawrence Erlbaum, 293–308.

Edmondson, A. C., Bohmer, R. M., and Pisano, G. P. (2001). "Disrupted Routines: Team Learning and New Technology Implementation in Hospitals." *Administrative Science Quarterly*, 46/4: 685–716.

Emirbayer, M. and Mische, A. (1998). "What is Agency?" *American Journal of Sociology*, 103/4: 685–716.

Essén, A. (2008). "Variability as a Source of Stability: Studying Routines in the Elderly Home Care Setting." *Human Relations*, 61/11: 1617–44.

Feldman, M. S. (2000). "Organizational Routines as a Source of Continuous Change." *Organization Science*, 11/6: 611–29.

Feldman, M. S. and Pentland, B. T. (2003). "Reconceptualizing Organizational Routines as a Source of Flexibility and Change." *Administrative Science Quarterly*, 48/1: 94–118.

Felin, T. and Foss, N. (2005). "Strategic Organization: A Field in Search of Micro-Foundations." *Strategic Organization*, 3/4: 441–55.

Felin, T. and Foss, N. (2009). "Organizational Routines and Capabilities: Historical Drift and a Course-Correction toward Microfoundations." *Scandinavian Journal of Management*, 25/2: 157–67.

Felin, T. and Foss, N. (2011). "The Endogenous Origins of Experience, Routines, and Organizational Capabilities: The Poverty of Stimulus." *Journal of Institutional Economics*, 7/2: 231–56.

Fiske, S. T. and Depret, E. (1996). "Control, Interdependence and Power: Understanding Social Cognition in its Social Context." *European Review of Social Psychology*, 7/1: 31–62.

Fletcher, C. (2001). "Performance Appraisal and Management: The Developing Research Agenda." *Journal of Occupational and Organizational Psychology*, 74/4: 473–87.

Fligstein, N. (2001). "Social Skill and the Theory of Fields." *Sociological Theory*, 19: 105–25.

Gersick, C. J.and Hackman, J. R. (1990). "Habitual Routines in Task-Performing Groups." *Organizational Behavior and Human Decision Processes*, 47/1: 65–97.

Giddens, A. (1986). *The Constitution of Society: Outline of the Theory of Structuration*. Berkeley, CA: University of California Press.

Goodwin, C. and Goodwin, M. H. (1987). "Concurrent Operations on Talk: Notes on the Interactive Organization of Assessments." *Pragmatics*, 1/1: 1–54.

Goodwin, C. and Goodwin, M. H. (1992). "Assessments and the Construction of Context." In A. Duranti and C. Goodwin (eds.), *Rethinking Context: Language as an Interactive Phenomenon*. Cambridge: Cambridge University Press, 147–90.

Hepburn, A. and Bolden, G. B. (2013). "The Conversation Analytic Approach to Transcription." In J. Sidnell and T. Stivers (eds.), *The Handbook of Conversation Analysis*. Cambridge, MA: Wiley-Blackwell, 57–76.

Heritage, J. (1984). *Garfinkel and Ethnomethodology*. Cambridge: Polity Press.

Howard-Grenville, J. A. (2005). "The Persistence of Flexible Organizational Routines: The Role of Agency and Organizational Context." *Organization Science*, 16/6: 618–36.

Huston, T. L. (1983). "Power." In H. H. Kelley, E. Berscheid, A. Christensen, J. H. Harvey, T. L. Huston, G. Levinger, E. McClintock, L. A. Peplau, and D. R. Peterson, *Close Relationships*. New York: Freeman, 169–219.

Hutchby, I. and Wooffitt, R. (1998). *Conversation Analysis: Principles, Practices and Applications*. Cambridge: Polity Press.

Kozica, A., Kaiser, S., and Friesl, M. (2014). "Organizational Routines: Conventions as a Source of Change and Stability." *Schmalenbach Business Review*, 66/3: 334–56.

Kuhn, T. (2012). "Negotiating the Micro–Macro Divide: Thought Leadership from Organizational Communication for Theorizing Organization." *Management Communication Quarterly*, 26/4: 543–84.

Labianca, G., Gray, B., and Brass, D. J. (2000). "A Grounded Model of Organizational Schema Change during Empowerment." *Organization Science*, 11/2: 235–57.

Lazaric, N. and Denis, B. (2005). "Routinization and Memorization of Tasks in a Workshop: The Case of the Introduction of ISO Norms." *Industrial and Corporate Change*, 14/5: 873–96.

LeBaron, C. (2008). "Microethnography." In K. Tracy (ed.), *The International Encyclopedia of Communication*. Cambridge, MA: Wiley-Blackwell, 1–5.

Leonardi, P. (2011). "When Flexible Routines Meet Flexible Technologies: Affordance, Constraint, and the Imbrication of Human and Material Agencies." *MIS Quarterly*, 35/1: 147–67.

Lindström, A. and Mondada, L. (2009). "Assessments in Social Interaction." *Research on Language and Social Interaction*, 42/4: 299–308.

McPhee, R. and Zaug, P. (2000). "The Communicative Constitution of Organisations: A Framework for Explanation." *Electronic Journal of Communication*, 10/1–2: 1–23.

Maynard, D. W. (2003). *Bad News, Good News: Conversational Order in Everyday Talk and Clinical Settings*. Chicago, IL: University of Chicago Press.

Metiu, A. (2006). "Owning the Code: Status Closure in Distributed Groups." *Organization Science*, 17/4: 418–35.

Mondada, L. (2007). "Multimodal Resources for Turn-Taking: Pointing and the Emergence of Possible Next Speakers." *Discourse Studies*, 9/2: 194–225.

Mortensen, K. (2013). "Conversation Analysis and Multimodality." In C. A. Chapelle (ed.), *The Encyclopedia of Applied Linguistics*. Cambridge, MA: Wiley-Blackwell, 1061–8.

Nathan, B. R., Mohrman, A. M., and Milliman, J. (1991). "Interpersonal Relations as a Context for the Effects of Appraisal Interviews on Performance and Satisfaction: A Longitudinal Study." *Academy of Management Journal*, 34/2: 352–69.

Nelson, R. R. and Winter, S. (1982). *An Evolutionary Theory of Economic Change*. Cambridge, MA: Belknap Press/Harvard University Press.

Parmigiani, A. and Howard-Grenville, J. (2011). "Routines Revisited: Exploring the Capabilities and Practice Perspectives." *Academy of Management Annals*, 5/1: 413–53.

Pentland, B. T., Feldman, M. S., Becker, M. C., and Liu, P. (2012). "Dynamics of Organizational Routines: A Generative Model." *Journal of Management Studies*, 49/8: 1484–508.

Pentland, B. T. and Rueter, H. H. (1994). "Organizational Routines as Grammars of Action." *Administration Science Quarterly*, 39/3: 484–510.

Pomerantz, A. (1984)."Agreeing and Disagreeing with Assessments: Some Features of Preferred/Dispreferred Turn Shapes." In J. M. Atkinson and J. Heritage (eds.), *Structures of Social Action: Studies in Conversation Analysis*. Cambridge: Cambridge University Press, 57–101.

Putnam, L. and Nicotera, A. M. (2009). *Building Theories of Organization: The Constitutive Role of Communication*. New York: Routledge.

Rerup, C. and Feldman, M. S. (2011). "Routines as a Source of Change in Organizational Schema: The Role of Trial-and-Error Learning." *Academy of Management Journal*, 54/3: 577–610.

Schegloff, E. A. and Sacks, H. (1973). "Opening Up Closings." *Semiotica*, 8: 289–327.

Schoeneborn, D., Blaschke, S., Cooren, F., McPhee, R. D., and Seidl, D. (2014). "The Three Schools of CCO Thinking: Interactive Dialogue and Systematic Comparison." *Management Communication Quarterly*, 28/2: 285–316.

Sidnell, J. (2010). *Conversation Analysis: An Introduction*. Chichester: John Wiley.

Sidnell, J. (2013). "Basic Conversation Analytic Methods." In J. Sidnell and T. Stivers (eds.), *The Handbook of Conversation Analysis*. Cambridge, MA: Wiley Blackwell, 77–99.

Sorsa, V., Pälli, P., and Mikkola, P. (2014). "Appropriating the Words of Strategy in Performance Appraisal Interviews." *Management Communication Quarterly*, 28/1: 56–83.

Stivers, T. and Sidnell, J. (2005). "Introduction: Multimodal Interaction." *Semiotica*, 156/1: 1–20.

Stolte, J. F. (1994). "Power." In M. Foschi and E. J. Lawler (eds.), *Group Processes: Sociological Analyses*. Chicago, IL: Nelson-Hall, 14–76.

Stolte, J. F., Fine, G. A., and Cook, K. S. (2001). "Sociological Miniaturism: Seeing the Big through the Small in Social Psychology." *Annual Review of Sociology*, 27: 387–413.

Streeck, J. and Mehus, S. (2005). "Microethnography: The Study of Practices." In K. Fitch and R. Sanders (eds.), *Handbook of Language and Social Interaction*. Mahwah, NJ: Lawrence Erlbaum, 381–404.

Taylor, J. R. and Robichaud, D. (2004). "Finding the Organization in the Communication: Discourse as Action and Sensemaking." *Organization*, 11/3: 395–413.

Thomas, D. L. (1972). "Role-Taking and Power in Social Psychology." *American Sociological Review*, 37/5: 605–14.

Van Riel, C. B., Berens, G., and Dijkstra, M. (2009). "Stimulating Strategically Aligned Behaviour among Employees." *Journal of Management Studies*, 46: 1197–226.

Zbaracki, M. J. and Bergen, M. (2010). "When Truces Collapse: A Longitudinal Study of Price-Adjustment Routines." *Organization Science*, 21/5: 955–72.

8

Teaming Routines in Complex Innovation Projects

Amy C. Edmondson and Tiona Zuzul

Abstract: Innovation projects thrive when they bring together individuals with diverse expertise. But, to succeed, such projects must support effective *teaming*: coordination and collaboration between experts working together in shifting, fluid ways across physical, status, or knowledge boundaries. In this chapter, the authors develop the idea of *teaming routines*: routines that enable coordination and collaboration *between* experts across multiple boundaries. The chapter draws on longitudinal data from Lake Nona, a novel mega-project in the built environment, to explore how leaders enabled the development of teaming routines that supported innovation. By theorizing the processes through which leaders can build teaming routines into complex, large-scale innovation projects, the authors add to the existing literature, which has largely focused on routines in the context of a single organization or an alliance between two organizations.

8.1 Introduction

Innovation projects thrive when they bring together individuals with diverse expertise. Individuals from a single area of expertise rarely possess all of the relevant experience and knowledge required to develop an innovative new product or service (Dougherty, 1992; Leonard-Barton, 1995). Building on this well-established idea, recent research has investigated complex, large-scale innovation initiatives that require collaboration across ever more diverse groups. In addition to including different functional expertise, such projects involve collaboration across different organizations, industries, and sectors (e.g. Lehrer and Laidley, 2008; Van Marrewijk et al., 2008; Davies et al., 2009; Edmondson et al., 2015). The output of these projects can be extraordinarily innovative: for example, a life-saving rescue (Rashid et al., 2013), or the rapid development of iconic, energy-efficient buildings (Eccles et al., 2010; Rashid and Edmondson, 2012). But, to succeed, such projects must support effective teaming across multiple boundaries.

Teaming, defined as coordination and collaboration between experts working together in shifting ways across multiple boundaries, is needed when stable teams are not feasible due to the complex, fluid, overlapping nature of work responsibilities (Edmondson, 2012). This kind of teaming is challenging: it may require collaboration across physical, status, or knowledge boundaries (Edmondson, 2012). Yet individuals located in multiple geographies, with different professional status and diverse expertise, hold differences in values, perspectives, and understandings that can block meaningful collaboration (Dougherty, 1992; Bechky, 2003; Nembhard and Edmondson, 2006; O'Mahony and Bechky, 2008; Kellogg, 2009). In complex innovation projects, developing processes that can encourage teaming across disciplinary and organizational boundaries, without the benefit of stable team structures and relationships, and for undefined and shifting periods of time, is as challenging as it is necessary.

In this chapter, we explore how organizational routines may support teaming activities. In so doing, we add to the existing literature on routines, which has largely focused on the context of a single organization (e.g. Edmondson et al., 2001; Howard-Grenville, 2005; Rerup and Feldman, 2011) or on partnerships and alliances between two organizations (e.g. Howard-Grenville and Carlile, 2006). We develop the idea of *teaming routines*—routines that enable coordination and collaboration between experts across multiple boundaries—and examine what leaders can do to build these routines into complex, large-scale innovation projects that involve multiple organizations, industries, and sectors.

We draw from case study data on Lake Nona, a novel mega-project in the built environment developed by a diverse group that included real-estate developers, medical experts, technologists, and government officials. We found that the diverse individuals developing Lake Nona developed robust routines that supported teaming across thick boundaries. Through analysis of interview and observation data collected from Lake Nona participants, we identified three leadership actions that enabled these teaming routines: *articulating a dynamic vision*, *structuring participation*, and *encouraging experimentation.* First, the project leaders actively articulated a vision for the project in a way that provided direction without a tightly specified blueprint (Edmondson et al., 2015). They made it clear that the vision was dynamic and would take shape gradually as a result of input from all participants, and ongoing shared experiences. Second, they provided structures to force conversation, co-creation, and coordination among the diverse individuals and organizations involved in the project. Third, they encouraged and facilitated experimentation—developing and testing new ideas in rapid feedback loops. Through their actions, leaders consciously enacted the *performative* aspects of the routines they hoped to inspire, in contrast to the *ostensive* aspects (Feldman and Pentland, 2003). This approach to leading the project helped build shared, project-wide understandings about the importance of communication and joint experimentation, and resulted in the development of teaming routines that allowed everyone working on the project to learn, contribute, and jointly discover new, innovative solutions. The routines thus provided a structuring system or scaffold (Valentine and Edmondson, 2015) that supported fluid teaming and innovation.

The remainder of the chapter is organized as follows. We first provide a theoretical overview of routines in teaming and collaboration for innovation. Next, we describe the Lake Nona project, and provide an overview of our data. We then examine the routines that enabled teaming, and the actions leaders enacted to develop them. Finally, we discuss the implications of this chapter for research on teaming, routines, and innovation.

8.2 Prior Research and Theory

Teaming—a kind of ad hoc coordination and collaboration among shifting participants, over unspecified periods of time—can be a powerful means of supporting innovation. When individuals from different disciplines, organizations, and industries recombine their specialized knowledge, they can create new connections, solutions, and outcomes (Henderson and Clark, 1990; Brown and Duguid, 1991; Dougherty, 1992; Leonard-Barton, 1995; Hargadon, 2003). But teaming is difficult (Edmondson 2012; Valentine and Edmondson, 2015). The very nature of the phenomenon is situation specific and unpredictable: teaming's interactions cannot be scripted (Edmondson, 2012). In contrast, routines are defined as "a repetitive, recognizable pattern"—one that brings together "interdependent actions" and "multiple actors" (Howard-Grenville, 2005: 618). At first glance, teaming and routines thus seem incompatible phenomena, and the idea of *teaming routines* appears to be an oxymoron. In this chapter, we present a different view, however, drawing on the recent literature on routines, which emphasizes their flexibility and dynamic nature.

8.2.1 Routines' Flexibility

Routines, increasingly, are seen as dynamic structures that allow flexibility. In particular, Pentland and Feldman emphasized that organizational routines can be dynamic and flexible (2005), and Howard-Grenville (2005: 618) noted, "Once regarded as stable and inflexible, organizational routines are increasingly seen as capable of being adapted to the situation at hand and a potentially important source of...change." Rerup and Feldman (2011) developed this idea further showing that routines can be vital for transforming the intention to innovate into action; that is, routines can provide a structure that enables dynamism, progress, and innovation.

Besides pointing to routines as a potential source of dynamism, recent research has suggested that routines can be flexible enough to accommodate change. Feldman and Rafaeli (2002) asserted that shared understandings between organizational members helps bring potential routines into action; as interpretations shift, routines shift, thus driving change in organizations. Similarly, Rerup and Feldman (2011) emphasized the dual nature of organizational routines as both enablers and products of change. As organizations conduct regular activities, members examine outcomes and revise routines accordingly. Finally, routines can be seen as the building blocks of organizational capabilities. Salvato and Rerup (2010), for example, described a complex relationship between routines and capabilities, in which they conceptualized capabilities as assemblages of routines.

We build on this dynamic perspective on routines to suggest that *teaming routines* constitutes a meaningful concept, which might play a vital role in complex innovation projects involving multiple organizations and areas of expertise. We define teaming routines as repetitive, interdependent patterns that support collaboration among shifting experts over unspecified periods of time. Precisely by providing a structuring system—a sort of temporary scaffold (Valentine and Edmondson, 2015) that can bolster coordination, knowledge-sharing, and joint innovation—these routines can support dynamic, fluid teaming and innovation.

8.2.2 Teaming Routines

Complex innovation projects that bring together diverse experts can benefit from routines to help ensure these experts coordinate their activities across the physical, status, and knowledge boundaries they face. For instance, architects designing a new, large-scale urban development are more likely to integrate the knowledge of local government officials to ensure the development is aligned with the needs of its intended population if systematic communication routines are in place. Similarly, engineers developing physical structures are more likely to embed them with information technologies (IT) that help lower the carbon footprint of the buildings once in use, when they develop solutions early in a project and regularly with experts in IT. Routines that help individuals coordinate and collaborate can facilitate successful innovation outcomes at the project level, and can also constitute a building block of new capabilities on the part of the innovators (Salvato and Rerup, 2010).

Developing routines to support teaming, however, may be difficult. Because teaming is by its nature time-limited, teaming routines are also. The same routines that govern knowledge-sharing, for instance, among teammates or co-workers who share a history, location, and unifying organizational culture might not work for individuals who have never met, work in different parts of the world, or lack shared norms of exchange and communication. Teaming might therefore call for the abandonment of old routines and the development of new routines to take their place. Neither is easy. Although some routines can be flexible enough to accommodate change, others are difficult to change or abandon without deliberate effort. In their study of the implementation of an innovative technology for cardiac surgery, for instance, Edmondson, Bohmer, and Pisano (2001) found that new routines only developed when individuals actively engaged in learning behaviors, took on new roles, and made numerous small adjustments in their modes of interaction. Disregarding old routines and developing new ones was extremely challenging for those who teamed up in the operating room, and disrupting and altering routines only happened through deliberate design and leadership action (Edmondson et al., 2001; Edmondson, 2003).

Because teaming also involves experts who come together across organizational, professional, and industry boundaries, routines that support it must be meaningful to and understood by individuals from diverse thought-worlds (Dougherty, 1992). But individuals with different identities (Levinthal and Rerup, 2006), from diverse professions (Howard-Grenville, 2005; Kellogg et al., 2006; Kellogg, 2009) and work domains (Howard-Grenville and Carlile, 2006), and situated in multiple geographies (Sole and Edmondson, 2002) often deploy different routines, or interpret or enact the same routines in incompatible ways. This can cause difficulties in knowledge sharing (Bechky, 2003) and integration (Lingo and O'Mahony, 2010): often, the difficulty in innovative, cross-boundary work "is not coming up with good ideas but sustaining the cooperation of others to synthesize and implement them" (Lingo and O'Mahony, 2010: 48). Shared routines can make connections between people that allow them to successfully work together, and to adapt and change their work over time (Feldman and Rafaeli, 2002). But developing these routines among diverse individuals with vastly different experiences and work histories is likely to be difficult.

Most of the existing literature on routines that enable coordination and collaboration focuses on the context of a single organization (e.g. Edmondson et al., 2001; Howard-Grenville, 2005; Rerup and Feldman, 2011) or on partnerships and alliances between two organizations (e.g. Howard-Grenville and Carlile, 2006). We draw on longitudinal data from a large-scale innovation project in order to explore the processes through which leaders can build routines that support teaming across boundaries. By focusing on *how* teaming routines are built, we adopt a process lens: we hope to extend current research by shedding light on the complex activities and practices that allow teaming routines to unfold over time in order to enable innovation in complex projects involving diverse organizations, professions, and industries.

8.3 The Lake Nona Project

We conducted in-depth case study research at Lake Nona to investigate the interdisciplinary opportunities and challenges in large-scale innovation projects. Lake Nona was a mega-project launched in 2006, located in Central Florida. Our qualitative research began in early 2011 and continued through the end of 2012. Lake Nona was envisioned as an innovative 7,000-acre residential and research cluster that would be developed by hundreds of collaborators from diverse organizations, professions, and industries to build a community with both a high quality of life and environmentally sustainable buildings and infrastructure. The project was spearheaded by Tavistock Group (Tavistock), an international private investment organization that formed Lake Nona Property Holdings and the Lake Nona Institute to lead the physical and social development of the community. Following the terminology of those we studied, we refer to the executives at these organizations as Lake Nona's leadership team.

The team's aim was to develop a master-planned community encompassing an innovation cluster focused on biomedical research, clinical care, and medical education in a healthy, eco-friendly environment. They aspired to develop an economically, environmentally, and socially sustainable community. They hoped the healthcare and research cluster would create many high-quality new jobs, would be master-planned and developed with sustainable principles in mind, and would include homes and public spaces suitable for a number of income levels.

When we ended our research, Tavistock and its partners had cultivated Lake Nona into an innovative, $2 billion medical and research campus and residential community that appeared well on its way to achieving its longer-term sustainability goals. In a speech on February 29, 2012, City of Orlando Mayor Buddy Dyer emphasized that Lake Nona was on track to create over 30,000 jobs and to have a major ten-year economic impact on the region. The projected economic impact had risen from the 2005 estimate of $5 billion per year to $7.6 billion. A diverse group of partners had moved onto plots of land at the development. The innovation cluster, dubbed "Medical City" by the local press, had attracted a number of private and public sector residents. Nemours Children's Hospital (Nemours), the first new Veterans Affairs (VA) hospital to be built in decades, the Sanford-Burnham Medical Research Institute (Sanford-Burnham), the University of Central Florida's (UCF) new medical school, and the University of Florida Research and Academic Center (UF) were open or slated to open within months. The leaders of Medical City residents maintained that Lake Nona's fusion of "clinics, classrooms and laboratories" would revolutionize the American healthcare landscape.

The residential community, too, was close to completion: three neighborhoods had been built and residents had begun to purchase houses in a brand new one. Lake Nona's master plan had been developed with principles of environmental sustainability in mind: in addition to the 44 linear miles of bike and walking trails on the development, every road had a bike lane, and all major buildings in the community were or were on track to becoming certified as LEED Silver or higher. The living spaces, the high-tech residential neighborhoods, and the schools had already begun to integrate feature energy-efficient technologies that would reduce energy consumption and encourage residents to lead healthier lives. Among other solutions, a technology company had developed custom LED streetlights for Lake Nona; the community would feature the largest single deployment of LED lights to date. Cisco had designated

Lake Nona as one of its Smart + Connected Communities, and hoped to deploy its sensor network to make the community connected and intelligent.

We collected data on Lake Nona's development through several means. First, we received archival data on the project, including early plans and presentations. Second, we visited the project site twice, and conducted twenty-nine formal interviews with twenty-six individuals from six of the organizations engaged in its development. Third, while on-site, we conducted informal interviews, probing individuals on their work, the challenges they faced, and how they resolved them; we asked them to reflect on positive and negative experiences they encountered in working together. Finally, we attended and observed a quarterly "project leadership dinner" where the leaders of the organizations involved in the project met for several hours to discuss their progress, challenges, and opportunities.

8.4 Teaming at Lake Nona

Recognizing the ambitious nature of their aims, Lake Nona's leadership team developed the project by coordinating and collaborating with hundreds of individuals from multiple organizations. This enormous, loosely bounded "team" comprised around seventy Lake Nona Property Holdings and Institute employees who worked with, among others, local government officials (who provided governmental support, assisted with zoning and regulatory issues, and assisted with funding), local school officials (who worked with the government and Tavistock to build new public schools for the cluster), multiple real-estate developers (who worked on the residential neighborhoods), individuals from several large technology companies, including GE and Cisco (who developed and provided "smart" sustainable solutions for the community), and employees and leaders of the healthcare institutions involved in the Medical City (who located to the cluster, helped recruit other institutional residents, collaborated to develop and negotiate the provision of technologies throughout the community, and began to work together to recruit shared employees and find opportunities for bench-to-bedside research).

Imagining, planning, and delivering the project involved highly complex interdependent work by all of these collaborators. The scope and novelty of the project aims necessitated the development of every aspect of the community from new schools to new solutions for sustainable urban buildings and spaces. At the same time, to develop a holistic, integrated community, the partners had to share their discoveries and ideas across boundaries: technology companies provided new solutions to be deployed by real-estate developers; developers developed real-estate solutions for medical institutions; medical institutions worked with Tavistock employees to think about the educational needs of the community; and so on.

8.5 Teaming Routines at Lake Nona

We observed two sets of routines that comprised effective teaming at Lake Nona. First, the diverse experts involved in the project developed routines for frequent and open communication. They routinely stepped away from their everyday work—located within their separate organizations—and came together in patterned ways to discuss issues and solicit feedback from beyond the bounds of the organizations. Second, the experts developed routines for joint experimentation. They generated and developed solutions in an iterative way: they would come together to brainstorm ideas, test those ideas within their organizations, then work together again to refine and improve them. We conceptualize these as teaming routines: frequent communication and joint experimentation allowed for ad hoc coordination and collaboration among shifting and diverse participants, and set the stage for the development of innovative solutions to benefit the project.

8.5.1 Routines for Fostering Communication

First, we discovered that the individuals working on Lake Nona developed routines that fostered open communication between partners from different organizations—even when these partners were not directly involved with a particular part of the project. Open dialogue, the exchange of ideas, and frequent feedback between individuals from different organizations characterized their interactions. A participant explained the open, generative nature of communication within the project:

> We [Lake Nona participants] are just continually asking each other the question, what can we do next? How can we make us better? What does the state of the art mean? What does collaboration mean? How do we integrate new organizations that join the project into this culture? How do we do develop kind of an on-boarding process?

A participant from a technology company collaborating with the Lake Nona team on the development of green technologies further explained:

> [People from] both companies have no problem showing their cards and saying, "This is why I'm interested in this," or "This is why I want to get this done," or "These are my priorities and here's why." So there's no surprises, you know, if something isn't going well . . . It's very easy for us to talk and I think we are very clear with all parties . . . It's been great.

Open discussions were the result of specific routines that encouraged communication. For instance, the leaders of the organizations involved in the project met in lengthy dinners every two months to share their progress, discuss issues, and solicit feedback from one another. During these dinners, the leaders would sequentially update others on their initiatives, and would seek feedback on both setbacks and opportunities. A participant described this routine as "think-tanking."

During the two-hour quarterly dinner we observed, for instance, after sharing stories about their families and personal lives, the leaders of four of the organizations involved in the project—three heads of Medical City institutions, three members of Lake Nona's leadership team—each spoke at length about and asked others to reflect on their progress within the project. A Lake Nona leadership team member updated everyone on his progress in real-estate development. The model homes, he explained, were nearly completed; he had managed to attract a number of hotels to the planned urban district. "That part," he explained, "is going OK." He also revealed a challenge: "we have not been able to sign retail yet—it has been skittish." This comment fueled a discussion where other attendees brainstormed ways to attract retail. Someone suggested that high-end retailers could be interested; others suggested finding a large grocery store to serve as an anchor retail tenant; the discussion eventually turned to the potential to attract temporary rather than permanent retailers, including food trucks. By seeking feedback about a real-estate challenge, the Lake Nona leader created space for a generative discussion of potential options.

Similarly, during the same dinner, a head of one of the medical institutions shared a hiring challenge: that few dual-career couples were attracted to Central Florida, given the limited employment opportunities outside of the Lake Nona development. She asked others what they thought; this request for feedback resulted in a long discussion of ways that other Lake Nona organizations could provide employment opportunities for Medical City employees' spouses.

Besides the leadership dinners, individuals involved with particular functions at each organization came together frequently (ranging from once a month to once a quarter) in lengthy, thematic "council meetings" to discuss ways to collaborate on issues including technology, communications, education, and operations. These councils—made up of a team of individuals responsible, for instance, for IT development across the different organizations involved in the project—provided a setting where open discussion dominated. A participant described the nature of council discussions: "We go in with kind of a loose agenda and then just let the conversation roll . . . That's the way we get the maximum flexibility on exploring and discovering stuff."

Participants pointed to the importance of leadership and council meetings for fostering communication and driving innovation in the project. In particular, council discussions generated a number of ideas for boundary-crossing innovations that could be deployed throughout the project. For instance, one of the major innovations—the development of a unifying distributed antennae system (DAS)—emerged out of discussions in the IT council. At an early council meeting, the IT specialists involved in Medical City discussed their desire to build a high-speed network. Through discussion, the team formed a distributed antennae system project to carry out together. In short, DAS would ensure 100 percent reliable cell phone coverage throughout Medical City's buildings. Although a number of the organizations involved in the Medical City had originally intended to build their own systems, discussions in the IT council convinced them of the advantages of a unified approach. Together, the members of the council created a timetable and a strategy to install DAS. One of the participants described how this innovation was fuelled by open discussion: "My colleagues around the table were always willing to seek the common good on this. They shared the limitations they faced—budgeting requirements, lock-ins from contracts with previous carriers—that posed barriers. But those have been resolved in a way that's probably the best possible outcome in terms of design."

8.5.2 Routines for Joint Experimentation

Second, we observed the individuals developing Lake Nona enacted routines for collaborative experimentation. These routines involved trying out and testing new ideas in iterative rapid feedback loops. Individuals from different groups would come together to brainstorm and discuss the potential for a particular solution or technology, return to their organizations to attempt to execute the ideas, and come back together to refine, improve, or abandon them. A participant from a large technology company described how this routine distinguished the project from others she had been involved in: "This isn't the first community that we've done, but this one just feels a little bit different... That's because there's always this level of brainstorm is going on. 'Hey, would this work? Hey, what do you think about this? Let's discuss it. Let's talk about it.' That, I think, helps us get to better results."

Experimentation routines characterized many of the partnerships within the development. The initial plans for Lake Nona, for instance, did not include the development of LED streetlights, but the idea emerged in conversations between Lake Nona leaders and their technology partners. A technology company developed new LED lighting systems for Lake Nona, compressing its product development period from eighteen to six months to fit the tight construction schedule. Participants from the company described this as a shared experiment. A technology executive from the partner firm explained:

> We had an LED streetlight solution that didn't quite match what Lake Nona was looking for. So, we said, "Okay, let's go back, let's go talk the factory. Let's see what they can do," and we did wind up coming up with a solution now that works for Lake Nona, but that we also can take and commercialize in other areas, as well... That's, I think, one of the great things about Lake Nona is they're willing to try things. "Let's just try it," and, honestly, from a cycle of innovation standpoint, that's how you get to innovations. Let's pilot, let's try, let's see what works, what doesn't work and then we can make the changes to get a product or a solution out.

As is often the case for experimentation, the experiments sometimes resulted in failure; for instance, after the technology company had already shipped and installed several LED fixtures, testing indicated a possibility of technical problems. Because failures were seen as opportunities for improvement, consistent with an experimental approach, the experimentation routines were not inhibited or cancelled by these outcomes. In contrast, failures were seen as data that informed innovation. A technology executive explained:

> [After the initial product was shipped], they [the Lake Nona leadership team] said, "Look, this is not going to work. It's not exactly what we're looking for... Let's think through it." After we went back and thought about what we could do and our schedule... We went back to them and said, "Look, here's what we

have to do. It's going to take this, this, this and this to do it. Can you guys work with that schedule?" And they were like, "Yeah, that works," and they were a part of the innovation cycle...It was this constant back and forth...It was very collaborative and understanding.

8.6 Leadership that Enables Teaming Routines

In examining the teaming routines at Lake Nona, we found that they were built deliberately by the Lake Nona leadership team from the outset of the project. Although many organizational routines emerge organically over time, in this case teaming routines were built deliberately by careful leadership (see Edmondson et al., 2001, for a similar finding). Our analysis suggested that Lake Nona's teaming routines were consciously and continually enacted and supported in the participating organizations. We uncovered three leadership actions that helped to build the eventual routines we observed in the context of the project.

8.6.1 Articulating a Flexible Vision

First, the Lake Nona leadership team focused on *articulating a flexible vision* for the community. A team member described how they spent significant time and effort developing a compelling vision for the project:

> We hired someone—an organizational behavior expert—and he helped us form and come up with this vision and got the team to really focus on it. We wanted the vision to be flexible and dynamic over time...because you never know where your final direction will be. Our vision has been to create a place that inspires human potential, but all of it through innovative collaboration.

The vision was notably bold (that is, it set challenging and unprecedented aspirations); however, it did not specify *how* its aims should be realized. Instead, it was flexible and dynamic: it left room to be informed by experimentation, iteration, and emergence.

When the leadership team communicated its vision for the project to partners or potential partners, the communication always included a request for feedback on the possibilities. That is, the team engaged a specific process for approaching partners. Instead of approaching partners with a specific plan for their collaboration, the leaders articulated a vision to generate a conversation about possibilities for adding to it. A Lake Nona leader described how partnering always began with the Lake Nona team asking a potential collaborator, "how can we create new, global models together?" Once they did this, members of the two organizations would sit together to think about how their capabilities could be combined to be innovative and add value to both organizations and the project. She elaborated:

> We give partners an opportunity to understand what we're doing. We get them in early on the ground floor so that they might even actually have some input into how we would shape our research or other studies . . . The opportunity [to do that] in a very casual setting is invaluable.

This early engagement both modeled and set the stage for the development of later routines for fostering communication. Because they saw themselves as jointly developing the vision, individuals working on the project recognized the need to come together, periodically, to seek advice from each another on their direction and progress. A member of Lake Nona's leadership team described how the early articulation of a vision—and the idea that participants should help shape that vision—resulted in a culture where people sought and shared feedback:

> We recruit people that are coming to an area to build this dream and be a part of this journey . . . We're recruiting collaborators, but those collaborators are coming here because they see the vision and they believe in that dream . . . And [they] will come to the table and be a group of action . . . We've got to get the folks in that see the vision, want to roll up their sleeves and jump in with us.

Similarly, an executive at Lake Nona Institute explained how the idea for one of Lake Nona's major health-related initiatives—a large-scale, longitudinal study on the health and wellness of community residents—emerged through conversations where she provided feedback to a major corporate partner that sought advice on ways to drive health-related initiatives. She attributed this evolution to the fact that Lake Nona's leadership team initially approached the partner with their dynamic vision:

> One of the things that I value is the creative process, and not having relationships fit within a box. I think that creates opportunities that could be really interesting . . . With [the partner], we initially came together at a strategic level. But the more we were talking and the more we were working, there are more and more initiatives that are being introduced and that are evolving that weren't discussed at the beginning. It's an interesting process—beyond just defining and working on a specific project, we allow time to have conversations on what else is happening, what other initiatives we need help with, how we

can be of assistance. Now there are about four different initiatives that have evolved that weren't even part of our original discussion.

8.6.2 Inviting Ongoing Participation

Second, the Lake Nona leadership team *invited ongoing participation* by actively creating spaces and opportunities for partners to meet and exchange ideas, thus further modeling and setting the stage for the development of the communication routines that built an effective teaming process. A team member described:

> A crucial realization at one of our early meetings was that collaboration just doesn't happen . . . you have to establish what they call a permissive platform for this dialogue to occur, where you establish times and venues to get people together and share their thoughts. That's when the "eureka" moments happen. I think too often people say, "We have a goal to collaborate" and then nothing happens. Well, it doesn't happen because you don't have this platform that we have established. It has to be a conscious decision of everybody involved that you are going to spend time periodically talking about things that matter to our long-term success.

For instance, one of the earliest executives hired to lead the Lake Nona Institutes was tasked with finding ways to foster discussion between the partners. He described how he came to the idea of councils as a way to create space for open discussion:

> One of the reasons I came aboard was because there was recognition that we have this opportunity and a need to do a better job connecting all the partners. So as I looked at that, I immediately saw that need . . . I started very informally, with lots of one-on-one conversations. I felt strongly that the real power was in getting the groups together. I wrote up a proposal internally about starting a leadership council and then getting some other councils . . . It laid out the mission of each of the councils to be set up. We started with the leadership group. We met several times and I came to them and proposed adding more councils. They all strongly endorsed it. We gathered suggestions on who should participate in them from the organizations.

He elaborated:

> This is something else that just made sense to us . . . If you're truly about collaboration—how do you make that happen? So we started with a leadership council. That worked well—it got people to know each other better, to trust each other, to share ideas and even expose weaknesses. And then out of that we created these other councils. It seems like an obvious idea, but when you show

this to people, they go—that's amazing! We consciously didn't create a lot of bureaucracy around that.

Importantly, to create space for open discussion, Lake Nona leadership team members put structures in place for inviting participation—but left ample room for emergent conversations. One leader described this process:

> We very quickly try to get out of the way and get the people who are deep down talking, because if we try to screen everything, we would lose a lot of potential ideas and thoughts. But we do the initial assessment and connect people as quickly as we can.

Another Lake Nona leader described how encouraging participation was critical in the development of the project's DAS system:

> You sound silly even saying this—but we just make people talk to each other. Would you believe—none of the IT heads here had talked to each other. And they're neighbors. We put them in a room—now, they don't want to leave each other. And they've realized they're more powerful as a group...But you can't leave them alone. The next day, they'll get into their lives again. This is where we come in. You've got to be after it.

8.6.3 Encouraging Experimentation

Finally, the Lake Nona team *encouraged experimentation* through their early support of new, untested ideas. A leadership team member explained:

> What we are looking for here are things that are not being done anywhere else. So, if [a potential partner] just wants to take an existing initiative and taking a different spin on it here, I don't think it would be quite as interesting. The idea is, can we model, research or pilot something.

In encouraging new projects and experimentation, Lake Nona's leadership team sought to lower the fears that they believed might inhibit partners' willingness to try out new things. This helped model and set the stage for the development of experimentation routines. For instance, a Lake Nona leader described how experimentation was encouraged within his own team:

> There's a remarkable mix of people on our team. We focus on throwing out crazy ideas, figuring out what's achievable and what makes sense. That's been part of our secret sauce. One of the things that's different about here than other places I've worked—there's sort of this culture of not being afraid to dream big ideas. Nobody here is afraid to come up with big ideas.

Table 8.1 Leadership actions associated with the development of teaming routines

Type of leadership	Example
Articulating a flexible vision	The leadership team at Lake Nona did not approach partners with a blueprint for the innovation, nor with specific plans of how each organization could contribute to the community. Instead, they articulated a vision for the community and engaged in a shared dialogue about possibilities. This early engagement of others in co-creation set the stage for the development of routines that fostered communication.
Structuring participation	The team invited participation by creating venues for partners to meet and exchange ideas. Rather than allowing partners to focus solely on their own role in the community, they fostered conversations between parties, setting the stage for a routine of open discussion and shared problem-solving.
Encouraging experimentation	The team regularly invited new, untested ideas, and modeled experimental behaviors, illustrating their acceptability in the new evolving community.

The team, in turn, encouraged experimentation amongst the partners. A Lake Nona leader explained: "We want to try things out, incubate them here, and if they work—great. If they don't, we'd rather fail fast and learn from them." Another described how he attempted to implement this approach in meetings with technology partners:

It's a mindset ... it's like, "Okay, let's sit down and figure out how to make this work." ... We [Lake Nona leaders and the technology company] probably have three or four different solar discussions [going on at the same time] on how to bring photovoltaics to the home. It hasn't worked out yet, but we sit down, "Hey, guys, let's make it work." Every quarter we kind of try to figure out, can we make it work? It's that mindset of trying to do as much as we can; I think makes a huge difference.

A participant from the technology company described the importance of this approach in fostering experimentation:

At Lake Nona you can be very creative ... [We are working on] green appliances, lighting, geospring ... We look [at the possibilities] and think, why not? Why don't we come up with a retrofit program to green out their homes? ... I mean, you can do creative things within the Lake Nona backdrop. It's almost like a playground for the different ideas you can come up with and the different solutions you can put together ... [The reason we can do this] is the team here and their culture. They're very innovative and they're open to new ideas and they move fast.

Together, these three leadership actions—summarized in Table 8.1—facilitated and set the stage for the development of teaming routines within the project. By articulating a flexible vision, inviting ongoing participation, and encouraging participation, project leaders acted as both architects that helped structure and coaches that helped model open communication and joint experimentation. Together, these persistent routines enabled individuals working on the project to both learn from each other, and to jointly discover new, innovative solutions not envisioned in the community's early plans.

8.7 Discussion

Novel, uncertain, complex work thrives when people know how to team on the fly—that is, how to work with a shifting mix of partners, share crucial knowledge quickly, ask questions clearly and frequently, make decisions, and make small adjustments as more is learned. Yet, valuable as it is for innovation, teaming is not a natural way of working. To do it well requires dealing with conflict and overcoming barriers created by jargon, competing interests, different timeframes, and more. Experts teaming up must integrate perspectives from different—and often unfamiliar—disciplines. Embracing these teaming behaviors requires letting go of common fears that limit transparency and openness, especially among people who don't know each other well, or who come from different areas of expertise, or different hierarchical levels (Edmondson, 2012).

In the present study, effective teaming among actors from diverse organizations, who shared neither reporting relationships nor formal team affiliations, was supported through deliberate management actions. The people we studied understood that what they were trying to accomplish required a new way of working that would not spontaneously emerge without effort. In our analysis, we found that teaming at Lake Nona was facilitated by a mix of new routines across organizations. These routines allowed individuals to openly discuss their ideas and experiment with new potential solutions, thus transforming *intended* teaming and collaboration into active, persistent teaming and collaboration behavior (Rerup and Feldman, 2011). Of course, teaming is, by its nature, not routine: it is about accomplishing work that cannot be scripted across thick and shifting boundaries. Yet teaming, this study suggests, benefits from routines that can provide an enabling structure to support communication and experimentation.

Our findings suggest that, although teaming across boundaries may be challenging, it can be built through deliberate acts of leadership providing the invitation to team, along with structures that help support it. Notably, our analysis suggested that the routines supporting teaming at Lake Nona did not develop organically—instead, they were mindfully built by leaders who invested in early actions that both modeled behaviors and provided a context in which teaming routines could emerge. Leaders acted as both process architects and coaches, and thus helped build an enabling system that supported teaming routines. By articulating a vision and inviting partners to help shape it, and by calling for participation in both formal and informal settings, Lake Nona's leaders created space for open discussion and communication. By encouraging experimentation, they built a culture where shared risks and small failures were both tolerated and encouraged, and experimentation routines could develop.

The idea that routines have both a mindful and a mindless, or automatic, component is well-established in the literature (Levinthal and Rerup, 2006; Turner and Rindova, 2012; Rerup and Levinthal, 2014). In studying routines in action, some scholars have described them as emergent (e.g. Rerup and Feldman, 2011); others have emphasized that new routines can develop through active adjustments and learning behaviors (Edmondson et al., 2001). We do not claim that routines that enable teaming cannot emerge over time through less mindful channels. However, our data suggest that leaders can invest in mindful processes to attempt to spur or direct that development.

Our data also suggest that these processes might revolve around modeling behaviors rather than setting out specific guides to action. Feldman and Pentland (2003) describe routines as having performative and ostensive aspects—comprising actions performed by project participants and task-specific patterns or structures to guide those actions. Notably, Lake Nona leaders did not specify the ostensive aspects of the routines they hoped would emerge: they did not, for instance, delineate strict targets or specific procedures for collaboration. Instead, they modeled the performative aspects of teaming routines: their actions signaled the importance of flexibility, participation, and experimentation in the project. These performances thus led to the emergence of a shared understanding about the importance of teaming, and eventual structures and patterns that supported it. That is, leaders' modeling of the performative aspect of teaming routines allowed their ostensive aspects to emerge within the project. Our analysis thus supports the idea that performative aspects can create and maintain the ostensive aspects of routines (Feldman and Pentland, 2003; Rerup and Feldman, 2011).

This finding is consistent with a growing body of research that suggests that dynamic, flexible collaborative routines—driven not by a shared patterns, script, or blueprint, but instead by a *learning logic*—can help structure innovation in novel or complex projects. This approach seeks to create routines out of that which is inherently not routine (Edmondson, 2012; Edmondson et al., 2015). According to this view, many organizational projects and work routines are organized according to a *blueprint logic*: leaders set out achievable targets and apply processes used elsewhere to meet those targets. A blueprint logic is ineffective in novel projects because it relies on a top-down, planned approach (Baron and Hannan, 2002). In novel contexts, setting targets can be challenging: often, there are no shared templates on what success might mean. And when multiple units or organizations are involved, new ideas might emerge from broad participation and experimentation (e.g. Henderson and Clark, 1990; Hargadon, 2003). In these settings, routines that encourage bottom-up learning, action, and experimentation aligned with a common vision can be critical in driving and supporting sustained innovation (Edmondson, 2012; Edmondson et al., 2015).

Of course, even effective teaming won't automatically lead to project success. The kinds of innovation projects that benefit from teaming—those that are characterized by novel or complex aims—present an intricate set of challenges. Goals are vague, and it is often unclear what success looks like (Weick, 1995). The novelty of these projects ensures the challenges are far more than interpersonal. Many technical challenges are likely. Internal risks and external risks, including financing problems and macroeconomic conditions, always loom large. Failure—at least along some dimensions—is inevitable (Edmondson, 2012). Although the Lake Nona project so far has resulted in an innovative, complex development, long-term success remains elusive. To reach their aims, leaders will have to ensure a sustained level of innovation. This will involve continual support of teaming, as well as the acceptance of inevitable failures along the way. As new partners—from institutions locating in Medical City to construction companies working on the still-developing residential cluster—join the project, friction might increase and even well-functioning routines might threaten to break down.

Nonetheless, we believe the Lake Nona case can give rise to several interesting questions to help guide future research. First, Rerup and Feldman (2011) distinguish espoused routines—the routines project leaders intend to build—and enacted routines—the routines that emerge in a project over time. At Lake Nona, we also observed a strong correspondence between the two; however, as Rerup and Feldman (2011) showed, they are not always perfectly aligned.

This leads to interesting questions about the boundary conditions of our study. Are there settings where the mindful articulation of a vision, inviting of participation, and encouragement of experimentation *will not* result in the development of routines that enable teaming? That is, when and why might leaders' intended routines fail to manifest as enacted routines? Perhaps Lake Nona's teaming routines were supported by additional factors—for instance, early project successes that provided leaders and participants with goodwill towards one another and positive emotions that encouraged them to jointly pursue their ambitious aims. If a project experiences significant setbacks early in its history, will these three actions prove sufficient? Failures can result in damaging spirals of blame (Edmondson, 2011) and negative emotion (Lawler, 2001), often directed toward others working on a project. Can early setbacks disrupt the development of routines that enable teaming? What additional processes or actions might prevent this possibility?

Second, we note that the leadership actions deployed by Lake Nona's team called for a subtle but constant balance between control and autonomy. The Lake Nona team set a vision that provided direction but did not specify how aims should be realized; they consciously created opportunities for open discussion but took care not to overtly manage that discussion; they hoped to encourage successful product or idea development but reconciled with the inevitability of small failures. Prior research has emphasized that traditional techniques of control are not suitable for highly uncertain, novel innovation challenges (see Sitkin et al., 1994, and Baron and Hannan, 2002, for further discussion), but at Lake Nona, a balance of control and autonomy was critical in supporting teaming. Future research can explore this tension between control and autonomy in teaming, and can attempt to generate propositions on how much of each is optimal at different stages in the innovation process.

Finally, future research can explore whether and how our findings can generalize to other innovation contexts. Will the actions we identified produce routines we observed and hence enable innovation in more bounded projects that involve only one team or organization? Will they be as important in repeated projects—if, for instance, the individuals developing Lake Nona come together to produce a second innovative urban cluster? Or will new processes and routines need to take their place?

8.8 Conclusion

Teaming is complex, temporary, ad hoc; routines are patterned, repeated, recognizable. Yet teaming routines are not an oxymoron but rather a necessity for complex innovation. By providing a structuring system that supports communication and experimentation, routines can support fluid teaming across boundaries. Our study of Lake Nona suggests leadership actions that can help guide the development of large-scale, complex projects that involve teaming between individuals from across organizations, professions, and industries. We believe such projects are an increasingly important source of innovation and large-scale change. We hope that future qualitative and quantitative studies will test and refine our ideas to benefit scholars, practitioners, and innovators.

References

Baron, J. N. and Hannan, M. T. (2002). "Organizational Blueprints for Success in High-Tech Start-Ups: Lessons from the Stanford Project on Emerging Companies." *California Management Review*, 44/3: 8–36.

Bechky, B. A. (2003). "Sharing Meaning across Occupational Communities: The Transformation of Understanding on a Production Floor." *Organization Science*, 14/3: 312–30.

Brown, J. S. and Duguid, P. (1991). "Organizational Learning and Communities of Practice: Toward a Unified View of Working, Learning, and Innovation." *Organizational Science*, 2/1:40–57.

Davies, A. C., Gann, D., and Douglas, T. (2009). "Innovation in Megaprojects: Systems Integration at London Heathrow Terminal 5." *California Management Review*, 51/2: 101–25.

Dougherty, D. (1992). "Interpretive Barriers to Successful Product Innovation in Large Firms." *Organization Science*, 3/2: 179–202.

Eccles, R. G., Edmondson, A. C., and Karadzhova, D. (2010). "Arup: Building the Water Cube." Harvard Business School Case 410-054.

Edmondson, A. C. (2003). "Speaking Up in the Operating Room: How Team Leaders Promote Learning in Interdisciplinary Action Teams." *Journal of Management Studies*, 40/6: 1419–52.

Edmondson, A. C. (2011). "Strategies for Learning from Failure." *Harvard Business Review*, 89/4: 48–55.

Edmondson, A. C. (2012). *Teaming: How Organizations Learn, Innovate, and Compete in the Knowledge Economy*. San Francisco, CA: Jossey-Bass.

Edmondson, A. C., Bohmer, R. M., and Pisano, G. P. (2001). "Disrupted Routines: Team Learning and New Technology Implementation in Hospitals." *Administrative Science Quarterly*, 46/4: 685–716.

Edmondson, A. C., Haas, M., Macomber, J. D. and Zuzul, T. (2015). "The Role of Multiplier Firms and Megaprojects in Leading Change for Sustainability." In R. Henderson, R. Gulati, and M. Tushman (eds.), *Leading Sustainable Change: An Organizational Perspective*. Oxford: Oxford University Press, 273–97.

Feldman, M. S. and Pentland, B. T. (2003). "Reconceptualizing Organizational Routines as a Source of Flexibility and Change."*Administrative Science Quarterly*, 48/1: 94–118.

Feldman, M. S. and Rafaeli, A. (2002). "Organizational Routines as Sources of Connections and Understandings." *Journal of Management Studies*, 39/3: 309–31.

Hargadon, A. B. (2003). *How Breakthroughs Happen*. Boston, MA: Harvard Business School Press.

Henderson, R. M. and Clark, K. B. (1990). "Generational Innovation: The Reconfiguration of Existing Systems and the Failure of Established Firms." *Administrative Science Quarterly*, 35: 9–30.

Howard-Grenville, J. A. (2005). "The Persistence of Flexible Organizational Routines: The Role of Agency and Organizational Context." *Organization Science*, 16/6: 618–36.

Howard-Grenville, J. A. and Carlile, P. R. (2006). "The Incompatibility of Knowledge Regimes: Consequences of the Material World for Cross-Domain Work." *European Journal of Information Systems*, 15: 473–85.

Kellogg, K. C. (2009). "Operating Room: Relational Spaces and Micro-Institutional Change in Surgery." *American Journal of Sociology*, 115/3: 657–711.

Kellogg, K. C., Orlikowski, W. J., and Yates, J. (2006). "Life in the Trading Zone: Structuring Coordination across Boundaries in Postbureaucratic Organizations." *Organization Science*, 17/1: 22–4.

Lawler, E. J. (2001). "An Affect Theory of Social Exchange." *American Journal of Sociology*, 107: 321–52.

Lehrer, U. and Laidley, J. (2008). "Old Mega-Projects Newly Packaged? Waterfront Redevelopment in Toronto." *International Journal of Urban & Regional Research*, 32/4: 786–803.

Leonard-Barton, D. (1995). *Wellsprings of Knowledge: Building and Sustaining the Sources of Innovation*. Boston, MA: Harvard Business School Press.

Levinthal, D. and Rerup, C. (2006). "Crossing an Apparent Chasm: Bridging Mindful and Less-Mindful Perspectives on Organizational Learning." *Organization Science*, 17/4: 502–13.

Lingo, E. L. and O'Mahony, S. (2010). "Nexus Work: Brokerage on Creative Project." *Administrative Science Quarterly*, 55/1: 47–81.

Nembhard, I. M. and Edmondson, A. C. (2006). "Making it Safe: The Effects of Leader Inclusiveness and Professional Status on Psychological Safety and Improvement Efforts in Health Care Teams." *Journal of Organizational Behavior*, 27/7: 941–66.

O'Mahony, S. and Bechky, B. A. (2008)."Boundary Organizations: Enabling Collaboration among Unexpected Allies." *Administrative Science Quarterly*, 53/3: 422–59.

Pentland, B. T. and Feldman, M. S. (2005). "Organizational Routines as a Unit of Analysis." *Industrial and Corporate Change*, 14/5: 739–815.

Rashid, F. and Edmondson, A. C. (2012). "Risky Trust: How Multi-Entity Teams Develop Trust in a High-Risk Endeavor." In R. Kramer and T. Pittinsky (eds.), *Restoring Trust*. New York: Oxford University Press, 129–50.

Rashid, F., Edmondson, A. C., and Leonard, H. B. (2013). "Leadership Lessons from the Chilean Mine Rescue." *Harvard Business Review*, 91/7: 113–19.

Rerup, C. and Feldman, M. S. (2011). "Routines as a Source of Change in Organizational Schemata: The Role of Trial-and-Error Learning." *Academy of Management Journal*, 54/3: 577–610.

Rerup, C. and Levinthal, D. (2014). "Situating the Concept of Organizational Mindfulness: The Multiple Dimensions of Organizational Learning." In G. Becke (ed.), *Mindful Change in Times of Permanent Reorganization*. Dordrecht: Springer, 33–48.

Salvato, C. and Rerup, C. (2010). "Beyond Collective Entities: Multilevel Research on Organizational Routines and Capabilities." *Journal of Management*, 37/2: 468–90.

Sitkin, S. B., Sutcliffe, K. M., and Schroeder, R. G. (1994). "Distinguishing Control from Learning in Total Quality Management: A Contingency Perspective." *Academy of Management Review*, 18/3: 537–64.

Sole, D. and Edmondson, A. C. (2002). "Bridging Knowledge Gaps: Learning in Geographically Dispersed Cross-Functional Development Teams." In N. Bontis and C. W. Choo (eds.), *The Strategic Management of Intellectual Capital and Organizational Knowledge: A Collection of Readings*. New York: Oxford University Press, 587–604.

Turner, S. F. and Rindova, V. (2012). "A Balancing Act: How Organizations Pursue Consistency in Routine Functioning in the Face of Ongoing Change." *Organization Science*, 23/1: 24–46.

Valentine, M. A. and Edmondson, A. C.(2015). "Team Scaffolds: How Minimal Team Structures Support Role-Based Coordination." *Organization Science*, 26/2: 405–22.

Van Marrewijk, A., Clegg, S. R., Pitsis, T. S., and Veenswijk, M. (2008). "Managing Public–Private Megaprojects: Paradoxes, Complexity, and Project Design." *International Journal of Project Management*, 26/6: 591–600.

Weick, K. E. (1995). *Sensemaking in Organizations*. Thousand Oaks, CA: Sage Publications.

9

Dynamic In-capabilities

The Paradox of Routines in the Ecology of Complex Innovation

Jacky Swan, Maxine Robertson, and Sue Newell

Abstract: This chapter identifies the routines enacted in complex innovation processes, specifically during drug development projects. Routines performed locally are nested in an organizational ecology constituted by multiple stakeholders, and in an innovation process characterized by "unknowability." Drawing from an extensive study of innovation projects in biotechnology firms, the authors identify strategic routines—protecting, evolving, and resourcing the science—that are enacted across organizations in order to develop new therapeutics, and three performative "guesswork" routines enacted within these firms—hedging, compressing, and reprioritizing. These routines reflect the influence of other organizations in the ecology—investors and potential investors, who demand to see swift progress and positive outcomes, and regulatory authorities that prescribe drug development as a linear process. This fosters a regime whereby guesswork routines at the project level simultaneously acquiesce to institutional pressures within the project ecology to demonstrate progress, yet may practically hinder the innovation process.

9.1 Introduction

A key aspect of organizational knowledge is constituted by routines (Dosi et al., 2008), defined as the "repetitive, recognizable pattern of interdependent actions, involving multiple actors" (Cohen et al., 1996; Feldman and Pentland, 2003: 96). Routines, it is argued, help to create a "truce" between conflicting parties and ideas because they establish the implicit rules about how to handle both the social (e.g. governance structures) and the physical (e.g. technological development) worlds (Dosi et al., 2008). Early work on routines suggested that they invoke a degree of rigidity and inertia that seems counterproductive in firms where the focus is on continuous innovation. More recently, however, research on routines, from both dynamic capabilities and practice-theoretical streams (see Parmigiani and Howard-Grenville, 2011, for a review), has emphasized their important role in promoting change as well as stability (Turner and Rindova, 2012). For example, more generative models of "routine dynamics" (Feldman and Pentland, 2008; Pentland et al., 2012) highlight the importance of routines for *all* organizations, including those whose main business is innovation. Moreover, even "routine routines" have been shown to exhibit considerable variation (Howard-Grenville, 2005; Pentland et al., 2011).

This research suggests that routines are important to study in firms whose core capability rests on their ability to innovate. Such firms include, for example, biotechnology firms—our main focus here—whose main (often only) work is to carry out projects that lead, ultimately, to the generation of new products and services. Quite what the relationship is between organizational routines and innovation processes at the level of projects is still not well understood, however. Bessant et al. (2011) argue that the "trick" for those firms that are in the business of innovation is to develop routines that allow for regular innovative activity. However, they also note a tension in that, the more innovation practices are routinized, the more difficult it is for firms to cope with the unexpected, and capitalize on emergent outcomes (cf. Obstfeld, 2012). Their solution is to suggest that such firms need to simultaneously follow routines, and acquire the ability to review their routines, and change them as required. However, while this normative idea seems plausible, we know little about what routines actually occur in innovation contexts and with what consequences. In this chapter, then, we address the following research question:

1. What are the routines that are enacted in organizations, in particular biotechnology firms, engaged in innovation processes?

In addition, innovation processes are complex; it is "through local interactions among people and technologies that diverse and novel outcomes emerge" (Garud et al., 2011: 737). Interactions are unpredictable, so organizations engaged in innovation must handle very high degrees of uncertainty. Often they rely on interactions with other organizations as well for knowledge and resources (Grabher, 2004; Swan et al., 2007). As Grabher

(2004: 1491) notes: "essential processes of creating and sedimenting knowledge accrue at the interface between projects and the organizations, communities, and networks in and through which projects operate." Most innovation projects unfold, then, within a complex "ecology" of organizations that generates significant interdependencies (Grabher, 2002, 2004; Dougherty and Dunne, 2011).

For biotechnology firms, for example, this ecology consists of multiple stakeholders, with different agendas: investors who want to see fast, high returns; clinicians who choose whether or not to enroll patients into clinical trials; regulators who set rules to ensure safety, and so forth. Thus organizational routines for developing innovation need to be understood as nested within this wider ecology. In relation to the regulatory approval process, for example, this depicts drug development as if it follows a linear progression through distinct, timed, phases and stage-gates that move drugs in development through clinical trials to commercialization (see Figure 9.1). These institutionalized rules are translated at firm-level into a

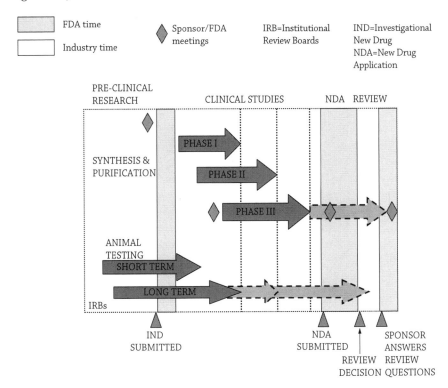

Figure 9.1 The new drug development process

set of processes that organize the firm's portfolio of products in development into a series of discrete projects, each with its own project management schedule and plan laid out according to regulatory approvals milestones. Together these projects constitute the firm's development "pipeline." However, in this complex innovation ecology, project teams encounter a great many unknowns because they are dealing with science that is still emerging and they have to interact with many potential stakeholders within the ecology (Swan et al., 2010; Dougherty and Dunne, 2012). Development processes "on the ground" are, therefore, far from linear and predictable (Newell et al., 2008; Styhre et al., 2010). How do those engaged in these projects practically cope with all of these unknowns and develop routines that can progress development while, at the same time, responding to institutionalized regulations that track a linear path to commercialization?

To answer such questions, and to better understand the dynamics through which routines operate in relation to complex innovation processes, requires an ecological approach that shows how being embedded in an ecology of interacting organizations shapes the enactment of routines at lower levels of project work. Previous theory on routines recognizes that they rely for their development on existing knowledge and repetition across contexts (Eisenhardt and Martin, 2000) and are therefore embedded in, and may even change, wider institutionalized practices. However, historically routines have been treated as more or less coherent "entities" that act as "building blocks" of organization capabilities. Such a view "has slowed efforts to bridge micro and macro understandings of routines and capabilities" (Salvato and Rerup, 2011: 469). More recently, the process/practice theoretical stream on routines has made great inroads into better understanding their dynamics, evolution, and generative effects (e.g. Feldman and Orlikowski, 2011; Dionysiou and Tsoukas, 2013). However, usually empirical work in this stream studies single, or occasionally multiple, routines in *single* organizations. In contrast, the "ecology of routines"—the way they are intertwined, both within organizations and with broader communities of organizations—is rarely examined (Salvato and Rerup, 2011). Hence, following from our first research question we ask:

2. How does the organizational ecology shape these routines and how do these routines shape the innovation process?

Our analysis identifies the performative routines at the project level that enable the team to cope with the unknowns that they face when innovating whilst adhering to institutional orders and the demands placed by other stakeholders in the project ecology, importantly, investor and potential-investor expectations. Our findings show that these performative routines can be characterized as "hedging," "compressing," or "re-prioritizing" and, more generally, that they are all enacted as forms of, what we refer to as, "guesswork" in the face of unknowability. Paradoxically, the guesswork routines, which are targeted at making progress while sustaining the order set by the wider ecology (the pipeline), often compromise the innovation process. Our contribution, then, is to show how performative routines, enacted locally in projects to deal with constant change and uncertainty, reinforce rather than challenge the institutionalized order and encourage practical actions that appear counterproductive to innovation processes. Thus, understanding the role of performative routines in generating both change and stability in complex innovation settings is not only important but also requires an understanding of the nested nature of the project and the firm within a wider, highly regulated, and market-sensitive ecology of organizations. Next we discuss critical facets of complex innovation contexts, and follow this with an overview of a practice-based view of routines, which we followed in our analysis.

9.2 Complex Innovation within a Project Ecology

Recently, Dougherty and Dunne (2011, 2012) have contrasted *complicated* with *complex* innovation, suggesting that, whilst similar, the latter needs to be theorized as a distinctive form of innovation and poses particular management challenges (Snowden and Boone, 2007; Dougherty and Dunne, 2011). Both forms of innovation entail a highly interactive process comprising multiple actors and organizations drawing together distributed specialist knowledge through a fairly lengthy development process. A good example of complicated innovation is the development of an aircraft, which typically takes several years, involves multiple organizations and stakeholders, including standards-setting bodies, and is accomplished by dividing the work into parts (e.g. parts of the aircraft) and then assembling the parts together. In these settings innovation is complicated but problem parameters are more or less known. In complex innovation processes, by contrast (e.g. new drug development), problem parameters and cause–effect relationships (e.g. the underlying science) are largely unknown or still being discovered (Styhre, 2006; Dougherty and Dunne, 2011). Dougherty and Dunne (2012: 1467) summarize the characteristics of complex innovation as: "nonlinearity, unpredictable interdependencies and the emergence of knowledge over long periods of time as innovators search the 'unknown unknowns'." This means that complexity is epistemic (how do we know what we don't yet know?) not just computational (how do we calculate solutions to known problems?). Moreover, as a result of "unpredictable interdependencies," unanticipated changes can occur at any step and can have significant and immediate effects on the development process. Complex innovation processes typically span many years and require significant financial investment, without any guarantee that a new idea will eventually turn into a commercial product or service, which is different to complicated innovation projects where costs may well overrun but a final product/service will be developed. Managers must therefore cope with paths to innovation that are not smooth and linear but uneven, iterative, and often unpredictable, with a very high risk of failure (Newell et al., 2008; Styhre et al., 2010; Obstfeld, 2012).

Put simply, the development of entirely new drugs requires different scientific specialists, typically spanning public and private sectors, to work closely together in order to identify "targets" (e.g. proteins) for possible diseases, as well as molecules, or chemical compounds, that might interact with the "target" for therapeutic effects. This specialist scientific knowledge needs to be brought together with commercial, management, and product development expertise if the financial and other resources needed to progress development are to be secured. In the early phases of drug development biotechnology firms are typically where this occurs, with the majority of these being small firms set up by those with specialist scientific knowledge in specific areas deemed to be exploitable (Swan et al., 2007).

In the early phases then, innovation is typically organized around projects led by biotechnology firms, which have been initiated to exploit some new area of science that appears to have commercial potential (Pisano, 2006; Gittelman, 2007). These firms are located within an ecology comprising multiple stakeholders and high levels of interdependencies (Newell et al., 2008). For example, these small firms are usually highly resource constrained and require private investment to resource projects. They often rely on partnering arrangements with larger pharmaceutical firms to take new products to market should the results from early development be promising. Senior managers in biotechnology firms are responsible for developing and overseeing a portfolio of development projects, indicated in their development "pipeline," which they use to attract investment and collaboration for ongoing and future projects. During development a series of increasingly large human clinical trials are required in order to test safety and efficacy through to commercialization. Given their limited internal resources, biotechnology firms usually work with an array of other organizations and stakeholders (clinical research sites and hospitals, specialist clinical research organizations (CROs) and manufacturing firms) in order to perform such trials. This all occurs within a highly regulated institutional context, which enforces strict requirements and a sequential ordering process for approvals and data reporting (e.g. the FDA in the USA).

The characteristics of the ecology and the challenges this poses for those managing complex innovation processes are well recognized, but the ways in which these challenges are routinely handled in practice is not at all well understood (Hodgson and Cicmil, 2006; Dougherty and Dunne, 2012). The role of routines in this context has not been much examined, perhaps because the very idea of routines has seemed at odds with the characteristics of complex innovation (Obstfeld, 2012). Nevertheless, as we shall see, routines are important because they make this unpredictable innovation process seem as if it were predictable.

9.3 Managing Complex Innovation and Routines

Dougherty and Dunne (2011) have begun to theorize the ways in which the ecology of complex innovation processes "should" be organized. Using a social practice lens, albeit not the language of routines, their propositional model for organizing complex innovation ecologies suggests that certain practices need to be performed repeatedly and on an ongoing basis in order to handle the degree of complexity entailed. Their study thus complements recent work on routines in that they take a "knowledge as practice" view (cf. Cook and Brown, 1999; Feldman and Orlikowski, 2011). Their model describes three sets of social practices necessary to foster and handle the ongoing collaboration and emergence necessary for innovation in the ecology: orchestrating knowledge capabilities (to support emergence and new product development efforts); enabling ongoing strategizing (to frame and direct new development efforts over time); and developing public policy (to ensure public welfare and safety). These practices, they argue, should be enacted at the level of the ecology in order to counter the "natural" tendency to focus on single-firm performance and on short-term, incremental innovations and benefits. From a routines perspective, we might argue that these constitute a capabilities view of routines (Winter, 2000) at the ecology level to explain the influences on sector performance, i.e. as "whole" entities (Rerup and Feldman, 2011).

Dougherty and Dunne's analysis is helpful in sensitizing us to the complex, and differently oriented, range of social practices needed at the level of an ecology to foster and sustain complex innovation. The model also alerts us to the need to understand innovation practices at project-level as nested within (cf. Schatzki et al., 2001), and simultaneously facing, a broader array of social and institutional practices; for example, around the regulation of science or the control of intellectual property (IP) and financing (Grabher, 2002, 2004). However, what are not explained, or studied, are the routines that are actually practiced within organizations developing innovation projects to handle the ongoing complexity and emergence they face (Feldman, 2000), or the ways in which these routines are intertwined with the broader ecology of organizations (our focal research questions). As Feldman (2000: 622) highlights, "Ostensive routines may be devoid of active thinking, but routines enacted by people in organizations inevitably involve a range of actions, behaviours, thinking, and feeling." It is these repeated thinking/feeling *actions* that constitute the performative routines that allow adaptation to change. This distinction between ostensive and performative alerts us to the role of agency and the messiness of day-to-day organizing, which is likely to be extreme within the context of complex innovation projects, and which underpins practice-based perspectives on routines (Parmigiani and Howard-Grenville, 2011). Here, then, we are interested, in particular, in identifying what performative routines are practiced within organizations developing innovation projects in order for drug development to progress in the face of ongoing unknowability. Given the nature of complex innovation, we want to develop, moreover, an ecological perspective that is sensitive to the ways in which performative routines are entwined with wider, institutionalized practices in the ecology. In developing this perspective we are in part responding to Dougherty and Dunne (2011: 1221) who note: "It is necessary to articulate the actual day-to-day process of complex learning and innovation in particular projects so that the ecologies can be organized to directly support these activities."

Existing literature suggests that, even in complex innovation contexts where it is pretty hard to plan anything, traditional project management tools/artifacts are used nonetheless to organize activities (Sheremata, 2000; Styhre, 2006; Andriopoulos and Lewis, 2009). For example, within biotechnology firms, it is a well-established practice in the industry as a whole for senior management to produce (typically in a Gantt chart) an overview of the firm's pipeline for the various products in development. This pipeline is routinely drawn upon to internally to plan development work at project level as well as to demonstrate externally to potential investors when they might expect different products to become commercially viable (Styhre et al., 2010). Any firm's pipeline is premised on development moving sequentially through the various stage gates laid out in the regulatory approvals process (e.g. Phase I to IV clinical trials—e.g. Figure 9.1). Here lies a puzzle. The pipeline, and specific project management plans that follow, prescribe a linear sequencing of activities and knowledge flows, and planning to predefined targets, timelines, budgets, and outcomes. They are based on an assumption that most activities can be predicted with a fair degree of certainty, so that they can be planned in advance and smoothly executed. Whilst these artifacts are certainly developed and applied by project teams, they do not accommodate the ongoing emergence they actually experience (Hodgson and Cicmil, 2006; Schreyogg and Sydow, 2010; Obstfeld, 2012). They give us little clue, then, about the performative routines actually practiced by project teams managing innovation processes. Given that the pipeline is common parlance and "currency" in development, however, and that it (and associated project management tools) tracks a regulatory process, it does suggest though that performative routines may be shaped in a very important way by institutionalized, ecology-level practices.

Our empirical study that follows therefore examines how senior management and project teams in biotechnology firms engage in routines to manage (or cope with) the unknowability that characterizes such projects whilst simultaneously following the linear path to innovation inscribed in development pipelines and approvals processes. Considering how routines are enacted at project level can contribute to theory on the organization and management of complex innovation because it allows us to move between more normative accounts of what "should" be done (e.g. Pisano, 2006; Dougherty and Dunne, 2011) to an analysis of how things are actually done, why, and with what possible consequences. It also allows us to consider the ways in which performative routines at the local level of projects are entwined with the broader ecology of interacting organizations and institutions within which they are nested.

9.4 Empirical Study

We use data collected from a longitudinal study of eleven projects entailing the early phase development of novel therapeutics in nine different firms (in two firms we followed two distinct projects). Firms were chosen to include both small and medium-sized biotechnology companies, facilitating a multi-case design that allowed us to provide robust insights about how routines are managed in the context of a complex innovation process (Eisenhardt, 1989). From the firms that we gained access to, we selected projects that were in Phase I clinical trials aimed at establishing safety (although basic science on the underlying mechanisms was still being carried out) and planned to begin Phase II safety and efficacy trials within the next twelve months. This is a point where "epistemic uncertainty" (Grandori, 2010) is very pronounced and where commercial and scientific pressures come together.

A key criterion for selecting projects was that we would be provided with excellent access to key projects and stakeholders, allowing us to conduct detailed longitudinal research (including observation of project meetings and access to documentation) so that we could capture the dynamics of routines and how these were influencing ongoing innovation processes (Feldman and Pentland, 2008). Access was key because drug development is notoriously secretive (and results can be shareholder sensitive). This meant negotiating legal confidentiality agreements that preclude us from revealing any details of the underlying science or firm identifiers.

We also needed to choose a period of time over which to observe and document practices that would bring "the everyday activity of organizing" (Feldman and Orlikowski, 2011) into focus and allow us to link this to innovation processes. In drug development, this poses special problems— it takes around eight to fifteen years to commercialize drugs and upwards of 85 percent of projects fail (Hay et al., 2014) so it is practically impossible to do a full live "tracer" study. Hence we chose development projects that had been "live" for at least two years and followed these projects over a thirty-month period. This allowed our longitudinal analysis to include both historic and live processes (Pettigrew, 1990).

9.4.1 Data Collection and Analysis

Data collection techniques comprised observations, interviews, and documentary analyses. Two of the authors visited each case site four to five times over a thirty-month period. The first visit to each company involved interviews with senior VPs, often including the CEO, and was focused on becoming familiar with the processes that were used in each company to manage drug development (Turner and Rindova, 2012), as well as to identify specific projects that were currently ongoing and that met our criteria. During subsequent visits, we focused on the particular projects we had identified, interviewing key actors in these projects, as well as undertaking repeat interviews, where possible, with senior staff. In this phase, our focus was on collecting systematic data on the way those involved in managing projects in this particular industry adapted to changing circumstances (the "systemization stage" of data collection, as described by Turner and Rindova, 2012). Visits were arranged so that we could observe project team meetings but during visits we also had the opportunity to observe informal meetings held on an as-needed basis to address project issues. We were provided access to project documents (e.g. company reports, minutes of meetings, trials plans and product development schedules, and drug pipelines) and also conducted repeat interviews with project team members (typically interviewing the same person on two to four different occasions). We conducted a minimum of fourteen interviews and observed four formal project team meetings in each case. When interviewing, we used the narrative interview convention (Jovchelovitch and Bauer, 2000), providing a time frame for structuring the interview ("Tell me what has happened in the project, both successes and failures and any unanticipated events, since we last met") and then encouraging uninterrupted storytelling. Each interview was recorded and transcribed verbatim. Detailed notes were taken during (and completed after) observed meetings.

From the first round of familiarization interviews, plus data we had on the process of drug development more broadly (e.g. from the FDA website), we identified the routines (repeated patterns of actions) that were common across our case organizations. To do this we deployed grounded theory analytical techniques used to good effect previously (Gioia et al., 2010). Specifically, we began, using open coding, by identifying across all our first phase interviews and documents actions that were taken to manage the development process, which related to, for example, the requirements of the regulatory process. We then organized our data to draw together any actions used repeatedly across all eleven cases, grouped as "first-order codes." From these first-order codes we clustered these recurring activities into three categories (second-order themes) that we refer to as the "strategic routines" used in the ecology (to distinguish them from routines performed locally within specific projects). These strategic routines are organizational-level practices that had been established to protect, evolve, and resource the science that formed the basis of the drugs in development (see Table 9.1). Although unusual for process/practice studies (which usually prefer to build from micro-analysis of routines in single organizations), we were interested at this stage in identifying common, repeated patterns of actions associated with drug development in the ecology, so this method of identifying routines seems warranted.

Table 9.1 Key recurring activities undertaken in all biotechnology firms and strategic routines

Recurring activities common to biotech firms	Strategic routines
Development teams, scientists, and IP/regulatory experts research existing and pending patents in one or more countries where drug expected to be marketed.	Protecting the science
File appropriate documentation with various patent offices around the world to protect own science.	
Development teams review all scientific data available from their own and other sources associated with different projects to establish whether there are sufficient valid data available to file for an IND and subsequent clinical trial applications; submit applications when sufficient data accumulated or to report trials results.	Evolving the science
Senior management construct pipeline of products in development and upload to website. Meet regularly with development teams to review projects' progress on against pipeline and (re)assess which projects to commit most resources to.	
Development teams (project managers) construct plans/schedules for their projects using associated artifacts (e.g. Gantt charts) to ensure progress against overall pipeline.	
Clinical teams design trials plan and study protocols (i.e. trials designs, e.g. whether testing for safety and/or efficacy, number of patients, preferred clinical investigators, etc.) and determine when and where to run trial. Estimate time/costs to run the trial against pipeline projections.	
Development team (chemical manufacturing control scientists) determine and document the raw materials, facilities required, and timings for manufacturing batches of product to align with trials plans and pipeline projections.	
Senior management identify new market opportunities for core technology and determine what resources/expertise are required to support new projects.	Resourcing the science
Senior/business development teams seek and negotiate deals with potential partners with appropriate expertise to resource development.	
Development teams review existing in-house capabilities and establish outsourcing required and review and decide upon external organizations to use.	
Development teams conduct due diligence on selected partners for particular projects.	

Given the strong regulatory environment, and the importance of intellectual property (IP) protection in this industry, it is perhaps not surprising that we were able to identify common routines across cases and that these were associated with different aspects necessary to develop and progress the science. These routines, in other words, are related to the strategic capabilities that are essential in this industry (hence our labeling "strategic routines"). This link between routines and capabilities was previously identified by Winter (2000: 991) who states that an organizational capability is "a high level routine (or collection of routines) that, together with its implementing input flows, confers upon an organization's management a set of decision options for producing significant outputs of a particular type."

From the data collected from subsequent visits and observations, we analyzed how these strategic routines were either followed or disrupted during the ongoing development projects that we were specifically focused on. To begin this part of the analysis, all data were entered into NVivo and we wrote detailed descriptions of each drug development case (around 13,000 words). These descriptions provided a rich, chronologically ordered account of key events in each focal project. Once we had these rich descriptions, we used open coding to identify all sections of text that related to actions taken by managers to protect, evolve, or approve the science for their focal project (Locke, 2001). During this stage, it became evident that a number of unknowns were regularly encountered in relation to protecting, evolving, and resourcing the science (see Table 9.2). We then organized our data by drawing together similar kinds of statements about how these unknowns were dealt with to form provisional categories (a second set of first-order codes). These broader categories were adjusted periodically throughout the analysis. Finally, we clustered these categories into three higher order, researcher-induced themes in order to produce our emerging framework (Eisenhardt, 1989; Gioia et al., 2010) of performative routines within projects. Thus, we identified three performative routines—hedging, compromising, and re-prioritizing. In order to ensure consistency in our analytical categories (Glaser and Strauss, 1967; Sole and Edmondson, 2002) we then went back to our original data and carefully examined whether any key issues were being ignored in the categories that we had established.

We used different techniques to verify the credibility and trustworthiness of our interpretation of the data (Denzin and Lincoln, 1998). First, while one author was responsible for conducting the initial analysis and (re) writing the case studies, fieldwork was conducted by two researchers so the second could help to discuss, and verify, the final account. We also presented the individual case narratives to project members who were able to verify (and occasionally correct) our interpretations. Finally, we held five scientific advisory board meetings over the duration of the research. Members of this board had extensive experience of drug development processes and confirmed that the problems and dynamics that we had identified were common in this context. For the remainder of this chapter we use two cases (SkinTech and AntibodyTech) as "revelatory cases" (Yin, 1994) to present findings. Selecting revelatory cases allows us to provide rich details of local practices and dynamics of routines in this complex innovation ecology.

Table 9.2 Unknowns encountered during project work and performative routines (Guesswork)

Typical unknowns	Examples of performative routines (Guesswork)
Protecting the science What IP will be needed? What countries to file in?	**SkinTech & AntibodyTech** 1. Extensive search of existing/pending patents across countries. 2. Prepare and submit enormous amount of documentation in order to comply with patenting requirements across multiple countries and avoid infringing existing/pending patents. 3. Majority of IP languishes on the shelf but considered necessary if projected development plans are to remain on schedule **in order to promote investor confidence** into the future as unsure where trials will be conducted or drug will be registered at this early stage of development. *Routine characterized as Hedging*
Evolving the science 1. What will be the most likely indication/treatment goal/trial to focus on to achieve positive results in the near future?	**SkinTech** 1. Review progress across all three projects. 2. Agree that all three face significant and different challenges. 3. Decide upon focal project based on opportunity to partner with high status but unfamiliar collaborator **as signal of confidence in the project to existing and potential investors.** 4. Revise (accelerate) product pipeline projections re milestone dates for this project to reflect change. *Routine characterized as Re-Prioritizing* **AntibodyTech** 1. Submit trial design documentation to gain approval for extreme/high risk phase II trial testing for efficacy instead of running further phase I safety trial. 2. Do not review or assess which sites to approach for patient enrollment as this would generate delays. 3. Revise (i.e. accelerate) product pipeline projections to reflect this proposed trial **to improve investor confidence in project.** *Routine characterized as Re-Prioritizing*
2. What data will be required to satisfy the regulator to register an IND?	**SkinTech** 1. Multiple teams produce documentation to file for an IND. 2. Senior management propose to file an IND recognizing that there is no possibility of gaining approval. However, this ensures that this milestone activity was within the time frame stipulated in the pipeline projection **to sustain current and possible future investor confidence.** *Routine characterized as Compressing*
3. When should we manufacture the product and in what form?	**SkinTech** 1. Development team establish that the dental product will require the manufacture of square cells. 2. Inform manufacturing of requirement. 3. Attempt to manufacture a square cell product, but this proves to be much more difficult than

Table 9.2 Continued

Typical unknowns	Examples of performative routines (Guesswork)
	anticipated—"*because cells don't grow in such an orderly pattern.*" Recognize that cannot overcome this problem in scheduled time scales for trials.
	4. Senior management agree to the manufacture of traditional round cell product instead for proposed trial.
	5. Trial for dental project goes ahead within stipulated time frame/plans recognizing that it will fail but ensuring it is on time in order **to sustain investor confidence in focal project.**
	Routine characterized as Compressing
	AntibodyTech
	1. Order raw materials for in-house manufacture.
	2. Manufacture significant quantity of product for high risk trial in-house *before* patients have been enrolled and despite the fact that the product has only a very short shelf life, to align with trial schedule plans **and sustain investor confidence in project.**
	3. Trial abandoned because patients cannot be recruited.
	4. Dispose of out of date but very costly product.
	Routine characterized as Compressing
4. What science/trials to perform in-house and what to outsource to academics/CROs?	**SkinTech**
	1. Development team attempt to monitor the work of selected but unfamiliar CRO for dental trial product.
	2. Produce documentation for the regulator based on CRO work but lack of understanding of CRO activities.
	3. Regulator rejects SkinTech documentation.
	Routine characterized as Compressing
	AntibodyTech
	1. Contract out high risk trial to unfamiliar CRO based on costs and their availability.
	2. CRO fails to recruit patients and trial aborted.
	3. Revert back to original plan for CRO to conduct a more conservative trial but only limited time to conduct it because of time lost on abandoned trial.
	4. Difficulty in "encouraging" CRO to prioritize trial.
	Routine characterized as Compressing
5. What will be the results of trials?	**SkinTech/AntibodyTech**
	1. Regulator approves some trial designs and not others (based on documentation or trial design) which create delays.
	2. Approved trials often delayed (significantly) because of problems with patient recruitment; expertise of external collaborators; competing priorities of collaborators/CROs and negative trial results.
	3. Pipeline projections for further trials reviewed but timelines typically *not* adjusted so planned future activities (trials, manufacturing, etc.) are reviewed and adjusted to "fit" with original timeline **in order to sustain investor confidence in project.**
	Routine characterized as Compressing

(continued)

Table 9.2 Continued

Typical unknowns	Examples of performative routines (Guesswork)
Resourcing the science	
1. What will potential investors and/ or partners want/expect to see in order to invest resources in the firm?	**AntibodyTech** 1. Design and seek approval for 2 trials simultaneously (i.e. ahead of pipeline projections): (i) a high risk (extreme) trial in hope of demonstrating high levels of efficacy to potential partners more quickly and (ii) a low risk trial to reduce chance of demonstrating problems with science (i.e. negative results) which could influence partnering process. 2. Both trials approved by regulator, including (unexpectedly) high risk trial. 3. Senior management agree to divert resources to the high risk trial **to promote potential partner confidence in project** (with deals now at a late stage), but trial fails to recruit patients and sets back project. 4. Resources diverted back to low risk trial. *Routine characterized as Re-Prioritizing* **SkinTech** 1. Senior management engage in ongoing, ad hoc, and opportunistic networking with strong and weak ties to support future development of core technology, e.g. contact head of research at major university Dental School, who used to be on the board of directors of SkinTech. 2. Facilitate a meeting with periodontal experts at the Dental School. 3. Members of the school agree to *informally* support a dental project with their expertise in periodontal science. 4. Senior management revise pipeline plan for periodontal project to improve pipeline plan **in order to promote investor confidence,** even though this reduces resources for other projects. *Routine characterized as Re-Prioritizing*
Who might be interested in licensing or partnering arrangement on focal project?	**AntibodyTech** 1. Business Development (BD) team produce a long list of potential partners and begin financial negotiations. 2. Development team request and assess phase II trial plans from long list of anonymous partners and compare to in-house phase II trial plans. 3. Produce shortlist of potential partners for business development based on their projected development plans but rather speculative as no knowledge of who potential partners might be. 4. BD request and assess all potential partner business plans. *Routine characterized as Hedging* **SkinTech** 1. Informal dinner with the Harvard scientists. 2. Produce an outline but nevertheless formal agreement between the parties for a number of preclinical and clinical trials for periodontal application. 3. Pipeline plan revised to reflect shift in focal project. *Routine characterized as Re-Prioritizing*

9.5 Overview of Cases

9.5.1 SkinTech

SkinTech is a regenerative medicine company that was originally formed in the 1980s as a spin-out from a university. Shortly after the spin-out the founders commercialized a biological "Skin" product, short-circuiting a lot of the normal regulatory approvals process because the product was classified as a medical device rather than a drug, for which there was, at the time, far less regulation. The product was marketed as a superior replacement for bandages because it contained biologically active ingredients that could stimulate wound healing, as well as protecting the wound. However, as the founders had very little business expertise, they licensed the product to Pharma who were responsible for sales and marketing. Pharma was interested in the regenerative technology because, at that time, this was seen as having the potential to revolutionize medical treatments, such as eventually being able to grow new organs for transplantation. However, the licensing agreement was dissolved after only a few years as Pharma found that marketing the product involved actively working alongside medics as they learned how to practically use the product and this was very costly. Coupled with the fading beliefs in the industry about the potential for regenerative treatments, Pharma pulled out of the venture.

SkinTech was making losses and filed for bankruptcy. However, two of SkinTech's founders decided to resurrect it by investing their own money into it. It emerged from bankruptcy, but as a much smaller company that was based on a business model focused upon outsourcing rather than extensive engagement in in-house research and development. SkinTech began working with a variety of academic researchers and organizations (e.g. CROs, manufacturing companies) to develop and expand its product portfolio based on its original technology in the development of medical therapeutics.

At the time of our study SkinTech had three actual and potential product lines in its portfolio:

1. "Skin" was the original and main product line aimed at wound repair, which was now profitable. However, SkinTech needed to develop the next generation of this product, which would be easier for medics to use and would not contain animal (bovine) products because of BSE risk.
2. "Dental Skin" was a potential dental application of the technology (regenerating gum tissue) for which SkinTech was setting up Phase I clinical trials.

3. "Cosmetic Skin" was a potential skin treatment developed from the waste products of the "Skin" manufacturing process. This waste contains biological material that it was thought could potentially regenerate skin and so reduce signs of ageing. During the time of our study the first Phase I clinical trial on this product was conducted.

9.5.2 AntibodyTech

AntibodyTech was set up by university researchers who had developed a core technology to develop monoclonal antibodies that could potentially be used in a range of areas, including the treatment of arthritis, allergies, and a range of cancers. The IP for the core technology was heavily protected so a range of pharmaceutical firms and other biotechnology firms had licensed the technology from AntibodyTech for their own development projects. This provided AntibodyTech with financial resources to invest in its own in-house projects, which included four cancer projects and a project to "cure" asthma called "Allergy." At the time of the research one of the cancer projects had just failed because the partnering agreement that the firm had entered into with a large pharmaceutical firm in order to conduct larger-scale Phase II and III trials had not progressed. This was because the pharma had shifted priorities and abandoned development in that particular cancer treatment area. This forced AntibodyTech to shift its priorities and focus upon Allergy as the basic science around this potential drug was advanced and the firm had successfully filed an IND (Investigational New Drug) with the regulator so it could commence Phase I trials. Whilst relatively well-financed, AntibodyTech did not have the resources or access to resources (e.g. patients) for large-scale trials and, hurt by their previous failure in later phase trials, looked to partner with a pharma if Phase I trials were successful. At the time we commenced research AntibodyTech had successfully conducted one Phase I safety trial and gained approval for both a further Phase I safety trial using different dosages and, surprisingly, a Phase II trial aimed at demonstrating efficacy which involved inducing a severe asthma attack in mild asthmatics. On this basis AntibodyTech believed it was an appropriate point in development to identify a partner who they could work with to take Allergy forward for future development.

The section that follows presents the way in which performative routines were enacted in projects as they attempted to satisfy the regulator and other institutional requirements (IPR) and how these involved considerable "guesswork." In the discussion we consider the reasons why guesswork was so central to the performative routines in this ecology as well as the outcomes and consequences for the innovation process.

9.6 Routines Enacted in SkinTech and AntibodyTech

Both firms were using development pipelines, which showed, stretching years ahead, when different phases of clinical work would be started and completed on each product. The milestones in these pipelines corresponded to dates (usually expressed as year quarters) indicating when clinical trials would be filed with the regulator for approval and, assuming positive results, when subsequent trial phases would occur. The product pipeline could be found on each firm's website and was focal to discussions with actual and potential investors as it is the generally accepted way in which firms in this sector communicate in order to forecast when different products will (potentially) be commercially viable.

Project teams used a variety of project management tools and techniques (e.g. Gantt charts) to plan their day-to-day activities needed to protect, evolve, and resource the science according to the milestones forecast in their pipeline. However, as time went on, setbacks and unanticipated problems inevitably occurred because of the many unknowns that were faced and, as more was learned about the scientific properties of the therapeutic itself, multiple adjustments had to be made. This meant project plans were revisited on a regular (i.e. weekly or sometimes daily) basis. As one project manager put it: "we have this Gantt chart that's a hundred pages long and I'm constantly tearing it up." At the same time, the time scales forecast in the overall development pipeline, stretching years ahead, were more or less immovable. Any proposed changes that would affect the pipeline projection always required approval from senior management, given that any "slippages" would be received negatively by investors and potential investors because they would dampen investor confidence.

9.6.1 Managing Unknowns

Our subsequent fieldwork identified how the strategic routines (organizational capabilities, in Winter's terms), when enacted, were regularly disrupted by "unknowns," which were either partly predictable but ignored or cropped up entirely unexpectedly. In the next part of our analysis, then, we focused on the routines performed within projects when attempting to enact strategic routines in the face of the unknowns. Not all the firms in our sample had to deal with all of these unknowns, but to be included in the analysis each "unknown" had to have been encountered by the majority, if not all of the projects across the sample of eleven case firms (including the two discussed in detail here).

9.6.1.1 UNKNOWNS ASSOCIATED WITH PROTECTING THE SCIENCE

Unless a biotechnology firm has, or is about to acquire, the IP for an IND then there is unlikely to be any investor interest or investment, hence protecting the science is fundamental from the outset and continues to be imperative as new discoveries emerge. Typical unknowns concerned exactly what aspects of the science to protect with IPR (intellectual property rights), what IPRs needed to be acquired based on existing patents, and what IPRs to license out to larger, better resourced firms (typically large pharma) to take development into later stages. Great care was required in order to precisely document IP protection for different aspects of the core technologies and/or therapeutics in development. For example if a biotechnology firm did not follow the specified production process precisely, IP protection would be invalidated so great accuracy was required and what might be missing, as far as the regulator was concerned, was often unknown at the time when IP was being amassed. In addition, IPR needed to be registered in each of the countries that a potential drug was likely to be marketed in, and each country had different requirements in terms of documentation. However, at this early stage, the exact choice of countries they (or, more accurately, the pharmaceutical firm that took the project through later development) would want to market to was unknown. Moreover, the biotechnology firms' managers also had to take decisions about who to partner with (e.g. which large pharmaceutical) and at what point, and for what financial return, they should license their IP out. Deals were being sought with potential partners and investors while, at the same time, the managers in our focal projects did not know how (or if) the science would actually evolve and so what to protect.

9.6.1.2 UNKNOWNS ASSOCIATED WITH EVOLVING THE SCIENCE

Typical unknowns here concerned what potential and actual investors wanted or expected to see in terms of scientific results in order to invest, or continue to invest, in the development project. This involved a consideration of what opportunities there might be to expand the scope of existing core technologies or products in development, what clinical trials to perform, when to start a clinical trial, and how to manufacture quantities of the product needed with the right formula to perform scheduled trials to the dosage and formula anticipated (e.g. concentration of solution, in Antibody, or square versus round "skin" in SkinTech). Within project work, unknowns frequently occurred when clinical trials did not yield positive results. Until further scientific work was conducted, or further trials were designed and conducted, it would often be unknown as to why a trial had produced negative results. For example, all firms encountered problems in orchestrating their manufacturing effort with their scientific work. This was because manufacturing work, needed to scale-up production for larger clinical trials, had to be scheduled many months in advance and, crucially, in advance of the results of ongoing trials (that would often yield unexpected results about the chemical formula) being available. In the Allergy project, for example, the Phase II trial designed to induce a severe asthma attack in patients failed (perhaps unsurprisingly) to recruit patients to the timeline anticipated, but the drug solution, which had a short shelf-life, had already been manufactured, resulting in very costly waste.

9.6.1.3 UNKNOWNS ASSOCIATED WITH RESOURCING THE SCIENCE

The main issue here was what indication/treatment goal(s) to focus on at any point in time given the inherent resource constraints they faced. If a firm was attempting to license its IPR and partner for future development then the major unknown would be about who to partner with (e.g. knowing who had the capabilities, resources, and motivation to take the project into large-scale trials). More generally, to conduct trials, firms often had to outsource much of the work required (e.g. patient recruitment) to clinical scientists and/or CROs. Often firms had little or no experience of dealing with this so would not know whether particular firms/clinicians could be relied upon to enroll sufficient patients and conduct trials within the firm's schedules.

9.6.2 Performative Routines

Our analysis then turned to assessing what performative routines were enacted within projects attempting to deal with the many unknowns and unanticipated outcomes (e.g. negative trials results) that they faced. Whilst project teams clearly needed to largely adhere to their firms' strategic routines because of the institutionalized (regulatory and market) pressures in the ecology, their performative routines varied in three ways as hedging, compressing, or re-prioritizing. Our summary analysis of the unknowns and the way performative routines were enacted in SkinTech and Antibody-Tech's development projects, with a range of examples from the data, is provided in Table 9.2.

Performative routines characterized by *hedging* occurred when various options available in relation to an unknown that all seemed relatively feasible, depending upon which external stakeholders would be mostly concerned with the outcome, were all pursued at once. In both firms, for example, in terms of protecting the science, firms had filed for extensive patents, typically covering more science than had been deemed "essential" for fulfilling IP requirements, and/or they had filed for IPR across multiple countries, even if there was no intention to market in some of them. In another example of hedging, in the Allergy team we observed a discussion during one project meeting over the number of patients to recruit for a trial. It was agreed that "from a scientific point of view" it could be run with twelve patients. However, after some debate the clinical trials manager concluded, "The magic number for subjects to be exposed (to antibodies) needs to be around fifty . . . you might as well stick your finger in the air as to how many patients you need . . . It's our guess against their guess, so let's stick with forty-two—it's the answer to everything isn't it." A trial with forty-two patients was designed, not just because it was "the magic number," but because this was the kind of sample size that the team were guessing that regulators might want to see if approvals of future, larger-scale, studies were to be eased and it might be a "more convincing number" to present to a partner, depending on who that partner might actually be. The performative routine of "hedging" entailed actions that were significantly more lengthy and costly compared to the strategic routine that, ostensibly, needed to be followed. For example, in SkinTech, a considerable amount of IP often "languished on the shelf" and in AntibodyTech it was much more costly to recruit additional patients. This performative routine of hedging had developed for two reasons. First, it was felt that future delays with regulation could be avoided if something unanticipated occurred (e.g. the partner decided they wanted to go to market in a different country) and, perhaps more importantly, investor confidence in the firm would be promoted/generated. However, in terms of time and costs this routine often created delays from the outset of the projects because of the work and time involved in holding open several options.

Performative routines characterized by *compressing* were probably most evident in our dataset. The routine evident here involved an underestimating and squeezing of the time needed to progress development built into each firm's pipeline. This meant that in the short term, when activities were delayed, often because hedging actions had not resolved problems or had actually created new ones, there were frantic attempts to compress or as one project manager put it, "squish-in," additional activities that were now required (e.g. the redesign of a trial because a regulator had rejected the trial design) or to attempt a short-cut in order to make up time that had been lost or actually attempt to be ahead of schedule. For example, in SkinTech's dental project there were attempts to manufacture a square molecular shape of "Skin," which periodontal experts had insisted was required and more suitable for gum healing. However, attempts to manufacture this had failed (because cells reproduce themselves into a circle rather than a square). Regardless of this fact, the team went ahead with a clinical trial "on schedule" using the round, original shape instead, whilst recognizing that this was not really workable for dentists. In so doing, it did mean, however, that there was no further slippage to the timeline! This action was therefore opportunistic and, from a scientific perspective, somewhat ad hoc. Moreover, the squeezing in of additional work to an already tight time scale often created new problems, for example, with manufacturers who were unable to supply the product to rescheduled, and often very tight, time scales and/or with project staff, who now had to juggle additional demands. Further examples of routines characterized by compressing are presented in Table 9.2.

Over time, and typically when compressing was no longer feasible, and it was clear that the pipeline projections were totally unrealistic, there would be a *re-prioritization* of projects and/or clinical studies. Thus actions would be taken to, either concentrate resources on a product line that, in relative terms, was considered to be more promising at that point in time, or to conduct a different trial that was likely to provide positive results more quickly. For example, in SkinTech, a clinical trial on Cosmetic Skin (which was expected to be a "blockbuster" aging product if it worked) failed to yield positive results from a clinical trial for reasons that were entirely unclear. At this point the project was de-prioritized and efforts of the project team switched back to a new version of the wound repair product that was, it was thought, more likely to meet its deadline.

Performative routines across all of our projects were, in effect, deviations from attempts to enact the organizations' strategic routines that reflected regulatory and market demands in the ecology, in the face of the inevitable, and ongoing, unknowns that projects were faced with. The overarching rationale for these performative routines seemed to be to maintain the timelines predicted in the pipeline and/or promote investor confidence in these projects, as highlighted in Table 9.2. However, all of these performative routines were characterized by what we refer to as "guesswork," which we define and discuss next as we consider the implications of our findings for innovation within complex organizational ecologies.

9.7 Discussion and Conclusions

Project planning and the product development pipeline, built around regulatory approval milestones, make it appear as if innovation in this context is a matter of following a smooth linear path from preclinical work, through phased clinical trials with increasing numbers of patients, and proving safety and efficacy of the drug in development, then eventual commercialization. However, we have seen that in complex innovation projects, where knowledge and outcomes are highly emergent (Newell et al., 2008; Dougherty and Dunne, 2012), the path is far from smooth— performative routines are enacted in ways that cope pragmatically with the many unknowns inevitably faced. Thus, one contribution of our study is to respond to calls to articulate the "actual day-to-day process" of managing complex innovation in particular project settings (Hodgson and Cicmil, 2006; Dougherty and Dunne, 2012).

The performative routines—hedging, compressing, and reprioritizing— identified in our study could be understood as "skillful accomplishments," insofar as they helped actors to behave as if things *were* predictable and, in so doing, they were focused on addressing the concerns of other stakeholders in the organizational ecology (e.g. responding to regulatory requirements or promoting investor confidence in the firm/project), even in the face of ongoing unknowns and highly emergent outcomes. These routines, collectively, can be referred to as "guesswork," since they all entailed actions taken to manage development projects based on "best guesses" in the face of unknowns. We define guesswork as routines enacted, using the collective experience of those involved, to establish and proceed through a course of action most likely to convince external stakeholders in the ecology that projects are progressing as anticipated, cognizant of the institutional requirements that exist. These enabled those involved to be pragmatic and to take action at points where decisions *had* to be made but where the outcomes were very difficult, if not impossible, to predict; hence the notion of "guesswork." We argue, therefore, that performative routines enacted within projects, that themselves are embedded within organization and a wider ecology of organizations, are significantly shaped by the actions and predicted actions of other stakeholders in the ecology.

One contribution of our study, then, in response to our first research question, has been to identify the locally-improvised performative routines actually manifest in firms and projects developing complex innovation processes. This complements more normative accounts of what "should" be done to "orchestrate" complex innovation ecologies (e.g. Pisano, 2006; Dougherty and Dunne, 2011) by providing an exploratory account of how things *are* actually done and why.

A second contribution, in response to our second research question, is to provide a multi-level account of routines that shows how performative routines at the level of projects develop in response to strategic routines used by organizations and reflect concerns of the wider ecology. By developing an empirically-grounded ecological view, that takes account of the heterogeneous, multi-layered nature of routines, we hope to have contributed, in a modest way, to organization studies on routines, which, as Salvato and Rerup (2011: 469) observe, "have long neglected the fine-grained, multilayered nature of routines and capabilities. Instead, they have opted to investigate them as truncated, collective, recurrent entities, or 'black boxes,' embedded in firms at micro or macro levels of analysis."

In terms of the consequences of these routines for the innovation process, our research suggested that those involved fully recognized the inherent uncertainties of development and the implausibility of following linear plans and predictions. Yet, their routines performed locally sought to sustain, rather than challenge, the timelines embedded in the product pipeline. In our case, then, albeit a very dynamic situation, we saw very little evidence of "dynamic capabilities" or "deviation" from established processes (Raman and Bharadwaj, 2012). The highly linear pipelines and timelines remained rigidly in place. Indeed, the performance of routines was actually geared toward affirming the "myth" of a manageable, and knowable, linear development process. Practically then, and somewhat paradoxically, the undoubtedly skillful accomplishment of these guesswork routines, set in motion in order to be able to *do something* when faced with relentless uncertainty, often significantly constrained those involved from actually developing new, or alternate, processes that might better support scientific development. For example, in SkinTech, in order to "keep things on track," trials went ahead with round-shaped dental material not suited to gums even though those involved recognized that any results from a trial designed in this way would be inconclusive.

These, outwardly counterproductive, activities can be understood when we consider the ways in which performative routines enacted within these firms are nested in the ecology of organizations implicated in complex innovation (Dougherty and Dunne, 2011). Thus, in this particular ecology the creation and revision of a development pipeline and detailed project plans were underpinned by a highly prescribed regulatory framework which embodies linearity and stage-gates, combined with strong pressures from investors who demand to see progress before committing to investment. Given products are still at the discovery stage, "progress" can only be demonstrated by showing adherence to project schedules that are aligned with the regulatory framework. For example, it is well known in the industry that, statistically, projects are much more likely to deliver commercial returns once Phase II trials have been approved (Kola and Landis, 2004). There is very little tangible evidence, aside from the results of successful approvals, to indicate progress.

In this context, then, market and regulatory pressures create a highly institutionalized set of norms and prescriptions in the ecology around the ordering of work that assumes linear development. This institutionalized "social order" is translated at the firm-level into an array of processes that involve creating pipeline and project plans that conform to the ideal of a linear development process. The guesswork routines that we identify, therefore, helped practitioners "fill the gap" between the linear assumptions of knowledge production imposed by the pipeline and the reality of a much more interactive (in the sense of moving back and forth between basic science and clinical work), messy, and emergent innovation process identified in previous work (Styhre et al., 2010; Swan et al., 2010; Dougherty and Dunne, 2011). In this way, we argue, the various performative routines enacted locally practically reproduce the institutionalized social order. Even though ultimately these may be counterproductive (in terms of development) and so appear to be not fit-for-purpose, for those involved in drug development, it is the practical way in which they can respond to the pressures to make drug development appear tractable (and so worth investing in). In this way, and following Turner and Rindova (2012), we argue that there is a high degree of consistency in the use of guesswork routines in the face of ongoing uncertainty and emergence across all our case study firms.

Thus, a final contribution of our study is to show how routines, enacted locally in order to handle ongoing change and uncertainty, are not only intertwined with, but might play an active role in reinforcing and stabilizing (rather than challenging or changing) the dominant social order (reflected in the development pipelines) in a wider organizational ecology. The sustained "myth" of the pipeline development model, in turn, appears to necessitate the further use of these guesswork routines to work around plans based upon this model that in many cases prove unworkable. These initial findings suggest an important dialectical process linking routines performed locally within firms and projects to wider institutionalized orders across the project ecology. It also suggests likely tensions between the mechanisms prescribed by Dougherty and Dunne (2012) to support complex innovation at the level of the ecology (e.g. developing public policy to ensure public welfare and safety) and those needed locally to manage emergence. Research from a routines perspective has not yet adopted an approach that recognizes this dialectical process.

Finally, rather than organizations designing processes to meet the demands of the emerging science (as suggested by Bessant et al., 2011, and others), we have demonstrated how the application of routines which are largely driven by regulatory and other (e.g. IPR) requirements to address unknowns can practically constrain innovation. In this sense, our findings build on earlier work that suggests that the biomedical innovation system fosters a technological regime that creates "lock-in" (Vanloqueren and Baret, 2009)—in this case to a set of routines that, whilst acceding to external regulatory and investment pressures, simultaneously hinder the development of novel therapeutics.

References

Andriopoulos, C. and Lewis, M. (2009). "Exploitation–Exploration Tensions and Organizational Ambidexterity: Managing Paradoxes of Innovation." *Organization Science*, 20/4: 696–717.

Bessant, J., Von Stamm, B., and Moeslein, K. M. (2011). "Selection Strategies for Discontinuous Innovation." *International Journal of Technology Management*, 55/1: 156–70.

Cohen, M., Burkhart, R., Dosi, G., Egidi, M., Marengo, L., Warglien, M., and Winter, S. (1996). "Routines and Other Recurring Action Patterns of Organizations: Contemporary Research Issues." *Industrial and Corporate Change*, 5/3: 653–99.

Cook, S. D. and Brown, J. S. (1999). "Bridging Epistemologies: The Generative Dance Between Organizational Knowledge and Organizational Knowing." *Organization Science*, 10/4: 381–400.

Denzin, N. and Lincoln, Y. (1998). *Collecting and Interpreting Qualitative Materials*. Thousand Oaks, CA: Sage Publications.

Dionysiou, D. D. and Tsoukas, H. (2013). "Understanding the (Re)Creation of Routines from Within: A Symbolic Interactionist Perspective." *Academy of Management Review*, 38/2: 181–205.

Dosi, G., Faillo, M., and Marengo, L. (2008). "Organizational Capabilities, Patterns of Knowledge Accumulation and Governance Structures in Business Firms: An Introduction." *Organization Studies*, 29/8–9: 1165–85.

Dougherty, D. and Dunne, D. (2011). "Organizing Ecologies of Innovation." *Organization Science*, 22/5: 1214–23.

Dougherty, D. and Dunne, D. (2012). "Digital Science and Knowledge Boundaries in Complex Innovation." *Organization Science*, 23/5: 1467–84.

Eisenhardt, K. M. (1989). "Building Theories from Case Study Research." *Academy of Management Review*, 14/4: 532–50.

Eisenhardt, K. M. and Martin, J. (2000). "Dynamic Capabilities: What are They?" *Strategic Management Journal*, 21/1: 1105–21.

Feldman, M. S. (2000). "Organizational Routines as a Source of Continuous Change." *Organization Science*, 11/6: 611–29.

Feldman, M. S. and Orlikowski, W. (2011). "Theorizing Practice and Practicing Theory." *Organization Science*, 22/5: 1240–53.

Feldman, M. and Pentland, B. (2003). "Reconceptualizing Organizational Routines as a Source of Flexibility and Change." *Administrative Science Quarterly*, 48/1: 94–118.

Feldman, M. S. and Pentland, B. T. (2008). "Issues in Empirical Field Studies of Organizational Routines." In M. Becker (ed.), *Handbook of Organizational Routines*. Cheltenham: Edward Elgar, 281–300.

Garud, R., Gehman, J., and Kumaraswamy, A. (2011). "Complexity Arrangements for Sustained Innovation: Lessons from 3M Corporation." *Organization Studies*, 32/6: 737–67.

Gioia, D. A., Price, K., Hamilton, A., and Thomas, J. (2010). "Forging an Identity: An Insider–Outsider Study of Processes Involved in the Formation of Organizational Identity." *Administrative Science Quarterly*, 55/1: 1–46.

Gittelman, M. (2007). "Does Geography Matter for Science-Based Firms? Epistemic Communities and the Geography of Research and Patenting in Biotechnology." *Organization Science*, 18/4: 724–41.

Glaser, B. and Strauss, A. (1967). *The Discovery of Grounded Theory: Strategies in Qualitative Research*. London: Weidenfeld & Nicolson.

Grabher, G. (2002). "The Project Ecology of Advertising: Tasks, Talents and Teams." *Regional Studies*, 36/3: 245–62.

Grabher, G. (2004). "Temporary Architectures of Learning: Knowledge Governance in Project Ecologies." *Organization Studies*, 25/9: 1491–514.

Grandori, A. (2010). "A Rational Heuristic Model of Economic Decision Making." *Rationality and Society*, 22/4, 477–504.

Hay, M., Thomas, D. W., Craighead, J. L., Economides, C., and Rosenthal, J. (2014). "Clinical Development Success Rates for Investigational Drugs." *Nature Biotechnology*, 32/1: 40–51.

Hodgson, D. and Cicmil, S. (eds.) (2006). *Making Projects Critical*. Basingstoke: Palgrave Macmillan.

Howard-Grenville, J. A. (2005). "The Persistence of Flexible Organizational Routines: The Role of Agency and Organizational Context." *Organization Science*, 16/6: 618–36.

Jovchelovitch, S. and Bauer, M. (2000). *Narrative Interviewing*. London: LSE Research online.

Kola, I. and Landis, J. (2004). "Can the Pharmaceutical Industry Reduce Attrition Rates?" *Nature Reviews Drug Discovery*, 3/8: 711–16.

Locke, K. (2001). *Grounded Theory in Management Research.* Thousand Oaks: Sage Publications.

Newell, S., Goussevskaia, A., Swan, J., Bresnen, M., and Obembe, A. (2008). "Interdependencies in Complex Project Ecologies: The Case of Biomedical Innovation." *Long Range Planning*, 41/1: 33–54.

Obstfeld, D. (2012). "Creative Projects: A Less Routine Approach Toward Getting New Things Done." *Organization Science*, 23/6: 1571–92.

Parmigiani, A. and Howard-Grenville, J. (2011). "Routines Revisited: Exploring the Capabilities and Practice Perspectives." *Academy of Management Annals*, 5/1: 413–53.

Pentland, B. T., Feldman, M. S., Becker, M. C., and Liu, P. (2012). "Dynamics of Organizational Routines: A Generative Model." *Journal of Management Studies*, 49/8: 1484–508.

Pentland, B. T., Haerem, T., and Hillison, D. (2011). "The (N)Ever-Changing World: Stability and Change in Organizational Routines." *Organization Science*, 22/6: 1369–83.

Pettigrew, A. (1990). "Longitudinal Field Research on Change." *Organization Science*, 1/3: 267–92.

Pisano, G. (2006). "Can Science be a Business? Lessons from Biotech." *Harvard Business Review* (October): 114–25.

Raman, R. and Bharadwaj, A. (2012). "Power Differentials and Performative Deviation Paths in Practice Transfer: The Case of Evidence-Based Medicine." *Organization Science*, 23/6: 1593–621.

Rerup, C. and Feldman, M. (2011). "Routines as a Source of Change in Organizational Schema." *Academy of Management Journal*, 54/3: 577–610.

Salvato, C. and Rerup, C. (2011). "Beyond Collective Entities: Multilevel Research on Organizational Routines and Capabilities." *Journal of Management*, 37/2: 469–90.

Schatzki, T. R., Knorr-Cetina, K., and Von Savigny, E. (eds.) (2001). *The Practice Turn in Contemporary Theory.* London: Routledge.

Schreyögg, G. and Sydow, J. (2010). "Organizing for Fluidity? Dilemmas of New Organizational Forms." *Organization Science*, 21/6: 1251–62.

Sheremata, W. (2000). "Centrifugal and Centripetal Forces in Radical New Product Development Under Time Pressure." *Academy Management Review*, 25/2: 389–408.

Snowden, D. J. and Boone, M. (2007). "A Leader's Framework for Decision Making." *Harvard Business Review*, 85/11: 68.

Sole, D. and Edmondson, A. (2002). "Situated Knowledge and Learning in Dispersed Teams." *British Journal of Management*, 13: 17–34.

Styhre, A. (2006). "Science-Based Innovation as Systematic Risk-Taking: The Case of New Drug Development." *European Journal of Innovation Management*, 9/3: 300–11.

Styhre, A., Wikmalm, L., Olilla, S., and Roth, J. (2010). "Garbage-Can Decision Making and the Accommodation of Uncertainty in New Drug Development Work." *Creativity and Innovation Management*, 19/2: 134–46.

Swan, J., Bresnen, M., Robertson, M., Newell, S., and Dopson, S. (2010). "When Policy Meets Practice: Colliding Logics and the Challenges of 'Mode 2' Initiatives in the Translation of Academic Knowledge." *Organization Studies*, 31/9–10: 1311–40.

Swan, J., Goussevskaia, A., Newell, S., Robertson, M., Bresnen, M., and Obembe, A. (2007). "Modes of Organizing Biomedical Innovation in the UK and US and the Role of Integrative and Relational Capabilities." *Research Policy*, 36/4: 529–47.

Turner, S. and Rindova, V. (2012). "A Balancing Act: How Organizations Pursue Consistency in Routine Functioning in the Face of Ongoing Change." *Organization Science*, 23/1: 24–46.

Vanloqueren, G. and Baret, P. (2009). "How Agricultural Research Systems Shape a Technological Regime that Develops Genetic Engineering but Locks out Agroecological Innovations." *Research Policy*, 38/6: 971–83.

Winter, S. G. (2000). "The Satisficing Principle in Capacity Learning." *Strategic Management Journal*, 21/10–11: 981–96.

Yin, R. K. (1994). "Designing Single- and Multiple-Case Studies." In N. Bennett, R. Glatter, and R. Levačić (eds.), *Improving Educational Management Through Research and Consultancy*. London: Paul Chapman, 135–55.

Part II
General Process Papers

10

Relational Power, Personhood, and Organizations

C. Robert Mesle

Abstract: Power is usually conceived as unilateral, as the ability to affect without being affected. Instead, this chapter proposes that we conceive of power as relational. Relational power may be seen as including three elements: the ability to be actively and intentionally open to the world around us; the capacity to create ourselves out of relationships with others; and the ability to sustain internal relationships, to influence others by having first been influenced by them. The concept of relational power arises directly from the process relational vision of reality and personhood in contrast to the traditional concept of the world as composed of self-existent and unchanging substances. Organizations founded on unilateral power undermine full personhood and community, while organizations which embody relational power lead to richer lives and more creative relationships.

10.1 We Have a Power

Martin Luther King, Jr., the great American Civil Rights leader, understood power, and he certainly understood how to organize. He preached:

> We have a power, power that can't be found in Molotov cocktails, but we do have a power. Power that cannot be found in bullets and guns, but we have a power. It is a power as old as the insights of Jesus of Nazareth and as modern as the techniques of Mahatma Gandhi....
>
> Somehow we must be able to stand up before our most bitter opponents and say: "We shall match your capacity to inflict suffering by our capacity to endure

suffering. We will meet your physical force with soul force. Do to us what you will and we will still love you." (King, 1983: 71, 72)

Reverend King wrote his doctoral thesis on Henry Nelson Wieman, one of the early process thinkers, especially Wieman's concept of Creative Transformation. It must surely have shaped King's thinking about power. Process thinkers have a long history of rethinking the nature of power as persuasive rather than coercive. But I believe we have not given enough attention to the work of Wieman's student, Bernard Loomer, who distinguished between unilateral and relational power, a distinction which includes the role of persuasion but moves us beyond it to a different vision of power.

The distinction between unilateral and relational power comes from Loomer, but his ideas and King's were both shaped by Wieman's idea of Creative Transformation. Not only was King a powerful preacher for what Loomer called relational power, but King's life, along with Gandhi's, proves that relational power is indeed *powerful*. It can transform the world in a way nothing else can. I offer King's words above as a preliminary explanation of relational power. To this we may add words of the Buddha:

> Hatred can never put an end to hatred;
> Love alone can. (The Buddha, 2005)

And finally, from Bernard Loomer:

> By S-I-Z-E I mean the stature of your soul, the range and depth of your love, your capacity for relationships. I mean the volume of life you can take into your being and still maintain your integrity and individuality, the intensity and variety of outlook you can entertain in the unity of your being without feeling defensive or insecure. I mean the strength of your spirit to encourage others to become freer in the development of their diversity and uniqueness. I mean the power to sustain more complex and enriching tensions. I mean the magnanimity of concern to provide conditions that enable others to increase in stature. (1976a: 70)

10.2 Unilateral Power

When most people think of power, they point to examples of what Loomer called unilateral power: winning sports teams, ultra-wealthy people and giant corporations, hurricanes and tornadoes, national leaders, the military, and especially nuclear weapons. All of these kinds of examples point to power as the ability to affect others without being affected by them.

Raymond Aron, in his book *Peace and War: A Theory of International Relations*, makes this common definition of power explicit in the political arena:

> On the international scene I should define power as the capacity of a political unit to impose its will upon other units.... This definition suggests several distinctions: between *defensive power* (or the capacity of a political unit to keep the will of others from being imposed upon it) and *offensive power* (or the capacity of a political unit to impose its will upon others. (1967: 47)

Unilateral power inherently flows one way, downward—moving the burdens of life from top to bottom of the power hierarchy, with few at the top and many at the bottom. It is frequently illustrated in the forms of social pyramids—like military ranks—where a few at the top can give orders to all those below. Those in the middle ranks receive orders from those above but can give orders to those below them. Those at the bottom receive orders from everyone above, but can give orders to none. Of course, those at the bottom search for someone to give orders to, so powerless men often give orders to even more powerless women, and adults to children, all in the same basic flow. The dog can be kicked by everyone, but gets to chase the cat, etc.

Unilateral power is woven deeply into our lives. We compete all the time in sports, games, grades, jobs, romance, and more. It is difficult for us to envision life without such competitive expressions of unilateral power. Even when we do not want to control and win, we do want to feel safe and secure. Most of all, we don't want to suffer and die. Understandably, we want to be "unaffected" by all the threats of the world.

Yet, consider what unilateral power looks like in the extreme. Given the realities of the world, no person has complete power over anyone else. But consider examples where people come very close to having absolute unilateral power over others. The starkest examples are deeply troubling: child abuse, slavery, rape, torture chambers, tyrants, and genocide. Unilateral power, in the extreme cases, shows itself as very dark, indeed.

Most disturbingly, if unilateral power is the ability to remain safely unaffected by others, then unilateral power seems to be the opposite of love in one important respect. Surely, to love someone is to be affected by them. The more deeply we love someone the more we are affected by them. Their joys and sorrows become our joys and sorrows. To have a child, it has been suggested, is to have your heart walking around outside your body. Unilateral power seems, in this respect, the opposite of love.

10.3 Unilateral Power and Personhood

Beyond its obvious origins in the human longing for safety and security, unilateral power has a long history in Western philosophy. Plato defined being in terms of power in his dialogue *The Sophist*:

> My notion would be that anything which possesses any sort of power to affect another, or to be affected by another, if only for a single moment, however trifling the cause and however slight the effect, has real existence; and I hold that the definition of being is simply power. (1937: 2:255)

I think Plato was right about this. Unfortunately, Plato did not weigh these two aspects of power equally. He modeled his eternal forms after mathematical ideas—as absolutely changeless, timeless, and impassive. In the *Republic*, Plato argued:

> Things which are at their best are also least liable to be altered or discomposed.... Then everything which is good, whether made by art or nature or both, is least liable to suffer change from without.... But surely God and the things of God are perfect in every way?...Then it is impossible that God should ever be willing to change; being, as is supposed, the fairest and best that is conceivable, every God remains absolutely and forever in his own form. (1937: 1:645)[1]

Western philosophers and theologians have followed Plato's lead. Aristotle's vision of the Unmoved Mover clearly prefers the power to affect over the power to be affected. Containing all possible values within God-self, the Unmoved Mover needed nothing, and got nothing, from the world. We can easily follow the Greek preference for the power to affect over the power to be affected through Christian theologians like Augustine, Anselm, Aquinas, Luther, and Calvin, and philosophers like Descartes, Leibniz, and Locke, and the Newtonian idea that atoms are self-subsistent.

Unilateral power, however, proposes a truncated vision of reality, personhood, and community. It invites us to conceive of the world in terms of purely "external relationships." In extreme forms, the vision of absolute unilateral power meant that God must exist totally independently of the world, controlling absolutely everything, and affected by absolutely nothing.

In early modern physics, following ancient Greek philosophers like Democritus, the natural world was believed to consist entirely of atoms moving in a void. These atoms were tiny hard things, indivisible, with no internal relations to each other. They only bounced off of each other, but nothing in their internal constitution in any way derived from the surrounding world. Each one was a model of unilateral power in the aspect of being unaffected by others. You could remove the entire universe except one atom and it would remain unchanged in any internal way. Hence, its relation to the universe was purely external.

Likewise, the self-subsistence of Aristotle's Unmoved Mover and the atomic vision of nature are glaringly evident in Descartes' vision of reality and personhood, and makes clear the link to Descartes' underlying philosophy of substance rather than relational process. Descartes thought of the human mind as a mental substance. What did he mean by a substance? Descartes explained, "By substance, we can understand nothing else than a thing which so exists that it needs no other thing in order to exist" (1955: 1:239). Amazing. Did Descartes think he had no mother? No teachers? No Galileo to excite his mind? Descartes further asserted that such substances, including the human mind, not only exist independently, but "endure unchanged through change." Did he truly imagine that the human mind would be the same if he stripped away every thought, idea, and belief, all of his love of truth and people, his emotions of hope, joy, and sorrow? What kind of self could possibly endure unchanged through such change? This vision of reality and of persons, as consisting of substances which exist independently and endure unchanged through all the changes of relationships, is a clear explanation of a reality envisioned in terms of purely external relationships. Descartes' philosophy asserted that none of your relationships with the world or the persons around you play any constitutive role in who you are. You are a purely atomic reality, as much as any of the Newtonian atoms moving in the void.

This illusion of independent existence expressed in the exercise of unilateral power can easily lead unilaterally powerful people to treat less powerful people as abstractions. Since, as Leibniz and others had argued, "A created thing is said to act outwardly insofar as it is perfect, and to suffer from another insofar as it is imperfect," inequality of power is believed to justify the master's position by showing the inferiority of the servant, wife, child, or worker (1973: 61–2). Thus, persons of great unilateral power—whether slave master, patriarchal husband and father, or simply the boss at work—need not deal with weaker persons in depth. They can treat them as mere tools—in Kant's language, as means *only*. The master seeks to have a relationship to the servant which is purely "external" to the master, having little or no effect on them. But it is "internal" to the servant because it imposes itself on their personhood, usually against their will. The masters are therefore free to pretend that true personhood, their own, is atomic, that they exist independently and that they are "self-made," needing nothing but their own power to exist. This pretense, however, is a lie. To affirm

239

reality as fully relational is to realize that all actual relationships are internal. We are always creating ourselves out of each other.

While relatedness is clearly a matter of degree, process relational thinkers ever since the Buddha have recognized that nothing in the world, and certainly no people in the world, exist independently. We all emerge out of and are constituted by our relationships. Whitehead understood that all actual entities, from the electron to the human soul are inescapably relational, arising out of our relationships with the world around us. To actively seek to cut ourselves off from being influenced by, and internally related to, the world and other persons is to impoverish our lives. As Desmond Tutu observed, "We can be human only together" (2007: 3). "If I diminish you, I diminish myself" (2007: 37) Thus we need a vision which draws us to be concerned with the concrete relational life of ourselves and of others around us, in all its depth and complexity.

We will return to the problem of internal and external relationships after looking at Wieman's vision of creative transformation and the corollary concept of relational power.

10.4 Creative Transformation and Relational Power

What, then, must we do to live richer lives, to capture a larger vision, to have souls and communities of greater SIZE? Bernard Loomer proposed a vision of relational power which emerged out of Wieman's concept of Creative Transformation. Pointing out that people can be transformed toward great good or great evil, Wieman asked what makes the difference. What transforms us away from evil and toward the good provided we give ourselves over to it? He described this active process of the growth of appreciative awareness in terms of four *ings*: emerg*ing* awareness, integrat*ing* insights, expand*ing* appreciation, and deepen*ing* community (Wieman, 1946: 68).[2] Loomer's concept of relational power, I think, describes the capacity and strength required to engage in creative transformation. The greater a person's relational power, the greater their openness to creative transformation and their capacity to enter into deeply mutual relationships.

Loomer defined relational power as "the ability both to produce and to undergo an effect. It is the capacity both to influence others and to be influenced by others" (1976b: 20). But we can clarify Loomer's intent if we think of relational power as having three dimensions, which can be seen as interwoven with Creative Transformation.

10.4.1 Active, Intentional, Openness

Active openness is the power to engage in what Wieman called Emerging Awareness. Children are wonderful examples of this aspect of relational power. They constantly explore the world with all five senses, literally stuffing the world into their mouths to learn more about it. Even we adults *must* engage in such openness just to survive and enjoy. We value those people with greater strength in openness. Stronger students and CEOs are precisely those most gifted at, and actively committed to, openness to new information, ideas, and visions. Artists are more open to the colors and shapes of the world, while poets are alert to the nuances of language. Musicians hear music all around us. Rather than the "picky eaters" of life, we admire people who can sit at any table and learn to enjoy the amazing array of flavors the world has to offer—in food, ideas, beauty, nature, language, people, and more. The best parents are those most sensitive and responsive to the changing feelings, hopes, fears, and dreams of their children. This fits the old saying that we should walk a mile in another person's shoes to learn who they are.

10.4.2 Self-Creativity

Relational power requires taking all that active openness and responding to it self-creatively. Loomer describes clearly and compellingly the relational character even of our self-creativity:

> In the relational viewpoint you begin life as an effect produced by the many others in the world of your immediate past. But you are not simply a function of these relations. You are an emergent from your relationships; and in the process of your emergence you also create yourself. Your life as a living individual consists of synthesizing into some degree of subjective unity the various relational causes or influences which have initiated your process of becoming something definite. Your concrete life is constituted by a process of deciding what you will make out of what you have received. This is your emergent selfhood. What you make out of what you have received is who you are. This is also your emergent freedom because you are your decisions. Your subjective life is your process of deciding who you are. (1976b: 22)[3]

Self-creativity is required for Wieman's events of Integrating Insight and Expanding Appreciation. We are not just putty in the hands of the world. Relationally powerful people don't just believe what we are told, or think as we are directed. Rather, we take in the new and thoughtfully integrate it with what we already have and value. We use our existing values and knowledge to sort out what we consider to be truer and better. But creative transformation demands that we sometimes recognize new truths and values as better than our old ones, requiring us to rethink, reconceive, revalue, and even reconstruct ourselves, our visions, and our actions in response to creativity. Walking a mile in the other person's shoes expands our range of appreciation by giving us a chance to integrate their wisdom with our own, and to see the world through their eyes—but without giving up our own wisdom or eyes. Active openness and self-creativity make it possible to see something creatively new.

Because truly Creative Transformation can transform our deepest vision and values, we cannot simply direct the process as we choose. It takes us places we cannot foresee, and hence cannot simply aim at. Wieman emphasized the demand that we open ourselves fully to this creative dimension of transformation, and that requires relational power and courage.

10.4.3 The Strength to Sustain Mutual Relationships

The Deepening of Community Wieman envisioned in Creative Transformation is expressed in the third aspect of relational power. It involves the willingness and SIZE to take in the new and then return to the world and our relationships with more openness, better questions, more sensitivity, and new understanding. It means being willing and able to go back and learn more, to sustain engagement with ideas, experiences, and people, especially when those relations are challenging. This step leads right back to the start in a creative spiral. We try to become more actively and intentionally open, and more self-creative. Having walked a mile in another person's shoes, we are in a better position to enter creative dialogue with them.

10.5 Relational Power and Personhood

Relational power, therefore, is what Loomer envisioned as the S-I-Z-E of a person, as quoted above. "By S-I-Z-E I mean . . . your capacity for relationships. I mean . . . the intensity and variety of outlook you can entertain in the unity of your being without feeling defensive or insecure. I mean the strength of your spirit to encourage others to become freer in the development of their diversity and uniqueness" (1976a: 70).

In stark contrast to unilateral power, where the extreme examples are found in tyrants, torturers, child abusers, rapists, and slave masters, the radical manifestations of relational power are found in people like Martin Luther King, Jr., Mahatma Gandhi, Jesus, and the Buddha. Relational power in the kinds of situations Gandhi and King faced takes enormous strength. It requires the willingness to endure tremendous suffering while refusing to hate. It demands that we keep our hearts open to those who wish to slam them shut. It means offering to open up a relationship with people who hate us, despise us, and wish to destroy us. Relational power requires the strength to say, "Father forgive them, for they know not what they do." King refused to let the hatred of others turn him into another hateful person like them. He understood that they needed and wanted to compel him to act hatefully so as to justify their own hateful actions. He wrote, "I'm tired of violence. And I'm not going to let my oppressor dictate to me what method I must use" (1983: 71).

> [S]o throw us in jail and we will still love you. Bomb our homes and threaten our children, and, as difficult as it is, we will still love you. Send your hooded perpetrators of violence into our communities at the midnight hour and drag us out on some wayside road and leave us half-dead as you beat us, and we will still love you.... But be assured that we'll wear you down by our capacity to suffer, and one day we will win our freedom. We will not only win freedom for ourselves, we will so appeal to your heart and conscience that we will win you in the process, and our victory will be a double victory. (King, 1983: 72)

Persons of relational power understand and embody the Buddha's ancient wisdom: "Hatred can never put an end to hatred; Love alone can" (2005: 78).

To return hate for hate is easy; but to respond to hatred with love is one of the most difficult things a person can do. Those who can do so are the saints, the true sages, the greatest hopes for our world. They have hearts, souls, and minds of enormous SIZE. Consequently, Loomer argues, "*Relational power is the capacity to sustain a mutually internal relationship*" (1976b: 23).[4]

10.6 Internal and External Relationships

We can understand the importance of relational power more deeply if we further explore the distinction between internal and external relationships. First, imagine yourself in a museum reflecting on a piece of sculpture, perhaps a Pietà. The statue, for most purposes, is only externally related to you. It has some effect on you, but is not affected by you. You don't make it feel happy or sad, or proud of its beauty. You, however, may be deeply changed by the sculpture, perhaps being moved to become a more compassionate and loving person. Your relationship to the statue is internal. It has become part of you.

Of course, as any museum curator knows, your very presence does affect the sculpture. The warmth of your body, the humidity of your breath, and the oil in your fingers, not to mention the flash of your camera or the hammer in your pocket, are dangers against which curators must be constantly vigilant. Nevertheless, you are able to engage in an internal relationship which is impossible for the statue. The stone is great at unilateral power, but has minimal relational power. Yet, we often seek to emulate the stone.

Unless we want lives as empty as the lives of stones we must understand that our very existence as selves is as creatures of internal relationships. We are constituted by our relationships. Without them we are nothing. There is not first a self which then has relationships. We *are* our relationships. Or, more precisely, we create ourselves out of our relationships with the entire world, including our bodies and our human relationships.

In the vision of reality proposed by the Buddha and also by Whitehead and modern process thinkers, everything in the world is constituted by its internal relationships. Modern quantum physics has demonstrated decisively that the old Cartesian/Newtonian view of reality as composed of self-existent atoms is simply false. Our physical universe is composed entirely of events, and these events, at the tiniest level called quantum events, are bundles of energy, of spatial-temporal relationships which cannot exist independently of the field of energy relationships out of which they arise. No event is truly "atomic" in the Newtonian sense because no event can exist apart from its relationships.

What is true of quantum events forming the physical universe is also true, and even more glaringly true, for us. The flow of experience constituting your sense of self arises because in each moment you are creating yourself out of all of your relationships. But there is not first a "you," and then an act of self-creativity. The event of self-creativity out of relationships *is* you, is who you are. You are constituted by your decisions within the network of your relationships—to your body and to the rest of the human and natural world.

This is why any effort to insulate ourselves from our relationships is ultimately self-destructive. To the degree that we succeed in such isolation we hollow ourselves out. As John Cobb, Jr., has so effectively expressed it, we are "persons-in-community" (2007: 577f.). We are social creatures from start to finish. To let fear of pain, insecurity, and death drive us to insular existence is self-defeating action of the deepest kind.

As I finish writing this essay, our grown children and their spouses and four young grandchildren are in our home for the Christmas holidays. The grandchildren are aged six months, and two, four, and eight years. It is wonderful—but not exactly restful, as you can imagine. It would be much easier to retreat into being purely externally related to everyone, letting others care for the crying children and read books and play games with them. External relationships are much less work. But then the whole point of family and holidays would be lost. Full immersion into the life of the family requires internal relationships—getting up at night with the crying baby and early in the morning with young children anxious to play, working together in the kitchen, talking about life and work and the emerging lives of children and adults alike. That is hard work—exhausting at times—with many failures. But the ability to sustain those relationships as internal, as mutually enriching, is what family life is all about. And, of course, we have to take turns giving each other naps and a little "work time" to keep up with the demands of our professional lives, even over the holidays.

So, given the joys of richly internal relationships, why do we so often retreat into purely external relationships? One reason is the hard work internal relationships require. But another is pain.

Pain is one very human reason why we idolize unilateral power and seek external relationships. We can respond to pain in many ways, moving toward either relational or unilateral power. Often suffering, like cancer, can draw families together and strengthen their mutually internal relationships. A person facing death may well come to celebrate each moment of life, each sweet strawberry, each hug of a child. Confrontation with their own mortality can intensify their hunger for truly internal relationships. Those are expressions of relational power—an active openness to the world by which we exert all our energy to reach out and embrace those relationships which make life truly worthwhile.

Consider, in contrast, a woman I know, who, after the death of her husband, collapsed into a bitter, angry, striking-out-at-everyone, ball of despair. She had always had a narcissistic streak, but the refiner's fire of emotional pain boiled her down to a prickly burr of self-centeredness. She drove everyone away. Like a burned cat, every human touch was so searing that she lashed out with her claws.

Gradually, the pain subsided and the claws withdrew a bit. Yet, the fear of hurt remained. In order to escape painful experiences, to avoid being vulnerable, she chose to forfeit nearly all power to engage with other people and the larger world. She increasingly shrank her world to three rooms of her two-story house and stayed at home, alone, 99.9 percent of the time. She stopped watching TV or reading, except old letters she knew to be happy. She abandoned nearly all relational power—all power to be actively and intentionally open to others, to create herself out of new experiences, or to enter into deeper community with anyone or anything.

I trust that you find her situation as sad as I do. But this is one strangely extreme expression of the "other half" of unilateral power. In a grossly convoluted way she sought the Cartesian ideal of pretending that she could exist independently, needing nothing but herself in order to exist. Ironically, of course, she was a black hole of need, utterly dependent on others.

An odd parallel to the illusion of independence can be seen in the political scene when a politician or corporate executive proclaims that they pulled themselves up by their own boot straps, never relying on handouts from anyone, and certainly never taking help from the government. We are left to wonder if they think they built all of the roads, railways, airports, or the Internet by which their commercial products move. Do they imagine that they built the municipal utilities, power lines, and sewer systems by themselves? Are they completely oblivious to the fact that public schools and universities, libraries, parks, police, the National Guard and military are supported by everyone in the polis? Do they imagine that they are the only customers whose hard-earned money buys their products and thus creates the jobs for which this entrepreneur takes credit? Even such capitalistic and self-motivated institutions as insurance companies are tools by which we collectively hire people to make it possible for us to share our resources so as to help each other out in times of great need. People who imagine that they achieve great wealth without the support and cooperation of larger communities on which they are deeply dependent live with immensely narcissistic blinders, bearing a strange resemblance to the woman described earlier.

Life requires work, effort, and the strength to enter into the relationships which make life rich and rewarding. We are finite creatures with finite capacity for such relationships. But even more narrowly than the limits of mere finitude, most of us, in varying degrees, seek to protect ourselves by fending off, or merely ignoring, a huge range of ideas, knowledge, people, self-awareness, and painful conflicts and engagements, by choosing to limit our exercise of relational power. In contrast, Loomer makes clear the difference between a life of relational power—the capacity to maintain internal relationships—and a life of unilateral power which seeks purely external relationships.

> The discipline demanded by the effort to sustain internal relationships is at least difficult. Its cost is large and sometimes enormous. The price to be exacted involves the expenditure of great energy in the form of an active patience, physical stamina, emotional and psychic strength, and a resilient trust and faith. Above all, the cost is measured in the coin of suffering. The capacity to endure a great suffering for the sake of a larger purpose is one of the decisive marks of maturity. (1976b: 28)

10.7 Relational Power and Organizations

Given the nature of creative transformation, Loomer argues that the "greatest possible good cannot emerge under conditions of control. The aim is to provide those conditions of the giving and receiving of influences such that there is the enlargement of the freedom of all the members to both give and receive" (Loomer, 1976b: 26). Consequently, in applying relational power to any organization, some questions are obvious. To what extent is an organization structured as a unilateral power pyramid with the flow of power from a few at the top toward the many at the bottom? To what extent does the organization assume, require, or unintentionally function so that those at the top are largely insulated from and unaffected by those further down the pyramid, only externally related to those below? Conversely, how well do the structures and culture of the organization encourage, require, reward, and/or educate people to be actively and intentionally open to mutually creative influence, self-creative in integrating that shared influence, and successful in using that self-creativity to sustain and deepen genuinely internal relationships within the organization?

In his thoughtful book *Reworking Authority: Leading and Following in the Post-Modern Organization*, Lawrence Hirschhorn explores some specific problems in what he calls the post-modern character of contemporary culture, selves, and organizations. While he makes no explicit reference to process relational thought, creative transformation, or relational power, his views clearly share much common ground with the perspectives I am presenting here.

Hirschhorn explicitly views the self as an interdependent process rather than an atomic and unchanging substance which exists independently and endures unchanged through change. He emphasizes the "openness" of relationships and the self, through which "we deepen our sense of inter-dependence" (1997: 89). Hirschhorn describes three interrelated ways of experiencing the self: "depth," "breadth," and "over a life span" (1997: 90). His approach offers important similarities with Wieman's description of creative transformation and my definition of relational power.

To experience yourself in breadth is to develop more emerging aware-ness that "A person's identity emerges from the widest set of relation-ships in which his or her life is embedded. The self is a social self. When thinking in breadth, we realize that our experiences are the echoes of other individuals' experiences, and that what we feel can represent truths about the system of relationships that surround us" (1997: 90). The depth dimension of self-exploration requires the self-creativity and crit-ical thinking to recognize the complexity of our own motives, and the potentially conflicting interpretations which stand in tension with each other, possibly obscuring each other, but potentially creating greater complexity of insight.

To be aware of the self over time connects to Wieman's hope for deep-ening community, because we recognize that creative transformation is a continuing and spiraling process:

> Each of these elements of the post-modern self helps us to become more open to one another. . . . I respond fruitfully to the other person when I become more aware of the quality of my own awareness. Similarly, to be aware in breadth is to find my own experiences in others' experiences and theirs in mine. And when I am aware of my evolving self, I know that another to whom I was impervious may now touch me. Through each of these orientations I become more open and vulnerable to others. (Hirschhorn, 1997: 90)

Those last sentences reflect essentially the same kind of creative trans-formation to which relational power seeks to open us. "When this happens people become more aware of the difference [*sic*] experiences that shape any moment of interaction. A sense of interdependence thus grows" (Hirschhorn, 1997: 92).

Hirschhorn observes that following World War II, Western capitalism actively sought to create "modern" unilateral hierarchical structures intended to create greater efficiency, and in some respects to protect senior executives and other supervisors from those below while creating clear structures for guaranteeing workers job security. In exchange, corporations required conformity, loyalty, and the sacrifice of individual expression. Authority—as unilateral power—flowed from top to bottom in a classic pyramidal form. Modernism offered some positive values, especially security, but required the sacrifice of much personal freedom.

Eventually, Hirschhorn argues, people rebelled. The cultural revolution of the 1960s and 1970s led to a new openness within Western culture at many levels. The roles of women changed. We began to abandon the idea that children should be "seen but not heard," in favor of more relational approaches to child-rearing. Minorities began to assert their voices, and large portions of even the mainstream workforce opted for a society of greater openness personally and in their communities. "Similarly," Hirschhorn observes, "we can say that the post-modern organization sustains a 'culture of being open to others'—in shorthand, a 'culture of openness'" (1997: 18).

Given the new "openness" of the post-modern self in a post-modern culture, Hirschhorn argues, organizations must function differently. We need a post-modern view of persons and of how persons function within organizations.

> Thus, to create a culture of openness, organizations must first and foremost build new relationships to authority. Leaders must make themselves more vulnerable to their peers and their subordinates. They must risk their *apparent authority* (the authority that announces that they are in charge) in the interest of deepening their *substantive authority* (the authority they gain from leading a successful team performance). Followers, for their part, must overcome both their excessive dependence on authority and their blanket hostility to it. In both challenging and accepting authority, one learns to *lead as a follower*. (Hirschhorn, 1997: 27)

It is easy to see how Hirschhorn's discussion of authority could be recast, perhaps with more clarity and depth, in terms or unilateral and relational power.

Hirschhorn believes that "The new openness, where it develops and flourishes, can help people work in such a setting. It creates enough psychological safety so that people will risk being more psychologically present and will use their thoughts and feelings to create new ideas and discover new solutions" (1997: 30).

However, just as Gandhi and King had to be utterly realistic in recognizing the deep-seated resistance they would face in bringing relational power into confrontation with the forces of unilateral power, and the purely human resistance to deep cultural change, Hirschhorn is honest and insightful in describing challenges to such a new kind of openness. He specially addresses chapters to the challenges of dependency, envy, "abdication" of authority, and fantasy heroism, as well as the roles of resentment and gratitude.

Given these deeply embedded forms of psychological resistance to the uncertainties created by greater openness, "How does a post-modern hierarchy help us become persons to one another, while allowing us to contain feelings that might undermine the work we have to accomplish?" (Hirschhorn, 1997: 41). We have to recognize, for example, that "Differences in talent, competence, or achievements can make people feel weak, insufficient, and vulnerable" (Hirschhorn, 1997: 44).

Hirschhorn does not call us to abandon hierarchy in such a way that leaders abdicate their responsibility for leadership. In the sense he means it, I think, I agree with him. As a university teacher, I cannot simply turn the entire class over to my students. I know more than they do about the subject matter at hand. I have to work to create a context in which I can share what I know in such a way that they increase their ability to do their own creative thinking, including the ability to thoughtfully challenge me. Similarly, parents cannot abdicate responsibility for being parents. But good parents must create relationships and opportunities for their children to develop their personal autonomy so as to increasingly become independent persons, capable of mutually internal relationships with their parents and others around them. Without treating workers as children or young students in a patronizing way, Hirschhorn calls for leaders at each level of an organization not to abdicate responsibility for leading, but to learn to do so in an open and relational way.

> The chain of command is a time-tested tool for delegating authority while not abdicating leadership. Today, the word "hierarchy" conjures up images of control and suppression. A hierarchy has another aspect, however. Although it creates a system in which some roles are vested with more authority than others (this is the "anti-democratic" aspect), it also facilitates delegation. It allows leaders to "lend" their authority to subordinates, thereby enabling the subordinations to participate in the leadership process. (Hirschhorn, 1997: 57–8)

Hirschhorn argues that hierarchy need not be the opposite of participation. Rather:

> well-functioning hierarchies are based deeply on the principle of delegation that, at bottom, stimulates and requires senior executives to share their leadership with their subordinates. When senior executives delegate leadership, they are lending their authority, never relinquishing it. This means that they remain deeply implicated in the workings of the organization so that they never abandon their subordinates to the mythical power of rules and procedures. . . . I suggest that the post-modern enterprise embraces hierarchy but enlivens it with feelings and passion. It strengthens hierarchy by personalizing it. (Hirschhorn, 1997: 67–8)

Hirschhorn provides compelling examples, using his own language, of how the ideas of relational power and creative transformation can be applied concretely to organizations of many kinds. He is definitely thinking within a process view of reality rather than a substance view, especially in how he understands the nature of the self, and the interdependent character of human relationships within organization structures.

10.8 The Inequality of Power

Hirschhorn's insistence that working for a more open culture within organizations does not mean the abandonment of hierarchies—of a more relational and participatory kind—requires us to examine what Loomer recognized as one of the great truths about human relationships. Power, whether unilateral or relational, is always unequal. Indeed, he insisted, "The fact of inequality is not just one consideration among many equally significant facts. It is a bed-rock condition" (1976b: 20).

There is a stark contrast between inequality of unilateral power, and inequality of relational power. In a unilateral relationship, the greater burden is clearly borne by the weaker partner, and unilateral power inevitably seeks to widen the gap and shift ever more of the burden of life downward. The current flow of wealth in the United States today is a glaring example. The rich get richer, and the poor get poorer. The blues singer, Billie Holiday, said it well, in her song, "God Bless the Child."

> Them that's got shall have
> Them that's not shall lose
> So the Bible says and it still is news
> Mama may have, Papa may have,
> But God bless the child that's got his own, that's got his own.

Relational power works very differently. The greater burden is borne by the stronger partners, who work actively to increase the relational power of the others. As Loomer observes, "The ultimate aim of relational power is the creation and enhancement of those relationships in which all participating members are transformed into individuals and groups of greater stature" (1976b: 26). This should be clear in what good parents and teachers do, but Hirschhorn is urging us to take the same approach to leadership within organizations, while examining deeply, broadly, and over a life span, the formidable psychological resistance we can expect to encounter.

Given the inherent inequality of power, life is unfair. Loomer reflects that we must:

> choose between two forms of unfairness. In the life of unilateral power the unfairness means that the stronger are able to control and dominate the weaker and thereby claim their disproportionate share of the world's good and values. In the life of relational power, the unfairness means that those of larger size must undergo greater suffering and bear a greater burden in sustaining those relationships which hopefully may heal the brokenness of the seamless web of interdependence in which all live. (1976b: 28)

Thus, when persons within an organization encounter reactions like envy, resentment, and abdication of responsibility, those of greater relational strength must be willing to carry the greater burden of interpersonal work. In practice, of course, we will need to take turns helping each other out since all of us have times when we burn out, feel threatened and insecure, and resent the demands of more mutually internal communities.

As Loomer repeatedly insisted, relational power is the capacity to sustain an internal relationship. "The sustaining," he argues further, "does not include management, control, or domination. Rather, it involves the persistent effort to create and maintain the relationship as internal" (1976b: 27). Obviously, Loomer uses "management" here in the negative sense suggested as domination. As Hirschhorn teaches us, "senior executives can succeed in guiding the enterprise only if they depend deeply on their employees' skills, their willingness to collaborate with one another, and their ability to recognize the impact of their work on the performance of the enterprise" (1997: 5). Likewise, Loomer urges, "Under the relational conception of power, what is truly for the good of any one or all of the relational partners is not a preconceived good. The true good is not a function of controlling or dominating influence. The true good is an emergent from deeply mutual relationships" (1976b: 21).

Here we may profitably return to John Cobb, Jr.'s insight that we are persons-in-communities: "Communities are societies held together by internal relationships" (2007: 567). Organizations with leadership and structures which nurture community within the organization can enrich our lives, create loyalty, and encourage mutual creativity. "If I understand myself as a person-in-community, there is a general harmony between seeking my own good and seeking the common good of the community. Benefitting the community benefits me" (Cobb, 2007: 577).

> If, however, the company has no appreciation for its role as community and treats its employees simply as functionaries working for their wages, the

community dimension will be weakened. Indeed, because people want a sense of belonging, the refusal of the employer to allow that sense to develop can cause resentment and withholding of effort. If one is treated as a cog in a wheel, one may act as a rather poor cog. (Cobb, 2007: 577)

10.9 Conclusion

In all of our human relationships, whether in families, classrooms, or corporate organizations, life is better when we work together, sharing the burdens and joys of relational life. Together, we are able to see more deeply and widely. Together, we solve problems more creatively. Together, we mutually increase our shared strength, shared wisdom, shared compassion.

Good parents, good teachers, good CEOs, and good leaders of cultural movements, of course, want their children, students, colleagues, and followers to grow in relational power. We want to help them increase their capacity to be actively, intentionally, open to the world around them. We want to nurture their self-creativity, and foster their capacity to engage in deepening community with the people, ideas, and world around them. In parenting, friendship, marriages, and many other relationships, this nurturing is the manifest expression of love. In larger organizations, relational living is an expression of common purpose, shared vision, and mutual respect.

When I think of the most extreme images of relational power, I always think of the vision of the Hindu *Bhagavad-Gita*:

> Those who burn with the bliss
> And suffer the sorrow
> Of every creature
> Within their own heart,
> Making their own
> Each bliss and each sorrow:
> Them I hold highest . . . (1972: 67)
>
> Their every action
> Is wed to the welfare
> Of other creatures. (1972: 61)

I am convinced that relational power offers us a vision with great spiritual depth because it shows us the way into the deepest dimensions of our own souls, and models the greatest kind of power we humans can have. Like the Golden Rule and the call to love our neighbor as ourselves, the depth of compassion envision by the *Gita* reaches far beyond what we can expect from human beings, but it reminds us that the vision of creative transformation through relational power is open-ended. There is no particular point at which we may not find ourselves feeling called to deeper mutual caring, even in the very heart of corporate capitalist organizations.

Let me return one last time to the words of the Reverend King. "We have a power, power that can't be found in Molotov cocktails, but we do have a power. Power that cannot be found in bullets and guns, but we have a power."

Whether or not we are tested in the fire as were Gandhi and King, I invite you to affirm that in our daily lives, we have a power. It is not the power of tyrants or torturers, but we do have a power. It is not the power of wrathful deities who send hurricanes and earthquakes to punish those we oppose. But we have power. It is the power of spiritual giants like the Buddha who knew that hatred can never bring an end to hatred, that love alone can do that. We preach the power of Gandhi and King, who, by their wounds, helped heal nations. We proclaim the power of gentle parents, imaginative teachers, compassionate counselors, creative CEOs, of babies exploring the world with all of their senses open. Let us nurture in our own lives, and the lives of those with whom we live and work, *relational power* as the strength, courage, and wisdom to creatively transform our hearts, our lives, our organizations, and our world.

Notes

1. See also the *Timaeus*: "What is that which always is and has no becoming; and what is that which is always becoming and never is? That which is apprehended by intelligence and reason is always in the same state; but that which is conceived by opinion with the help of sensation and without reason, is always in a process of becoming and perishing and never really is" (Plato, 1937: 2:12).
2. Italics original.
3. Paraphrased from Loomer, shifting "he" to "you" and editing accordingly. In 1975, Loomer was aware of the problem of sexist language, but I have elected to follow his spirit of creative transformation by revising "his or her" into smoother, more contemporary forms.
4. Italics are original. Paraphrased for inclusive language.

References

Aron, R. (1967). *Peace and War: A Theory of International Relations*. Trans. Richard Howard and Annette Baker Fox. New York and Washington: Praeger.

Bhagavad-Gita: The Song Of God. Trans. Swami Prabhavananda and Christopher Isherwood, with an introduction by Aldous Huxley. The Vedanta Society of Southern California, 1944, 1972 [edited for inclusive language].

Billie Holiday (1939). "God Bess the Child."<http://www.metrolyrics.com/god-bless-the-child-lyrics-billie-holiday.html, 3/25/2014>.

Cobb, J. B. (2007). "Person-in-Community: Whiteheadian Insights into Community and Institution." *Organization Studies*, 28/4: 567–88.

Descartes, R. (1955). *Philosophical Works of Descartes*. Trans. Elizabeth Sanderson Haldane and G. R. T. Ross. New York: Dover.

Hirschhorn, L. (1997). *Reworking Authority: Leading and Following in the Post-Modern Organization*. Cambridge, MA: MIT Press.

King, M. L. (1983). *The Words of Martin Luther King, Jr.* Comp. Coretta Scott King. New York: Newmarket.

Leibniz, G. W. (1973). *Discourse on Metaphysics/Correspondence with Arnauld/Monadology*. Trans. George Montgomery. La Salle, IL: Open Court.

Loomer, B. (1976a). "S-I-Z-E Is the Measure." In H. J. Cargas and B. Lee (eds.), *Religious Experience and Process Theology: The Pastoral Implications of a Major Modern Movement*. New York: Paulist Press, 70.

Loomer, B. (1976b). "Two Kinds of Power." *Criterion* (Winter): 20.

Plato (1937). *The Dialogues of Plato*. Trans. B. Jowett. New York: Random House.

The Buddha (2005). *Buddhism: The Dhammapada*. Trans. E. Easwaran. Berkeley, CA: Nilgiri.

Tutu, D. (2007). *Believe: The Words & Inspiration of Desmond Tutu*. Boulder, CO: Blue Mountain Arts.

Wieman, H. N. (1946). *The Source of Human Good*. Edwardsville and Carbondale, IL: S.I.U.

Index

Tables and figures are indicated by an italic *t* and *f* following the page number.

Printed and bound by CPI Group (UK) Ltd, Croydon, CR0 4YY